Comparative Theory and
Political Experience

Mario Einaudi

Comparative Theory and Political Experience

Mario Einaudi and the Liberal Tradition

PETER J. KATZENSTEIN

THEODORE LOWI

SIDNEY TARROW

Editors

Cornell University Press

Ithaca and London

First published 1990 by Cornell University Press.

International Standard Book Number 0-8014-2368-6
Library of Congress Catalog Card Number 89-39112

Printed in the United States of America

*Librarians: Library of Congress cataloging information
appears on the last page of the book.*

⊗The paper used in this publication meets the minimum requirements
of the American National Standard for Permanence of
Paper for Printed Library Materials Z39.48–1984.

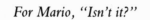

For Mario, "Isn't it?"

Contents

Preface

THIS volume has grown out of a conference held in November 1987 at the Society for the Humanities at Cornell University, in honor of Mario Einaudi, Goldwin Smith Emeritus Professor of Government. Sponsored by Cornell's Western Societies Program, with the support of the Center for International Studies and the Government Department, the conference brought together a group of Einaudi's friends, former students and colleagues whose connections with Cornell spanned four decades. They shared three convictions that are central to Einaudi's work and thought: that the study of politics must be embedded in history; that Europe and the United States have much to teach each other about the practice of democratic politics; and that the classics of political theory must inform the study of contemporary democratic states.

The conference presentations subjected each of Einaudi's six major books in political theory and comparative politics to analysis, praise, exegesis, and occasionally criticism. Einaudi listened in silence as his works were examined. When the celebration ended, the final word was his: "Thanks!" he responded, and he would say no more.

The papers from the conference, with the addition of a new contribution by Martin Schain, have been refashioned and expanded into the essays in this book. Tarrow's Introduction greatly profited from the contributions of Katzenstein and Lowi and of an invited critic who must remain nameless but to whom we tender our thanks.

We also thank the Cornell Western Societies Program, the Center for International Studies, and the Government Department for the financial help that made the conference and this publication possible. Further, we are grateful to the friends and colleagues who participated in the conference and to Rose Zakour, who helped in its organization. Finally, we extend our thanks to Robin Blakely, Tammy Gardner, Martha Linke, Lawrence Kaplan, and Cynthia Witman who helped to make this volume a reality.

P.K., T.L., S.T.

Ithaca, New York

Comparative Theory and
Political Experience

⤞⤞⤞⤞⤞⤞⤞⤞⤞⤞⤞⤞⤞⤞⤞⤞⤞⤞⤞   ⤝⤝⤝⤝⤝⤝⤝⤝⤝⤝⤝⤝⤝⤝⤝⤝⤝⤝⤝

Introduction

SIDNEY TARROW

In 1948 Mario Einaudi published an article that was to be for many years the standard introduction in English to the new Italian constitution. The article's concerns went well beyond the language of the document. Einaudi compared the new constitution to its historical predecessor, the Albertine *statuto* of 1848, analyzed its development out of the 1946 constituent assembly, and assessed its relation to the constitutional tradition of the West.[1] Einaudi doubted that the constitution's more detailed policy provisions could be implemented and was amused by its references to a variety of conflicting constitutional schools.[2] But he attributed these to the confusion of the domestic and international climate—this was, after all, the period of the early cold war. He was worried about the influence of the Left over the consti-

I am grateful to Cynthia Witman for the preliminary research on which this chapter is based. I am also grateful to all of my collaborators who commented on an earlier draft and especially to the care and diplomacy of a reviewer who must remain nameless.

1. Mario Einaudi, "The Constitution of the Italian Republic," *American Political Science Review* 42 (August 1948):661–76.
2. Ibid., 662.

tutional text, but noted that the final version retained few signs of "Eastern," or Soviet constitutionalism.[3]

The constitution makers appeared to Einaudi to have built on solid theoretical foundations. As he put it: "The framework and the means, the procedural as well as the substantive requirements, appear to be all at hand to get the Italian experiment in constitutional and progressive democracy in motion under conditions as favorable as this tragic postwar era will allow." The constitution's prospects, he thought, would profit from the postwar environment of European-American cooperation. "The Marshall Plan," he wrote, "will presumably place at the disposal of the Italian government means of unprecedented size which—if wisely used—should guarantee the creation of a more sound and just economic system."[4]

But good theory and a propitious environment do not suffice: they have to be implemented through practical politics, and that meant the party system. Einaudi noted that "the Italian people have now turned over the primary responsibility for governing the country to one political party, the Christian Democrats." And as theory was shaped by experience, it would clash with human weakness. He observed ironically: "Looking at the problem purely within its national boundaries, one must conclude that if the cumulative result of these forces shall not be such as to lead to the gradual establishment of a free and advancing political and economic society, the folly of man must indeed be adjudged immeasurable."[5]

Theory and experience, constitutional doctrine and democratic politics: these are the two poles of Einaudi's interest. His belief in the liberal constitutionalism that is the main heritage of the eighteenth century is one of the themes of this volume. But in his assessment of the 1948 Italian constitution there was also the political realist's caution not to take the words of the text as gospel, in a world in which words have often been used to justify the opposite of their accepted meaning.

When he writes, for example, that the Christian Democrats in the Constituent Assembly quoted Stalin while the Communists approv-

3. Ibid., 661.
4. Ibid., 676.
5. Ibid.

ingly cited George Washington,[6] it is more than irony that we hear; we also hear the skepticism of the student of constitutions who had seen his country's 1848 *statuto* betrayed without even the dignity of abrogation.[7] And when he observes that even the best constitution may not triumph over "the folly of man," the tradition of eighteenth-century political constitutionalism meets head-on the empirical observer's eye for the erosion of institutional rules by ordinary politics. Einaudi's analysis of the postwar Italian constitution embodies the synthesis of political theory and comparative politics.

There is also a hidden tension in the article: between an obvious devotion to constitutional democracy and the thorny problem of the role of the Marxist Left in the future of democratic Italy. Indeed, although Einaudi admits that there are few signs of "Eastern" constitutionalism in the final text, he deals with the Partito Comunista Italiano (PCI) more as an irritant and as a threat to what others might consider the constitutional parties than as the legitimately elected representatives of a class that had contributed blood to the liberation of Italy from Facism. This too embodies a typical dilemma of comparative politics as it encounters democratic theory.

Einaudi's 1948 discussion of the new Italian constitution is a good place to begin a volume that recalls both his contribution to comparative politics and its relation to political theory: first, because this book embodies important themes present throughout his work; and, second because it pinpoints the central tensions in the study of politics as the field emerged from the Second World War. The themes are the interdependence of Europe and America, the role of the comparative method, and the centrality of the eighteenth-century heritage to both of them. The tension is between the theorist's belief that constitutions are the site in which freedom and democracy are fought over and the realist's understanding of the frailty and contrariness of ordinary people when faced with overriding questions of values.

This tension between theory and experience is as central to Einaudi's work as it is to the political science of the postwar period. With-

6. Ibid., 662.
7. Mario Einaudi, "Constitutional Government: France and Italy," in Fritz Morstein Marx, ed., *Foreign Governments: The Dynamics of Politics Abroad* (New York: Prentice-Hall, 1949), 210.

out theory, the study of politics becomes merely descriptive, as most of it was in the 1950s and 1960s. But in the absence of reality, theory remains sterile, a situation that dismayed Einaudi in certain strains of recent political philosophy. He was thus at pains (and he was one of the few major figures in recent American political science to do so) to combine classical political theory with comparative politics in his work and in his teaching—even when, as in his 1948 article on the Italian constitution, an integrated synthesis proved elusive.

It is the combination of theory and experience that explains Einaudi's fascination with the eighteenth century, where he found the historically rooted political philosophy of a Burke preferable to the abstract theoretical theorems of a Locke. The same synthesis produced the richest insights in his work, for example, on the New Deal. But the tension between theory and experience was responsible for some puzzling lacunae in his writings as well. This synthesis and this tension will turn up repeatedly in the three themes that constitute the core of Einaudi's contribution.

EINAUDI, EUROPE, AND AMERICA

I first met Mario Einaudi when I came to Cornell to teach in its government department in 1972. Though officially retired from full-time service since 1965, Einaudi was still teaching Gov. 104, which had been "his" course for three decades. Inheriting even a piece of Einaudi's mantle was not a comfortable prospect. I looked forward to our first meeting with some trepidation, for we had both written about French and Italian communism, a subject on which our views were very different.

We met in the Center for International Studies, which Einaudi had helped found in 1960 and which he ran for most of that decade. The center was then lodged in Rand Hall, which looked more like the annex of a gun factory than an academic building. I had not expected to find the Goldwin Smith Professor Emeritus of Government holding court in such an undignified setting. But such was the aura surrounding Einaudi that, from the moment he began to speak, we might as easily have been in a European atheneum as in the brick pile of Rand Hall.

We went to lunch at the Cornell faculty club, and there, as I watched him munch a bacon, lettuce, and tomato sandwich and sip a cup of very thin coffee, it became apparent that Mario Einaudi was as at home in America as in Europe. He offered a wager on the forthcoming presidential election (a bet that he won, incidentally, as he did most of his bets on American politics). He then proceeded to instruct me on the current real estate values in Ithaca and to predict with amazing accuracy what I would have to pay for a house there. Einaudi in America was a man who stood on native ground.

Recalling this first experience of Einaudi helps introduce a major theme in his contribution to comparative politics. During a period that was marked, on the one hand, by the impact of central European exiles burned by totalitarianism and, on the other, by Americans' almost naive discovery of "behavior," Einaudi combined a European's appreciation of the state with an American's political realism. This gave his work its transatlantic character, which is the major source of its success.

On the other hand, there was a tension between America and Europe in his work, for Einaudi saw postwar European politics through a lens that had been crafted in the United States. For example, although recognizing the major changes reflected in the New Deal, he insisted, with Tocquevillean fervor in *The Roosevelt Revolution*, on the need for decentralization to protect freedom and democracy.[8] And in the books that make up the "French-Italian Inquiry,"[9] he assumed an Atlanticist credo that could leave the impression that his comparative work was part of the polemics of the early cold war.

It is not that Einaudi's intellectual roots did not go deep into European culture or his work range broadly across the ideological spectrum before he came to America. A graduate of the University of Turin's distinguished law faculty, he had earlier come to know Roberto Michels, who moved to Turin when his Socialist opinions made it impossible for him to win a permanent academic appointment in Germany.[10] After graduation, Einaudi went to Berlin, where

8. Mario Einaudi, *The Roosevelt Revolution* (New York: Harcourt, Brace, 1959). Although, like Tocqueville, he regards decentralization as necessary for democracy to survive (p. 355), Einaudi does not really grapple with the implications of the New Deal for the centralization of the American state (p. 356).

9. See n. 26, below.

10. In 1908–9 Michels (1876–1936) came to Turin, where he became close to

he met the great German jurists Friedrich Meinecke and Carl Schmitt, before spending two years at the London School of Economics, where he worked with William Beveridge, Harold Laski, Graham Wallas, and A. D. Lindsay and gathered material for his doctoral thesis on Burke.[11]

It was in London that Einaudi had his first exposure to the tragic side of real politics, as he began to meet with exiles from Fascism. Two of the most important were Don Luigi Sturzo and Gaetano Salvemini. Sturzo had founded the Catholic Popular party after World War I, when the Vatican was moving in a direction favorable to allowing Catholics to participate in democratic politics. After 1922, with the consolidation of the Fascist state, he tried at first to find a role for the party within the institutions, but refused to follow the church into an accommodation with Mussolini and was forced into exile. His progressive Catholicism had a profound influence on this son of a distinguished Italian liberal.

It was also in London that Einaudi consigned a first small contribution to the archive of freedom, following the murder of Giacomo Matteotti. Matteotti was a Democratic Socialist who had enraged the newly installed Fascist party by trying to rally the anti-Fascist forces in Parliament against them. The outcry following Matteotti's murder forced the government to undertake an official inquiry. Salvemini, who had been associated with Einaudi's father through the journal *La critica sociale*, brought a record of the proceedings to London when he too was forced into exile. Einaudi consigned it to the library of the London School of Economics, where it still may be found.[12]

Then, in 1927–29, Einaudi went to Harvard as a Rockefeller fellow. There he worked with William Yandell Elliott, Carl Friedrich, and Charles McIlwain and did research on the United States Supreme Court. The experience was electrifying. When he was fired from the

---

Einaudi's father, Luigi (1874–1961), one of Italy's great economic thinkers and historians and the first president of the future Italian Republic from 1948 to 1955. In 1933, in Dogliani, the family home, Mario Einaudi was married to Michels's daughter Manon.

11. Published as *Edmondo Burke e l'indirizzo storico nelle scienze politiche* (Turin: Istituto Giuridico della Reale Università, 1930).

12. From the author's conversation with Einaudi in Ithaca, on 14 May 1988. On Matteotti's importance in the opposition to Fascism before his murder, see Einaudi, "Constitutional Government," in Morstein Marx, *Foreign Governments*, 210.

University of Messina for refusing to take out a Fascist party card, Harvard gave him refuge, first as a tutor and then as an instructor. Many of his most enduring ties (and the birth of his first son, Luigi) date from those years in Cambridge.

Einaudi stayed around Harvard Square long enough to imbibe the best of American academic life, but not so long as to forget that there was a country outside its rarefied atmosphere. In 1938 he was hired by Fordham University as an assistant professor. He moved his young family, first to Greenwich Village and then to Washington Heights, and plunged into the exciting world of New York exile politics. It was here that his second and third sons, Robert and Marco, were born, and that he renewed his earlier acquaintance with Sturzo, who had meanwhile moved on from London. Einaudi later used his good offices to get Sturzo's book *L'Italia e l'ordine internazionale* distributed in Italy almost as soon as the Allies reached Rome.[13]

When the war came, Einaudi was the father of three and, at thirty-eight, too old to enter active service. But he undertook assignments both for the Office of War Information and for the Council on Foreign Relations. It was to help in preparing future Allied Military Government personnel for service in Europe that he was brought to Cornell in 1943, commuting to Ithaca one day a week on the Lehigh Valley railroad, to teach about European government. Like many a European academic, he worked on his lectures on the train. At the war's end, he was asked to stay on as associate professor of government.

In those days of small faculties with broad interests, Einaudi was hired to teach both political theory and European politics, but unlike that of most native-born comparativists, his teaching reflected his interest in the United States as well. From 1945 to 1956 he taught "The Comparative Study of the Public Regulation of Economic Life," using continental, British, and American materials. Few comparativists in the decade of the cold war imagined that the United States could

13. Luigi Sturzo, *L'Italia e l'ordine internazionale* (Turin: Einaudi, 1944). There was no Einaudi book publisher in New York in 1945. The book was printed privately and rushed to Italy on one of the first ships to cross the Atlantic after Italy was liberated. Sturzo, however, never regained his prominence in the Catholic movement. The Christian Democratic party that became politically dominant failed to embody his vision, as Einaudi reluctantly had to admit in 1953. See his "Italy in Crisis," *Behind the Headlines* 13 (August 1953): 56.

be compared to other nations—many still have trouble with the idea—and few Americanists looked outside of the United States.[14] Without fanfare, Einaudi had accomplished in 1945 what it would take political science three more decades to recognize—the inclusion of the United States in comparative politics.

Einaudi's institution-building efforts at Cornell also revealed a clear understanding of American reality. He was the government department's longest-lasting chair, from 1951 to 1956 and again from 1959 to 1963, presiding over the department's expansion from five to twelve members. When Cornell decided it was time to venture into interdisciplinary research in international affairs, Einaudi was quickly brought into the founding of the Center for International Studies, where he emerged as its first director. His tenure left a permanent mark on the center, in its continuing role in teaching American students about modern Europe.

His experience with American institutions of higher learning has left a permanent mark on his native Italy as well. As Italian universities entered the turbulent 1960s, Einaudi saw that European scholars were without the necessary relief from teaching and administration needed to devote themselves to research. With the creation of the Fondazione Luigi Einaudi of Turin, Einaudi successfully transplanted the American model of the independent research institute to Italy. Built around his father's extensive library, the foundation offered fellowships to hundreds of young Italian and foreign scholars over the next twenty years.[15]

It was Einaudi's *Roosevelt Revolution* that best revealed the synthesis of the European and American traditions in his thought. It was, he wrote, "a book aimed at those Europeans who think and worry about modern America and are confused about its meaning." Europeans, Einaudi worried, have forgotten—if they ever knew—that the price America pays for its present way of life results from daring "to identify and accept some of the unavoidable conditions for the survival of

14. Only after disciplinary boundaries loosened in the 1960s would the American Political Science Association admit to its annual convention the Conference Group on Political Economy. Not coincidentally, the group was co-chaired by a former Einaudi student and current Cornell professor of government, Martin Shefter.

15. See Fondazione Luigi Einaudi, *Cronache della Fondazione*, extract from *Annali della Fondazione Luigi Einaudi* 27 (Turin: Fondazione Einaudi, 1983).

a democratic community in the twentieth century." Those conditions demanded that liberal theory be reformulated to support positive government—not the collectivist state he abhorred, but the creative interventionism that Einaudi saw in pathbreaking New Deal agencies such as the TVA.[16]

In the decade of McCarthyism, Americans too were in danger of forgetting how the New Deal had saved American democracy by expanding it. Reviewers understood what Einaudi was about. The *Nation* wrote: "To readers abroad, he can bring the fruits of years of study and teaching in the United States; for Americans he provides the perspectives of centuries of European civilization."[17] For Einaudi, the completion of the heritage of the liberal constitutionalism of the European tradition was the positive state of the New Deal.

It is paradoxical that Einaudi's most widely reviewed book was written on a subject an ocean apart from either his European roots or his formal teaching interests. But like the man, his choice of subject matter was rigorously logical: for the Roosevelt that Einaudi cherished in *The Roosevelt Revolution* was not the victorious war leader, the patrician liberal, or the scheming professional politician. His greatness lay in his "efforts to re-establish the sense of community in a free industrial society" and "to affirm the validity and the central role of the political instruments of democracy in facing the crisis of our times."[18] Only a scholar with a foot on both continents could have highlighted the relevance of the New Deal to the European experience so well.

EINAUDI AND THE COMPARATIVE METHOD

Einaudi the comparativist was before all else a teacher. At our faculty club luncheons, he would turn to the role he liked best: that of the interested teacher examining a bright but temporarily uninformed

---

16. Einaudi, *Roosevelt Revolution*, v, vi, chap. 4. This line of analysis was prefigured in a short article by Einaudi: "In Defense of the Economics of TVA," *New York Sun*, 3 February 1945.

17. *The Nation*, 29 August 1959, 95.

18. Einaudi, *Roosevelt Revolution*, vii.

student. At that first lunch in 1972, he quizzed me carefully about the unstable political situation in Italy, a condition that—since I had recently returned from sabbatical—he expected me to understand as if I had just left the corridors of Montecitorio.

I cagily explained that I had spent my sabbatical in France, not Italy, thereby trying to disguise, or at least excuse, my ignorance of recent Italian events. In that case, he wanted to know, what was my opinion of the recent Pompidou devaluation? Was it not a more intelligent strategy than the Bank of Italy's willingness to print money endlessly to cover its government's profligate ways? And would this fellow Mitterrand (this was 1972) put together the modern Socialist party that France needed to achieve a true alternation in power, thereby completing France's evolution to a modern democratic state?[19]

There was no place to hide! I could sympathize with the generations of graduate students who had shivered before Einaudi's Socratic method, and had to endure his kindly but fixed gaze as they responded to his questions with facts and interpretations. Worse than the probing questions were the ironic echoes he provided to one's uncertain answers. For whenever Einaudi had doubts about your information or interpretations, he would restate and correct your naive utterances, followed by the equivocal but penetrating, "Isn't it?"

Einaudi's Socratic method was not only how he drew information from others; it was also how he taught. The range of his teaching was breathtaking. Looking back at his first year at Cornell, 1945–46, we find him responsible for the basic courses in both modern political thought and comparative politics. In addition, he was teaching courses in contemporary political thought and public regulation of economic life and a seminar in political theory. In the following years he added to his teaching repertoire a seminar in comparative constitutional law and a seminar in political and economic change in contemporary Europe. There were iron men teaching in the stone academic buildings of those days!

Einaudi's students had little doubt that they were being taught by

19. As early as the 1962 referendum on the direct election of the presidency, Einaudi had realized that the constitution of 1958 was an interim document between the Fourth and a putative "Sixth" republic. I am grateful to Ted Lowi for this recollection.

an intellectual heavyweight. In the Cornell course critique for 1947, we find the following comment on Gov. 104:

> *Lectures*: stimulating and well-organized;
> *Assignments*: fair and useful;
> *Examinations*: Fair and rather difficult . . . marked hard.[20]

The comments in the course critique that was published almost twenty years later were remarkably similar:

> *Assignments*: extensive and exhaustive;
> *Exams*: rather difficult;
> *Lectures*: witty and brilliant;
> *What impressed you most about the course?* Einaudi.[21]

Einaudi's teaching was never far from his research interests. When he helped found Cornell's Center for International Studies, one of the themes central to the proposal that gained Ford Foundation support for the initiative was the role of the center in linking international to domestic affairs. Einaudi argued that international studies should be "an integral component in the education of our children and an element in our attempts to solve domestic problems."[22]

Under Einaudi's successors—and not without resistance from some quarters—the center has continued to devote considerable efforts to undergraduate education and to link international affairs to domestic problems. This is especially true of its Western Societies Program, founded with Einaudi's help; its very title was designed to reflect both the unity of the Atlantic community and the importance of studying the problems of advanced industrial democracies comparatively. As he wrote in *The Roosevelt Revolution*, "Europe and America must realize that only a balanced and reasoned understanding of the respective grounds upon which they stand can provide an authentic basis for the solidarity so needed in their future relationships."[23]

20. Cornell University, *Student Guide to Courses* (Ithaca, 1947), 22.
21. Cornell University, *Insight* (Ithaca, 1963), 20.
22. From a memorandum to the author by one of Einaudi's successors, Davydd Greenwood, summarizing the center's two founding proposals, June 1988. I am grateful to Greenwood for his help in preparing this section.
23. Einaudi, *Roosevelt Revolution*, vi.

But the European heritage had a cost: even as a plethora of new nations freed themselves from colonialism, Einaudi's courses on comparative government remained stubbornly culture-bound. They first appear in the Cornell catalog in 1946–47 as "Comparative Government, with a major emphasis on Europe." The course description changes only slightly until 1964–65, when Russia is added. Even as a host of new nations were added to the world and the term "political development" passed into the lexicon of political science, Einaudi never ceased to teach some version of this course—which to him meant mainly Western Europe.

Einaudi's Eurocentric compass arose from the close identity he held between comparative politics and political theory, and the centrality of the eighteenth-century European heritage to both. His first widely read work in English, his contribution to Fritz Morstein Marx's *Foreign Governments*, came out of this mold. It was a skillful synthesis of the French and Italian political traditions, designed to reintroduce Americans to these countries after the hiatus of Fascism and to show how their new constitutions might work. But it did not deal with more general issues of political development, and—like the 1948 article on the Italian constitution—it did not come to grips with the tension between constitutional government and the role of the Left.[24]

The books in the French-Italian Inquiry that he organized in this period—*Christian Democracy in Italy and France, Communism in Western Europe*, and *Nationalization in France and Italy*—were the result of both his liberal agenda, as Roy Pierce shows in his contribution to this volume, and of his conviction that Americans needed to know much more than they did about the countries of Western Europe.[25]

24. "Constitutional Government," in Morstein Marx, *Foreign Governments*, 262–63, does deal with the Communists' views of the new constitutions of Italy and France. Although Einaudi believed that both parties had real domestic sources of strength—and were not simply Russian transplants—he does not confront the constitutional rights of minorities who reject liberal constitutionalism. The PCI, in fact, not only accepted the Republican constitution, but ultimately became one of the most stalwart defenders of its "guarantist" principles, according to an interpreter who is far from sympathetic to communism. See Giuseppe Di Palma, "Establishing Party Dominance: It Ain't Easy!" in T. J. Pempel, ed., *Uncommon Democracies: One-Party Dominant Regimes* (Ithaca: Cornell University Press, 1990).
25. Mario Einaudi and François Goguel, *Christian Democracy in Italy and France*

As a mine of information, those three books still stand up well today, although they are much weaker in drawing explicitly comparative conclusions from the national materials. These weaknesses—but also the books' fundamental strengths—go back to the unity of political theory and comparative politics in Einaudi's approach. If they reflected a fear of European communism that seems, with the virtues of hindsight, somewhat exaggerated, it was Einaudi's vision of a free society which explained it—and not the cold-war mentality that was more intense in his contemporaries. And if he saw Christian Democracy as a way to combine freedom with positive government, as the New Deal had done, it was the progressive vision of a Sturzo—who in the meantime had been politically defeated—and not the sterile anticommunism of Italy's leaders that inspired him.

Einaudi's comparative method could seem old-fashioned to those who were experimenting with new approaches to political behavior in the 1950s and 1960s, for his approach was not driven by a particular analytical formula or based on any global model. Instead, it was carefully built of the accumulation and synthesis of a mass of facts and ideas derived from prodigious reading and knowledge. For Einaudi, only a deep knowledge of other countries, rather than a magic theoretical or methodological key, was the basis on which comparison had to be carried out.

This explains, among other things, the curious lack of attention he gave to the differences in the environments of the French and Italian Communist parties in *Communism in Western Europe*,[26] differences that are clear from Chapters 5 and 6 in this volume. For one who knew France and Italy as well as he did, it went without saying that France was Jacobin and that Italians lacked a sense of the state; to rehearse these points was to belabor the obvious. But this did not help the young scholars who were trying to explain the growing differences

---

(Notre Dame, Ind.: University of Notre Dame Press, 1952); Mario Einaudi, Jean-Marie Domenach, and Aldo Garosci, *Communism in Western Europe* (Ithaca: Cornell University Press, 1951); Mario Einaudi, Maurice Byé, and Ernesto Rossi, *Nationalization in France and Italy* (Ithaca: Cornell University Press, 1955). A fourth book—*France under the Fourth Republic* (Ithaca: Cornell University Press, 1952)—was wholly written by François Goguel.

26. See "Communism in Western Europe," pt. 1, in Einaudi, Domenach, and Garosci, *Communism in Western Europe*, 6–35.

between the two parties, as these differences emerged more clearly in the 1960s.[27]

Einaudi also underexploited the potential for comparison in his treatment of the Christian Democratic parties of France and Italy, the Mouvement Républicain Populaire (MRP) and the Democrazia Cristiana (DC).[28] He treated them as variants of the same progressive Catholicism he had encountered in Sturzo, a factor that made it difficult to predict the rapid demise of the MRP and the remarkable persistence of the DC as a governing party, as T. J. Pempel points out in his contribution to this volume. The understatedness in Einaudi's comparative work was a defect that did not escape the reviewers when the book appeared.[29]

But if Einaudi's comparative work seemed behind the times to some reviewers in the 1950s, its creative blend of politics, institutions, and history was a trait that comparative politics—under the new weight of statistics and sociological jargon—came close to losing. The careful accumulation and synthesis of facts and ideas at which he excelled was no more old-fashioned than Tocqueville's *Democracy in America* or Bryce's *Modern Democracies*, two of the enduring classics of comparative politics.[30] It is no accident that, of all the writers on American or European political history, the one Einaudi cited with the most approval was Tocqueville.[31]

Einaudi's method, like Tocqueville's, consisted in training a fine logical mind on a few countries with the lens of a vast amount of historical, institutional, and political knowledge. Einaudi dealt with institutions and history during a period in which political scientists were discovering behavior and ignoring history. He carried out and organized paired comparisons when multicountry studies based on aggregate data profiles were becoming fashionable. And he plunged

27. See, e.g., Donald L. M. Blackmer and Sidney Tarrow, eds., *Communism in Italy and France* (Princeton: Princeton University Press, 1975).
28. Einaudi, "Constitutional Government," in Morstein Marx, *Foreign Governments*, 222–28.
29. See, e.g., Gordon Wright's review of *Christian Democracy in Italy and France* in *Annals of the American Academy* 284 (November 1952):218.
30. The comparison with Tocqueville may seem excessive to some, but a reviewer of *The Roosevelt Revolution* called it "a book that may well stand beside Tocqueville's *Democracy in America.*" *Kirkus* 27 (1 April 1959):287.
31. See, e.g., the final chapter of *The Roosevelt Revolution*, esp. 356–60.

into the technical complexities of economic planning when voting studies and surveys were the rage.

If this methodology seemed old-fashioned in the 1950s and 1960s, it is far more modern today. For as comparative politics has retraced its steps from behavior to institutions (or better, to the study of behavior *within* institutions), and from voters and opinions to laws, constitutions, and political economy, Einaudi's work appears to have anticipated later developments. For example, the inclusion of a section called "Extending the Public Sector" in his 1949 essay in the Morstein Marx volume[32]—almost unique for textbooks of the time— would not raise an eyebrow among today's political economists, as Peter Katzenstein shows in Chapter 7 of this volume.

The true timeliness of Einaudi's comparative work was not due to its rehearsal of contemporary issues or to its once again fashionable configurative methods, but to the timeless nature of the issues that it dealt with: institutions and institution building, the impact of history on politics, the relations between freedom and community. And this takes us to the central theme in Einaudi's thought—the eighteenth-century heritage.

THE EIGHTEENTH-CENTURY HERITAGE

We can learn a great deal about what is central to a scholar's interests from the chronology of his or her work. Einaudi completed his thesis on Burke in 1926 and his essay on judicial review in America in 1931. His first book in English, *The Physiocratic Doctrine of Judicial Control*, appeared in 1937.[33] All three works were about the eighteenth century. Then came the four books in the French-Italian Inquiry and *The Roosevelt Revolution*, which occupied him from 1938 to 1958. In 1967, after devoting his writing to comparative politics for twenty years, he returned to the eighteenth century with his last published work, *The Early Rousseau*.[34]

32. Einaudi, "Constitutional Government," in Morstein Marx, *Foreign Governments*, 271–86.

33. Mario Einaudi, *The Physiocratic Doctrine of Judicial Control* (Cambridge: Harvard University Press, 1938).

34. Mario Einaudi, *The Early Rousseau* (Ithaca: Cornell University Press, 1967).

None of Einaudi's works on the eighteenth century had the immediate appeal that the comparative work of the 1950s would have, nor did they enjoy the critical acclaim of *The Roosevelt Revolution*. But they demonstrate the hold that the eighteenth century had over his thought and the relationship in his mind between political theory and comparative politics. The eighteenth century was as important to Einaudi's political thought as it had been to his father's economic theories. But he refracted it through his own personal and political experiences, and thus emphasized only a part of that century's heritage and exaggerated its unity.

We first see Einaudi's passion for the eighteenth century in his thesis on Burke, which was completed in Turin in the mid-1920s. Though he claimed in the characteristically laconic preface of the published version that the book was nothing but a "particularistic analysis of those specific characteristics of Burke's thought that relate to the historical approach to political science,"[35] it was in fact a study of the reciprocal influence of ideas and politics in this turbulent century of British life.

The same can be seen in Einaudi's first article in English, in *Political Science Quarterly* in 1934, on the British background of Burke's philosophy.[36] In it, he strove to show how deeply Burke was rooted in the tradition of his country and his century.[37] He contrasted the Irish statesman to Locke, not for his greater conservatism, but for his ability to root political theory in historical reality. But what was the historical reality in which Einaudi would root his own work—that of the century he wrote about or the one he was living in? When Einaudi began his American career, it was to study the eighteenth-century origins and subsequent development of judicial control in America. The research he did there resulted in a published monograph in Italian on the theoretical and historical origins of judicial control in the United States.[38] This was not a subject likely to stimulate great inter-

35. Einaudi, "Preface," in *Edmondo Burke*, 5.

36. Mario Einaudi, "The British Background of Burke's Political Philosophy," *Political Science Quarterly* 49 (1934): 576–98.

37. For Burke's reflections on Bolingbroke, see, e.g., ibid., 593–96.

38. Mario Einaudi, *Le origini dottrinali e storiche del controllo giudiziario sulla costituzionalità delle leggi negli Stati uniti d'America* (Turin: Istituto Giuridico della Reale Università, 1931).

est in the United States of the early 1930s, but he saw it as of crucial importance in Western Europe.

The depth of Einaudi's interest in constitutional theory must be gauged not from the tone of this early essay, which lacks the lightness of touch of his later writing, but from its date and place of publication. Italy under the Fascist state was not the most politic place for a young scholar to write about the judicial control of government. Einaudi's brief survey of the experience of judicial review in Western Europe in fact included exactly six words on Italy,[39] for the Fascist regime, with its institution of special tribunals to deal with political dissent, had made a mockery of the independence of the judiciary.

Although it takes an expert in Aesopian writing to find any criticism of the corporate state in Einaudi's essay, it must have taken conviction for a young man trying to begin his career in the Italian university system to devote a book to "the law that is above ordinary laws."[40] If nothing else, Einaudi's friendship with liberal anti-Fascists such as Piero Gobetti,[41] and his later refusal to become a member of the Fascist party, prove what his convictions were at the time. The subject of *Le origini dottrinali* was American, but it refracted the Italian reality that was still central to his preoccupations.

Einaudi's early work on Burke and on judicial review in America was followed by an excursion into French political theory, *The Physiocratic Doctrine of Judicial Control*. This was a curious book in some ways. In its densely packed ninety-six pages, Einaudi dealt with the theme of the judicial review of the executive by a group of scholars who are more typically associated with the doctrine of legal despotism. On the surface, the book seemed to be tangential, if not contradictory, to physiocratic political thought. But it was more than an

39. Ibid., 14.
40. Ibid., 9.
41. Piero Gobetti (1898–1926) had been one of Luigi Einaudi's students; he entered the University of Turin in 1918, four years before Mario. Like the elder Einaudi, he was a liberal, but unlike him, he believed that classical liberalism could survive only by accepting the working class as its true heir. Though he remained personally close to Luigi Einaudi, he worked in the early 1920s with the young Antonio Gramsci, as well as with the Democratic Socialist Salvemini. His boldest challenge to the Fascists was to found a journal, *La Rivoluzione liberale*, which marked him for Mussolini's vengeance. He was so savagely beaten by Fascist thugs in 1925 that he collapsed and died in Paris the following year.

intellectual hors d'oeuvre; it established how metaconstitutional limits could be important even to the eighteenth century's most enthusiastic proponents of enlightened despotism, and it helped win Einaudi
his first permanent post, at Fordham.

Was it the obvious parallel between the physiocratic thinkers and
the American doctrine of judicial supremacy which whetted Einaudi's
interest? Apparently not, for he was at pains to make clear that the
physiocrats' belief in legal despotism led the American founders to
ignore the entire corpus of their work. It was, rather, to underscore
the unity he thought he found in eighteenth-century constitutional
thought that he turned to the French school.[42] But as Steven Kaplan
shows in Chapter 1 of this volume, Einaudi ignores the deep cleavages within the eighteenth-century "party of humanity" and under-
plays the extent to which the physiocrats derived their political pre-
cepts from economic premises.

Einaudi's underlying interest was, in fact, not in the physiocrats
themselves but in the process by which the men of the eighteenth
century sought to combine freedom and social regulation. That the
relation between the two was Einaudi's abiding passion is hinted at in
the last paragraph of the book, where, with apparent irrelevance to
his topic, he adds a reference to the twin goals of freedom and community in Jean-Jacques Rousseau.[43]

Einaudi's return to these themes in *The Early Rousseau* in 1967
shows that they were no mere coda in a brief early sonata, but the
overture to a far more serious engagement that would take him thirty
years to complete. In the conservative 1950s, Rousseau was confirmed as the cult scapegoat of the critics of mass democracy, by
people who claimed to see in his work a premonition of our own
century's totalitarianism.[44] By the 1960s, as Isaac Kramnick points out
in Chapter 2 of this volume, Rousseau was enlisted as the ally of
another twentieth-century theory—the politics of "authenticity."

For Einaudi, Rousseau had to be reclaimed for the eighteenth century from a false contemporaneity: both from those who would
transform him into an advocate of totalitarianism, and from those

42. Einaudi, *Physiocratic Doctrine*, 87.
43. Ibid., 90.
44. The major exponent of this view is Jacob Talmon, whose *Origins of Totalitarian
Democracy* (New York: Norton, 1970) was first published in 1952.

who claimed him for the politics of the radical New Left. As a result, though dealing only with Rousseau's early writings, he presents a more balanced and more historical picture of Rousseau than either Jacob Talmon or the advocates of "authenticity." If Rousseau is relevant to the people of the twentieth century, wrote Einaudi, it is because he teaches that "there is nothing inevitable about the future."[45]

But rather than confront Rousseau's critics with the meaning of his oeuvre tout court, Einaudi attacked them by focusing on the early work. With characteristic understatement, he wrote that he wished "to show how much of decisive importance Rousseau had said in the course of these twenty years, how indeed most of what he was to say later in his major works is to be found in this early period."[46] But he tried to do so in the absence of an integrated treatment of Rousseau's oeuvre. Although one astute reviewer realized that Einaudi's real goal was more fundamental—to restore "Rousseau's preeminent place in the history of egalitarian radicalism"[47]—many others would miss the underlying intent.

It is only in recent years, as Kramnick observes, that Einaudi's service to the complete Rousseau has been recognized and that "no student of political theory reads only Rousseau's Social Contract and Emile. The Discourse on Arts and Sciences, the Discourse on the Origin of Inequality and A Discourse on Political Economy are now essential reading due, to a great extent, to Einaudi's seminal study of the early Rousseau."

The eighteenth century produced the twin incubators of freedom for the next two hundred years: Western Europe and North America. From Burke and the physiocrats, to Roosevelt and Rousseau, passing through the struggle for constitutional democracy in postwar Italy and France, the heritage of the eighteenth century was as central to Einaudi's work as it has been to the Western experience.

First, biographically: the century produced the economic doctrines that, in modernized form but spiritually unchanged, Einaudi had imbibed in his father's library. Second, intellectually: it produced most

45. Einaudi, Early Rousseau, 278.

46. G. H. McNeil, review of The Early Rousseau in American Historical Review 17 (January 1968):1539.

47. Judith Shklar, review of The Early Rousseau in Political Science Quarterly 83 (September 1968):477.

of the major schools of political theory that Einaudi taught to generations of Cornell students. Third, historically: we owe to it, as Einaudi
wrote, man's first organized attempts to "recover control over his
own life."[48]

THE EINAUDIAN HERITAGE

Not all of Einaudi's contributions are immediately obvious as we
go through the various stages of his career, in part due to the extraordinary understatedness of his claims, and in part because he devoted much of his time to empirical issues. As a political theorist in
the 1930s and 1940s Einaudi did not go very far beyond eighteenth-
century constitutional and political thought. Einaudi the comparativist brought his European experience to bear for American students
but was also looking at Western Europe's reconstruction through Atlanticist lenses. It was only Einaudi the student of the New Deal,
showing Europeans what the American experience had to offer Europe, who integrated theory with contemporary reality, and Einaudi
the Rousseau scholar who brought it all together, emphasizing the
role of politics in mediating between freedom and community.

Looking back at Einaudi's work as a whole, we find in it a creative
tension between theory and experience. Like all creative tensions, it
has its more dated and its more resilient aspects. On the one hand,
Einaudi's classical idea of freedom produced the uncompromising opposition to communism and the optimistic view of Christian Democracy of the French-Italian Inquiry. On the other, his passion for the
eighteenth-century heritage, tempered by forty years of teaching and
research, produced both the progressivism of *The Roosevelt Revolution* and the strongest passages of *The Early Rousseau* and enabled him
to transcend the sterile cold-war atmosphere of the postwar years.

If Einaudi's work is a testament to the eighteenth century's quest
for freedom, it was heir to that century in another sense as well—in
its discovery of politics as the central activity of modern life. He
writes: "Rousseau is anxious to upgrade politics, and because of that
to believe that man might recover to some extent control over his

48. Einaudi, *Early Rousseau*, 278.

own life. Everything depends on politics, Rousseau tells us, and we must find a way of creating a community in which men, assisted by new institutions and acting upon the principles of a new civic virtue, can manage their life better than in the past."[49]

Not every episode of Einaudi's work was as synthetic or as aware of the integrating role of politics as this passage. If in *The Physiocratic Doctrine* he emphasized a generic economic theory to the detriment of political experience, in *Communism in Western Europe* and *Christian Democracy in Italy and France* he seemed caught up in the political experience of the early cold war. It was his classical idea of freedom, combined with the vision of his adopted country, that made it impossible for Einaudi to accept what he considered anticonstitutional parties as legitimate players in the democratic game. As long as communism remained a danger to freedom, Christian Democracy, despite sordid practices and uninspired leadership, had to be embraced as freedom's best hope.

If *Communism in Western Europe* and *Christian Democracy in France and Italy* reflected the political issues of their time, *Nationalization in Italy and France* and *The Roosevelt Revolution* had a more enduring message. In *Nationalization*, the theme of the centrality of politics attained a new level of understanding. As Peter Katzenstein shows in Chapter 7 of this volume, Einaudi was ahead of the economists in his understanding of economic policy, because he saw nationalization in essentially political terms. This allowed him to understand its role historically in the postwar reconstruction of Europe.

It was in *The Roosevelt Revolution* that Einaudi moved forward most boldly in his understanding of both freedom and democracy, for he saw in the New Deal the state as steward of society. Constitutionalism, he writes, is "the regulated application of humane and rational faculties to the task of guiding the political community toward common goals in an atmosphere that will recognize the supreme moral values inherent in the individual."[50] Through positive government and economic management, Einaudi argued, the New Deal brought about a revolution in American politics and (we may interpolate) a truer implementation of the idea of freedom than the false

49. Ibid., 277–78.
50. Einaudi, *Roosevelt Revolution*, 359–60.

centrism of either the Fourth French Republic or the Italian Christian Democratic regime.

Viewed from this perspective, Einaudi's early writings laid the theoretical groundwork for the empirical work of the French-Italian Inquiry, and the inquiry is best seen as an extended examination of the search for freedom within politics. Einaudi remains the dedicated constitutional liberal he had been in his early writings, and as *The Early Rousseau* proves, he is still devoted to an idea of constitutionalism which embraces both freedom and community. But in the interim, through experience, he recognized the primacy of politics to economics, and in representative democracies that means recognition of the need for a positive state.

Politics, for Einaudi, is the realm of experience in which humankind's capacity for folly is most apparent and can be most dangerous to constitutional government. But as for Rousseau, politics is also the realm in which the highest claims of theory can be realized. For the eighteenth-century philosophers, freedom had to be sought within institutions, and the highest quest was for institutions that would embody both freedom and civic virtue. What was true for the eighteenth-century philosophers, Einaudi teaches, must also be true for the twentieth-century political scientist—and so it is for our teacher, colleague, and friend Mario Einaudi, to whom we dedicate this book.

I

Physiocracy, the State, and Society: The Limits of Disengagement

STEVEN L. KAPLAN

IN THE WAKE of one bicentennial (American constitutional) and on the eve of another (French revolutionary), in the aftermath of the tumultuous Bork nomination and at the end of the Gallican experiment called cohabitation, it is particularly appropriate to reflect on the nature, the vocation, and the limits of state power. In his elegantly crafted and penetrating monograph *The Physiocratic Doctrine of Judicial Control*, Mario Einaudi explores the ways in which these reformers tried to shelter their system against error and excess.[1] That system was predicated upon absolute deference to the imperious laws of nature, as revealed by the irresistible force of *évidence*, accessible to anyone's rational contemplation. The first laws of nature were the "holy" right of property ("without which the other laws could not exist") and the concomitant power to dispose of property with "total liberty." Every form of social and political relation followed from

1. Mario Einaudi, *The Physiocratic Doctrine of Judicial Control* (Cambridge: Harvard University Press, 1938). My essay in this volume draws heavily on several of my earlier works: *Bread, Politics, and Political Economy in the Reign of Louis XV*, 2 vols. (The Hague: Martinus Nijhoff, 1976); *La Bagarre: Galiani's "Lost" Parody* (The Hague: Martinus Nijhoff, 1979); and "The Famine Plot Persuasion in Eighteenth-Century France," *Transactions of the American Philosophical Society* 72 (1982).

these "immutable laws of divine justice." The discovery of natural law showed people the range of their options (what they could do through positive law) and the scope of their errors (what they must do in order to make the best use of their lives, individually and collectively).[2]

As a consequence of their "science of the natural order," the physiocrats proposed ideas for changes in economic policy, financial administration, modes of political participation, education, and the structure of society—reforms that imposed themselves, in Einaudi's words, "as a rigid deduction" from certain unassailable principles.[3] For them the bulk of fundamental legislation was already accomplished, as Mirabeau phrased it, "ready-made, wholly natural, divine, universal, immutable, to which men can only add disorder."[4] The test of the validity of positive law, which governed everyday actions, lay in its compatibility with the standard of natural law. Only the "tutelary authority" of royal power would be strong enough, reckoned the physiocrats, to realize this natural order. But the authority of this prince, whom they styled "legal despot," would be severely circumscribed: it consisted merely in "announcing laws already necessarily made and arming them with coercive force."

The physiocrats worried, however, about the risks of princely abuse. In order to forestall the despot from transgressing the limits inscribed in nature, they envisioned in particular two ways to force him to comply. The first involved the mobilization of public opinion through education, propaganda, and incentives of reward and punishment. But the physiocrats were themselves not at all sure about which

2. See P.-P.-F.-J.-H. Lemercier de la Rivière, *L'Intérêt général de l'état* (Amsterdam, 1770), 49–65, 271, 377–78; Nicolas Baudeau, *Avis au peuple sur son premier besoin* (Amsterdam, 1768), 2–3; P. S. Du Pont de Nemours, "Vrais principes du droit naturel," *Ephémérides du Citoyen* 3 (1767): 102–3, 131–33, 160–61, 167; Etienne Bonnet de Condillac, *Le Commerce et le gouvernement considérés relativement l'un à l'autre* (1776), in E. Daire and G. de Molinari, eds., *Collection des principaux économistes* (Paris, 1868), 14:421; André Morellet, *Mémoires inédits de l'abbé Morellet* (Paris, 1821), 190; J.-P.-L. Luchet, *Examen d'un livre qui a pour titre "Sur la legislation et le commerce des bleds"* (n.p., 1775), 17, 40–41; anon., "Mémoire sur le commerce des grains," ca. 1788, Bibliothèque de l'Arsenal (hereafter cited as Arsenal), manuscrit (hereafter ms.) 7458, fol. 30; "Observations sur les effets de la liberté du commerce des grains, par l'auteur des *Ephémérides du Citoyen*," *Journal économique* (August 1770):348.

3. Einaudi, *Physiocratic Doctrine*, 10.

4. Cited in ibid., 24–25.

public to target, about the educability of opinion, especially in the short run, and about the implications of an appeal to opinion. The most supremely confident physiocratic exegetists, such as Lemercier de la Rivière, pretended not to doubt for an instant the ineluctable coalescence of opinion around the correct (that is, the natural) principles. His confidence was grounded in a tautological conceit familiar to all students of politics: if opinion does not embrace the truth, it can only be because it is inadequately or improperly enlightened. Du Pont was far less sanguine—at least in his early years of militancy—about the wisdom of counting on opinion, especially in moments of social stress. In terms of political practice, the physiocrats were committed to the right of publicists to explore all the aspects of public affairs and of the public to read about them.[5] But I suspect that at times they lamented with their archenemy, Séguier, advocate-general of the Paris Parlement, the loss of "the veil with which the prudence of our Fathers had enveloped all that which pertains to Government and Administration."[6] For the physiocrats public opinion meant apprehending and rehearsing the ABC's of *évidence*, not debating the options in the flawed language of contingency and relativism. Curiously Einaudi spares the physiocrats any reproach on this account, perhaps in part because he himself subscribed to an abstract and ahistorical notion of what he variously referred to as the "public mind" and the "popular mind."[7]

Because citizens could not be relied on to resist princely encroachment on natural law, the physiocrats—most of them, Einaudi gingerly reminds us—settled on the idea of judicial control, on the institution of a supreme magistracy charged with the task of declaring void those acts contrary to the first principles.[8] In some of his sharpest and most subtle pages, Einaudi defends first the general concept of judicial review "as an indispensable safeguard of the rights of individuals in a state" (remember the political, intellectual, and

---

5. André Morellet, *Réflexions sur les avantages de la liberté d'écrire et d'imprimer sur les matières de l'administration* (Paris, 1775). On this question, see the probing discussion of Keith Michael Baker, "French Political Thought at the Accession of Louis XVI," *Journal of Modern History* 50 (June 1978):289–91.

6. Arrêt du Parlement de Paris, 30 June 1775, cited by Baker, "French Political Thought," 291.

7. Einaudi, *Physiocratic Doctrine*, 47, 53.

8. Ibid., 22, 27–28, 88.

moral conditions of production of this study, published in 1938), and then the specific physiocratic version of it.[9] He evinces no patience with the failure of commentators to see the true character of the infelicitously baptized doctrine of legal despotism. Neither Tocqueville, with whom one should not uncritically identify Einaudi, nor Weulersse and Schelle, the foremost scholars of physiocracy, are absolved. Like himself, Einaudi's physiocrats were deeply suspicious of the power of the ruler and resolutely determined to hedge it rigorously: "it is clear that their monarch was a limited one . . . existing only for certain well-defined purposes and no others."[10] Instead of viewing legal despotism as an error and/or an aberration within the logic of physiocracy, Einaudi rehabilitated it as a necessary consequence of Quesnay's founding doctrine, the *Tableau économique*, and the means of realizing "radical changes in the economic system." In restituting legal despotism to the central place it had to have, Einaudi no less adamantly insists on the equally capital role of the "judicial guarantee" built into the system and devised to make it safe and trustworthy.[11]

There is a double polemical charge here: first, on the broadest plane, a challenge to pay more attention to political doctrine (if not yet to ideology tout court); second, a specific argument about the crucial articulation of legal despotism-*cum*-judicial control within the physiocratic system. The first point, prophetically sage, I hasten to accord (even as we historians have finally overcome the absurd and pernicious malediction that the new history—or was it the new new history?—cast on politics). The second point remains to be sorted out by scholars. I only address it obliquely, in terms of Einaudi's preoccupation with the theoretical problem of preventing and sanctioning overgovernment—the aggrandizement and perversion of power by the prince. In *The Physiocratic Doctrine* Einaudi largely restricts himself to the realm of ideas. His efforts to ground them historically in social and economic context are cursory and generally not convinc-

9. The quotation comes from Charles H. McIlwain's foreword to Einaudi, *Physiocratic Doctrine*, x.

10. Writing in an uncharacteristically polemical tone, Einaudi deplores the failure to seize "the real extent to which the physiocratic school identified itself with the doctrine of judicial control" (*Physiocratic Doctrine*, 8).

11. Ibid., 4–6, 8–10, 28.

ing.[12] The bulk of his corpus, however, testifies to a keen sensitivity to the play between theory and experience, and to the imperative of historicizing in order to explain. In what follows I shift the focus drastically to the actual itinerary of the physiocrats as reformers. In practice, "physiocratic power" posed a very different problem in the eyes of many French men and women drawn from the masses as well as the elite of eighteenth-century society. They complained not that the physiocratic prince was too despotic, but that he was insufficiently so. They dreaded not the violation of first principles, but the abandonment of the stewardship of the social order to the whimsy of nature. They reproached the physiocratic prince for being a spectator king—an oxymoronic, solecistic, and dangerous conception. The limit of royal disengagement in the 1760s and 1770s, at the apogee of physiocratic influence, was a bitterly experienced counterpoint to Mario Einaudi's study of the problem of shackling the legal despot.

As Einaudi stresses, the political theory of the physiocrats emerged from their economic analysis. Indeed, the physiocrats were known to contemporaries as the *économistes*. Virtually all of the major threads of their thinking converged on the question of the grain trade. No issue was more urgent, more pervasively felt, and more difficult to resolve than the matter of grain provisioning. Cereal dependence conditioned every phase of social life. Beyond its paramount role in agriculture, grain shaped the development of commerce and industry, regulated employment, and generated a large part of the income of the state, the church, the nobility, and substantial segments of the third estate. Subsistence needs gave cereal dependence its most telling expression. The vast majority of the people derived the bulk of their calories from cereals, in bread or some other form. Because this was an economy of scarcity and uncertainty, the dread of hunger haunted everyone. While cereal dependence buttressed deep cleavages between the haves and the have-nots, the consumers and the producers, and the city and the countryside, the subsistence obsession forged curious ties of solidarity between the governors and the governed. For a host of reasons connected with its own survival and expansion, the state

12. I am thinking, inter alia, about Einaudi's treatment of the genesis of physiocracy, his picture of French economic development, his neglect of the problem of social organization, his view of the parlements in monolithic terms, and his serious underestimation of the political impact of parlementary filibustering.

had traditionally pledged itself to the protection of the consumer interest through an elaborate policy of regulation and intervention. Consecrated by legend (the *héros nourriciers*) and religion, this commitment was symbolized by the king and embodied in the idea of king as father-to-his-people. Assuring their subsistence was not merely something the king did for his people; it was something he was expected and in some sense required to do. Victualer only in the last resort, the state depended on the grain trade to meet the needs of consumers. But it construed the trade as a quasi-public service and it subjected it to what was called its police.

In the view of the physiocrats, this policy was directly responsible for many of France's gravest ills: agricultural stagnation, commercial lethargy, fiscal devastation, rural depopulation, proliferating misery, political impasse, and more. Paternalism and *dirigisme* were onerous and counterproductive because they systematically violated the laws of nature. The physiocrats argued that grain was a commodity like any other, and should be so treated; that "police" was tantamount to theft; that low prices and real abundance were mutually exclusive and contradictory ambitions. Only a rigorous application of all-azimuth laissez-faire could transform the structure of production and distribution in such a way as to make painful shortage highly unlikely and famine virtually impossible. The emancipation of the grain trade represented the precondition and the take-off stage for their program to reinvigorate the economy and the management of public affairs. Joined in a powerful liberty lobby by other publicist-reformers, many officials at various levels of public administration, merchant interests, and landowners and grain growers and collectors, the physiocrats pressed the government to renounce its old, flawed fidelities and policies and to embark on a fresh, scientific course.

For various reasons the government was ready to venture such a new departure in 1763. Surrounded by a half dozen physiocratic advisers, Controller General Bertin had the king pronounce the most radical reform of the old regime: the dismantling of the entire apparatus of market control and the overt repudiation of the traditional social contract guaranteeing subsistence. The following year another dramatic measure permitted unlicensed exportation. By desacralizing grain in the name of nature and efficacy, the king changed fundamentally the relation between state and society. The old system was niggardly, pessimistic, suspicious, and prohibitive; the new would be generous, sanguine, trusting, and permissive. Oblivious to the social utility of economic egotism, the police approach stunted growth and initiative; liberty, through the harmonious concourse of self-interests and in conformity with "the order established by divine providence," would release constructive energies and encourage progress. Here was absolutism in the service of liberalism: the exercise of central authority to eradicate popular habit and expectation, administrative arbitrariness, anachronistic privileges and concessions, and widespread parochialism.[13] Liberalization presaged the eclipse of the marketplace as the regulatory bastion and the *idée force* of the old regime and foreshadowed the triumph of the market principle as the new ideology of economic exchange and social relations.[14] The liberal press hailed the new age and the new king with unbridled enthusiasm.

The buoyant climate in which liberty was greeted soon gave way to a mood of uncertainty and apprehension as the kingdom became engulfed in acute subsistence difficulties that, in many places, persisted in a more or less severe form for almost a decade. The period was characterized by the most serious and widespread outbreak of disorder in the long reign of Louis XV. The consumers/people became desperate as prices doubled and tripled, supplies became scarce, wages lagged behind prices, unemployment spread, and "panic terror" erupted. What began as a subsistence crisis swelled into a general economic and political crisis as well. A run of mediocre-to-catastrophic harvests triggered and then sustained the dearth. As the crisis widened and deepened, however, more and more contemporaries linked its onset and its virulence to the implementation of the radical grain reforms of 1763–64. If the new liberty itself did not cause the disarray, it dramatically exacerbated it by authorizing suppliers to withhold goods, to speculate, to export, to betray their traditional commitments. Unencumbered trade mimicked on its own the dislo-

13. On the "police" tradition, the physiocratic critique of that tradition, the formation of the liberty lobby, and the origins of the radical reforms of 1763–64, see Kaplan, *Bread, Politics, and Political Economy*, vol. 1.

14. Steven Laurence Kaplan, *Provisioning Paris: Merchants and Millers in the Grain and Flour Trade during the Eighteenth Century* (Ithaca: Cornell University Press, 1984), 23–33.

cating consequences of dearth, inducing many observers to wonder whether the shortages were not "artificial" (that is, man-made) rather than "real" (natural).

Even as the police and the consumers, often arrayed on the same side against the suppliers, turned the marketplaces into battlegrounds over liberalization, so the war over liberty broke out in the salons as well. While their critics denounced the reckless extremism of the liberal measures, the *économistes* deplored their timidity: the automatic export cutoff when the statutory ceiling price was triggered, the exceptions accorded to Paris to facilitate its provisioning, the insufficiently draconian policy of implementation at the local level. Nevertheless, despite these reservations, the physiocrats publicly defended the reform program with their usual ardor. Hoping to rally the support of the whole family of philosophes, they made the grain issue into *the* litmus test of enlightenment: those who adhered to the cause of liberty and to lean kingship constituted the forces of light, science, and progress; those who opposed it represented darkness and backwardness, and a specious and obsolete conception of bloated kingship. The *économistes* wrote letters, pamphlets, and articles exhorting and apologizing for the increasingly harried liberal ministry. They denounced the obstinate stupidity of the misguided consumers/people; the demagogy, venality, and ignorance of local officials; the tepidness and/or outright treason of many high officials and magistrates; and the perversity, blindness, and opportunism of their intellectual rivals.

There were grounds for hostility to physiocratic policy as expressed by three different groups: the people, the police, and the parlements. (Were I not constrained by space I would add a fourth category, the philosophes, in order to show how violently the grain debate buffeted and divided the putatively monolithic "party of humanity.") The most powerful cues for opposition came from below rather than from above. They were embodied in riots and *émotions* that battered the entire realm, especially the northern half, during the years following the reforms. I have counted over sixty within the jurisdictions of the Parlements of Paris and Rouen between 1765 and 1768; elsewhere there are scores of others to be noted. Though the cadence of disturbances abated during the following year, it rebounded smartly in 1770 and continued to jolt many parts of the kingdom through 1775.[15]

These risings shared a number of traits. They occurred in substantial towns as well as in more modest bourgs and hamlets. They struck towns located on or near rivers more frequently than those remote from water transportation. Most of the towns were entrepôt markets integrated more or less formally into a larger chain of provisioning serving a metropolitan center or feeding river traffic to the coast. For the most part the disturbances were indigenously and spontaneously generated, albeit the geographical and commercial relations of the towns sometimes suggested a process of contagion and emulation. Panic and rising prices were both causes and effects, though in the beginning panic often seemed to precede and to prime rising prices. Grain movement that once passed imperceptibly now aroused resentment and fomented resistance. Opposition to what contemporaries called "removals" and "exportation" of grain (which in this context meant nothing more than the transfer of grain from one community for use elsewhere, within the kingdom or abroad) was the form these risings habitually took. As long as grain seemed to be available it was merely a question of intercepting it and diverting it to the market, in most cases for relatively orderly distribution by sale to local consumers. When the grain seemed to disappear from circulation, consumers felt more desperate; instead of lying in wait for grain that might never materialize, they went after it where they suspected it was hidden. Women played a strikingly prominent role in these riots. It is not clear if they were predominantly wage earners themselves, if they were married or single, if they were housewives and mothers as well as partial providers; and if they participated with the approbation of their husbands, brothers, fathers, and sons. But these subsistence "furies" were in the forefront everywhere, and the authorities seemed to concede that in times of suffering and hunger, the women had an imperious mission to fulfill.

While the rioters, men and women, ascribed their misery at first to avid, profiteering merchants, ultimately they held the public authorities accountable for the irregular and threatening situation. When

15. See Kaplan, *Bread, Politics, and Political Economy*, 1:164–214, 2:563–82.

spontaneous and direct pressure on the traders failed to win tangible, immediate redress, the insurgents expected the police to intercede. Indeed, some of the *émotions* seemed to have aimed not so much at humbling the merchants as at making a point to the constabulary and providing it with a pretext for action. More often than not the grain riot of the sixties was a self-conscious political gesture rather than a tropismatic act of desperate frustration. It was the only mode of expression available to the bulk of consumers, and its demands were usually moderate and straightforward: the constant availability of grain (or bread) at a price within the means of the majority of the laboring poor. The rioters could not understand how public officials could allow the situation to get so far out of hand. In the past officials had tended to intervene preemptively. Now they appeared to stand by idly as their "constituents" were submerged in hardship. The aim of the rioters seems to have been to force the officials to assume their traditional responsibilities.

The local police comprehended the message clearly, and in many instances collaborated, overtly or covertly, with the rioters, at considerable professional risk to themselves. In these cases the police cited imminent threats of bloodshed and chaos as justification for embargoing or requisitioning grain, or imposing a generally recognized "just" price. At Bar-sur-Aube in May 1770 the police and the people together prevented the removal of supplies designated for shipment to Besançon. Shortly afterward officials at Libourne in the southwest, moved by the "desperation" of the people, visited private granaries in quest of grain, ordered merchants to declare their stocks, and "opposed the circulation of grain passing through the city."[16]

According to the royal procurator of Meaux in the summer of 1770, the combined effect of the protracted shortage and "a vice of commerce" which siphoned grain from the market was "terrible." The yawning "disproportion" between need and supply was "breaking up households of workers and country folk," reducing upright men to beggary, and threatening to detonate a wave of crime. Every day more and more people thronged about the marketplace aimlessly and nervously. One morning in the third week of July a phalanx of

16. Laroi to intendant of Champagne, 11 May 1770, C. 299, Archives Départementales (hereafter AD) Aube; procurator Lesberat to intendant of Bordelais, August 1770, C. 1431, AD Gironde.

famished consumers "made themselves masters of the sale and of the price of the grain." Patently sympathetic to the crowd, the procurator coolly portrayed the stand taken by the authorities: "Thus despite all the coordinated attention and vigilance of the police, the rural gendarmerie, and the subdelegate [of the intendant], it was necessary, while appearing to command, to cede to the populace and engage the grain-sellers to give their goods at forced discounts in order to prevent pillage." Similar action by authorities in Reims issued in an outburst of joyous relief and fraternization: "The people and the lowest people gathered in a crowd around the police commissaires and universally applauded the measures taken." The victims of such action pointedly denounced the league between the police and the people.[17]

The rioters made a riveting impression less because of their violence than because of their relative restraint, their suppleness, their lucidity. Manifestly, they were not brigands, riffraff, or outside agitators. They were well-known local consumers, most of whom had more or less spotless records. They arose in anger but not with mindless malevolence. They acted with the conviction that their grievances were just and that their right to existence—which was the state's business to guarantee—had been trampled. If many officials responded warmly, it was because they recognized the legitimacy of popular demands; or because they viewed price fixing as a conventional emergency tactic that could be applied exceptionally without establishing precedent—a relatively cheap and effective vehicle of social control. This perception was vigorously contested by the ministry, which enjoined officials to indulge none of the people's weaknesses. Impetuously and erroneously the people believed that their right to subsist took precedence over all the rights prescribed by natural law as the basis of social organization, lamented Bertin's successor as controller general, Laverdy. The people misconceived the role of government and its proper relation to the citizenry. "The people," Laverdy bemoaned, "hardly used their reason in matters of subsistence."[18]

17. Canelle to procurator general, 21 July 1770, Bibliothèque Nationale (hereafter BN), Collection Joly de Fleury (hereafter Joly) 1151, fols. 55–56; lieutenant of police to intendant of Champagne, 12 July 1770, C. 414, AD Marne.

18. Laverdy to Cypierre, September 1768, cited by Camille Bloch, "Le Commerce des grains dans la généralité d'Orléans," in *Etudes sur l'histoire économique de la France (1760–1789)* (Paris: Picard et fils, 1910), 43.

Surely the bulk of police officials who dealt with these problems day to day would have found it singularly fatuous to rebuke the people for being unreasonable when they were hungry, impoverished, or simply anxious. It was the job of the authorities to be reasonable about provisioning; for the public, especially in time of stress, it was virtually impossible to avoid subsistence terror. Insofar as popular fears were often imaginary—a fact that had little bearing on the clinical state of fright or its consequences—and popular solutions were illegal and myopic, Laverdy would not acknowledge them either as manifestations of an authentic problem or even as genuine symptoms of a congenital psychosomatic disorder.

To vanquish this mentality, the controller general opted to deprecate and insult it with all the sophistry of progressive thinking. It consisted of nothing more than a crazy quilt of "prejudices." "Prejudice" was one of the harshest epithets in the political vocabulary of the Enlightenment; it acquired added force when accompanied by Laverdy's favorite metaphors, light and sight. Their prejudices "blinded the people" not only to the "veritable principles of things" but also to "their true interests." Though he knew that it urgently had to be done and that it would be extremely difficult, he had no concrete plan for "breaking the old chain of prejudices." Only a tough, unbending stance would produce results. "By stiffening against the prejudices of the people," he predicted, "they will gradually weaken and we will succeed in accustoming them to a *bien*," though, he conceded, "they will continue to misjudge [it] for some time to come." The specter of bullying them into submission was the only real incentive the controller general offered the people to embrace the liberal program.[19]

Persuaded that liberalization was salutary and necessary, Laverdy rejected the notion that it could be materially responsible for the host of riots and disruptions. In none of the uprisings was there "any [au-

19. Laverdy to procurator general, 11 November and 4 December 1765, BN, Joly 1131, fols. 9, 24; Laverdy to same, 23 October 1766, Joly 1109, fols. 145–46; Laverdy to Miromesnil, 31 December 1767, in *Correspondance politique et administrative de Miromesnil, premier président du Parlement de Normandie*, ed. P. Leverdier (Rouen: Picard et fils, 1899–1903), 5:70; Laverdy to Lescalopier, intendant of Touraine, July 1764, C. 94, AD Indre-et-Loire.

thentic] motive for fear," only the "frivolous and illusory pretext" for precipitate action. Or, as a liberal journal serenely put it, the riots "are not and *cannot* be the effects of real need" because in a regime of laissez-faire "the dearth that the enraged minds fear, or feign to fear, is patently impossible."[20] To dispel the idea that consumers could riot without cost Laverdy instructed the police after every episode to repress and punish with dispatch and without pity.[21] To disabuse the public of the idea that popular demonstrations would compel the fatherly king to renounce liberalization, the controller general asked officials at all levels of administration to make it plain that nothing could induce the government to waver. Publicize the point, he enjoined them, that the liberal laws are "fixed and invariable," "perpetual and irrevocable." Even if the people did not understand the laws, they must realize that the laws cannot be changed under any circumstances.[22]

No wonder that an increasingly bitter, suspicious, and subversive strain marked expressions of popular opinion. In September 1768 a badly spelled and crudely worded wall poster in Paris "warned" the king "to get rid of Messrs Choiseul [foreign minister] and Laverdy, who, with a troop of thieves, cause grain to be removed outside the kingdom" or else thirty thousand men would do the job for him "at an unexpected moment." Similarly devised posters, ascribed to *"gens de peu de chose,"* threatened to torch "the four corners of Paris" unless the king put a stop to "eating dear bread." At the end of October authorities found "a large, badly written poster containing horrors and imprecations against the King." Betraying deep disenchantment

20. Laverdy to procurator general, October 1766, BN, Joly 1132, fol. 12; Laverdy to same, 13 September 1765, Joly 1131, fols. 92–93; Laverdy to same, 23 October 1766, Joly 1109, fols. 145–46; Laverdy to Miromesnil, 9 February and 2 March 1768, *Correspondance*, 5:82, 135; "Supplement aux Journaux de l'agriculture, du commerce et des finances," September 1765, C. 80, AD Somme.

21. Laverdy to procurator general, 22 June and 12 July 1767, BN, Joly 1136, fols. 179, 181; Laverdy to bishop of Angers, 13 September 1765, Archives Nationales (hereafter AN), F¹²* 150; dépêche to B. de Sauvigny, intendant of Paris, 10 April 1768, AN, O¹* 410, fols. 219–20; Laverdy to procurator general, 23 October 1766, Joly 1109, fols. 145–46.

22. Laverdy to procurator general, 13 September 1765, AN, F¹²* 150; Laverdy to Lescalopier, 28 August 1765, AN, F¹²*; Laverdy to Lescalopier, September 1765, C. 94, AD Indre-et-Loire.

with Louis XV, it reproached him for abdicating the traditional pa-
ternalistic kingship, and it hinted bodefully that he had a venal interest
in prolonging the suffering of his subjects:

> Under Henri IV we suffered a dearth of bread occasioned by the wars,
> but during this time we had a king; under Louis XIV we similarly
> experienced several other dearths of bread, produced sometimes by the
> wars, sometimes by real shortages caused by bad weather, but we still
> had a king; in the present time the dearth of bread can be attributed
> neither to wars nor to a real shortage of grain; but we don't have a
> king, for the king is a grain merchant.

The poster concluded by recalling Damiens's attempt to assassinate
the king in 1757, intimating that such a fate would not be unworthy
of the apostate-monarch and that men capable of such a murder were
prepared to strike.[23]

The liberal laws deprived the local police of the basic tools they felt
they needed for the maintenance of public order. By permitting anyone to enter the grain trade, to form associations or companies, to
circumvent the official market, and to deal secretly, and by openly
encouraging speculation and higher prices, the new regime legiti-
mized practices that had till now been considered heinous antisocial
crimes. Henceforth the authorities could not take action to guarantee
the supply of the market and the docility and honesty of the suppliers.
Local officials did not conceal their malaise over the deepening subsistence crisis and their misgivings about government policy. Significantly they did not focus on crop failure as the primary source of
unrest, though there was considerable empirical evidence to support
such a hypothesis and the allure of a clinical explanation that largely
absolved human agencies from responsibility. The immediate causes
to which the local police ascribed the upheavals of the sixties were
abrupt grain exports and removals, bristling resentment of grain and
flour traders, prolonged penury, misery, and high prices. But they
also described a general state of mind, a pervasive and terrible anxiety—they called it "agitation" or "fermentation"—and a state of so-

---

23. Roland, commissaire of police, to procurator general, 21 September 1768, Joly
1139, fol. 54; Leblanc, commissaire, to same, 28 September 1768, Joly 1139, fol. 55;
Roland to same, 21 September 1768, Joly 1139, fol. 56; Hardy's Journal, 31 October
1768, BN, manuscrit français (hereafter ms. fr.) 6680, fol. 183.

cioeconomic anarchy, both of which they linked to the new liberal regime.

The dismantling of the regulatory apparatus frightened, perplexed, and sometimes shocked the administrators. Very few of them simply turned their backs on the new legislation, though it was often tempting and circumspect to claim ignorance. Rather they faced it, tried to cope with it, and found that it prompted for them a crisis of conscience as well as one of authority. For it seemed dangerous and wrong-headed to undermine the public order and security by abandoning the grain trade to a concourse of self-interests. Despite its shortcomings, the old system engendered for the community a semblance of solidarity and a sense of accountability, and it frequently managed to attenuate the margin of unpredictability and mitigate the consequences of accidents. Now wheat, which habitually furnished a given market, succumbed to strange blandishments. New dealers pullulated in grain commerce, brandishing the liberal code as if it were a special royal patent, thereby exacerbating the standard dearth-syndrome fears of plots and maneuvers. Ordinary people, with neither criminal dispositions nor antisocial motives, arose in revolt. A refrain of frustration and anomie arose from the police, chanted by the intendant of the region as well as by the fiscal procurator of the town: "Our hands are tied"—what should we do? Many of the disturbances of the sixties were police as well as popular revolts, riots for rather than against an ostensibly dated version of the *chose publique*. In this sense popular behavior and administrative attitude constituted the foundations of a grass-roots movement for the recall of the reform measures of 1763 and 1764.

Though a cynical observer might advance that they were merely contriving pretexts to justify their intractability, many local authorities appear to have viewed the liberal laws with genuine bafflement and incredulity. Like the people, the police had certain expectations and beliefs about the conduct of government. There were certain steps that they simply could not believe the government—personified in their minds by the king himself—would take. "If, by the Declaration of 1763," the fiscal procurator of Châtillon-sur-Loire wrote his intendant, "the King seems to have given commerce a certain liberty that it did not have heretofore, *His intention surely was not* to strip the police officers *of the right* they have to prevent grain from being sold anywhere but in the public marketplaces. . . . the sole precaution capable of procuring abundance in the markets and, consequently, the just price of grain." Similarly, the interim royal procurator at Montargis rejected as "a false interpretation" of liberalization the claim intoned by the traders that the new laws authorized transactions outside the marketplace. These were "abuses" that were certainly "contrary to the intentions of His Majesty," for Louis XV "had no less in view [the aim] of providing for the provisioning of the markets and the needs of His people" than of favoring commerce. Despite a welter of contrary evidence, a subdelegate in the Hainaut persisted in thinking that "the intention of His Majesty was never to alter the general police established to procure abundance."[24]

Building on the same premises, a Beauce procurator drafted an interpretive brief in which he argued that the reform laws did not grant as much liberty as everyone supposed. "The Declaration of 1764 [*sic*]," he maintained, "gives liberty of commerce, but it does not give that of buying and of selling grain clandestinely, in the taverns, or on a mere sample." Though in fact the liberal legislation licensed all these practices, it was inconceivable to the procurator that this could be. Groping to make sense of the events that were threatening to engulf their community, the municipal officers of Châlons-sur-Marne wishfully forecast that liberalization could not last much longer because it was so wildly at odds with the functions of kingship. "It is still true," they comforted themselves, "that the King is the common father to his subjects and that His heart is repelled by the idea that some of those who have the good fortune to live under His laws are exposed to another bread shortage by the inability to meet the price to which grain is being pushed by the continuation of exports."[25]

The most common feeling expressed by the local officials was a mélange of confusion and impotence. Convinced that there was a

24. Cypierre to Trudaine de Montigny, 18 October 1768, and Montargis police register, October 1768, cited in Camille Bloch, *Le Commerce des grains dans la généralité d'Orléans d'après la correspondance inédite de l'intendant Cypierre* (Orléans, 1898), 135–38, 153–55; subdelegate at Valenciennes to intendant, 22 July 1770, C. 6690, AD Nord.

25. Procurator of Angerville-la-Gaste to procurator general, BN, Joly 1148, fol. 65; municipality of Châlons to Laverdy, 29 December 1767, C. 413, AD Marne.

mistake in the legislation that could be administratively rectified, that the central authorities lacked information about the true state of affairs, or that, as in the past, exceptions would be readily made to accommodate local peculiarities, they besieged the procurator general of the Paris Parlement and their intendants with petitions for clarification and precise instructions. In the fall of 1766 the lieutenant general of police of Vitry-le-François painted a dismal picture of his town's provisioning situation. A swarm of merchants descended on the market, stripping it bare; others prowled the countryside, buying, hoarding, and propelling prices up. He complained that the Declaration of 1763, by introducing freedom of commerce everywhere, crippled him. Within the confines of the law, he could do nothing, but he knew exactly the sort of measures that the circumstances required: "I dare not undertake anything without the authority of My Superiors; consequently, I have the honor of supplicating Your Grandeur to please authorize me to have a sufficient quantity of grain brought to the market to be sold to the people."

Four years later the situation had not substantially changed. Without workable powers of police, the city administrators could do nothing to ease misery or preempt revolt. Faced with an "extremely urgent" predicament, the royal procurator asked Joly de Fleury for permission to use old-fashioned constraints, darkly hinting that whatever his response the force of circumstances would compel the municipal officers to defy the liberal regime:

> We will soon be reduced to having no more bread if you do not have the kindness to support the officers of police. We cannot do otherwise than to interdict the transport of grain; we no longer have any choice. In 1768 the Parlement overturned a sentence of the lieutenant of police of this city which condemned to a fine several individuals who had refused to bring grain to the market. *We respect the arrêt without being able to understand it.* Nevertheless, Monseigneur, we cannot take any other course; we are forced to do it in order to prevent some excessive outburst on the part of the people.[26]

In 1767 the police at Mantes told the procurator general that they no longer knew how to fulfill their functions. Liberalization severely disrupted commercial transactions in this busy market port. In exe-

26. Deballidart to procurator general, 6 July 1770, BN, Joly 1152, fol. 175.

cution of the laws, the police suspended prohibitions on purchasing, selling, and regrating; a host of newcomers plunged into the grain trade; and consumers lost the right to meet their needs before traders entered the market. Convinced that the dearth and misery of the times were a direct result of the new system, the authorities of Mantes wanted to know if there were any loopholes in the reform bills. Are all "prosecutions of evil doers forbidden?" they inquired. The liberal laws perplexed the lieutenant general of Dreux. Have they changed all the old rules and definitions? he wondered. Does the "great liberty" of 1763 permit the purchase and resale of grain at the same market, a price-swelling practice rigorously prohibited according to traditional ways? Do I treat men who commit such abuses as "monopolists?" queried the lieutenant. Do we understand correctly, asked the municipality of Angers, that "according to the current System of the Council it must no longer be a question [for the police] of taking measures to assure the subsistence of the people?" The fiscal procurator of Tournan in the Brie testified to the success of liberalization from the point of view of the suppliers. "Ever since the Declaration of the King which authorizes freedom of trade," he related, "all the merchants, *blatiers*, and regraters have considered themselves to be free to disregard the regulations of the police." In order to overcome the subsistence crisis the procurator contended that it was "of an indispensable necessity" to implement those rules. A Breton subdelegate warned of serious disorders unless the police were rearmed to battle the "avarice" upon which the new legislation has bestowed a "total liberty." Ganneron, royal procurator of Dammartin, a market near the capital, watched helplessly as the suppliers traded privately and irresponsibly, inflated the prices, and created a situation likely to produce famine, crime, and dire hardships. "Because the Declaration of the King ties my hands," he wrote, inviting the procurator general to unbind him, "I can do nothing without new orders."[27]

The most daring critics within the local administration spoke out

27. Chedde to procurator general, 26 September 1767, BN, Joly 1146, fols. 143–44; lieutenant general of police of Dreux to same, 9 January 1769, BN, Joly 1146, fols. 104–5; municipality of Angers, mémoire, 1769, C. 96, AD Indre-et-Loire; fiscal procurator of Tournan to procurator general, 22 December 1770, Joly 1155, fol. 18; Pravalon of Lannion to intendant of Brittany, 6 October 1768, C. 1652, AD Ille-et-Vilaine; Ganier to procurator general, 18 June 1770, Joly 1149, fols. 118–19.

vehemently against the system spawned by "Modern Philosophy." "The *cherté* of grain seems to me to have its origin in the dispositions of the edict of the month of July 1764," argued the subdelegate of Avesnes in the Hainaut. The key test for him was that "the unlimited liberty accorded by this law has made more *malheureux* than *heureux*." "The frantic license, the avarice, and the cupidity" unleashed by the liberal reforms, he affirmed, "have shattered and sundered all the ties and the chains that should naturally link one part of the nation to the other, that is to say, the owners of the land, the farmers, and the country folk [on the one side] with the businessmen, the artisans, the workers, and the dwellers of the towns and cities [on the other]." Even as it emancipated grain, the liberal laws enslaved the majority of the French: "Three-quarters of the French nation has become within a year tributary to the other quarter." Bertinière, *substitut* at Melun, held the new legislation directly responsible for the widespread scarcity and turmoil: "The awful circumstance to which the people find themselves reduced by the abrupt *cherté* of grain . . . is prompted neither by the penury of grain nor of harvests but solely by the rapacity of evil-intentioned men who use the general liberty of the trade to buy at any price in order to hoard." Profoundly shocked by the fruits of liberalization and the ostensible indifference of the government toward them, the royal procurator at Meulan confided in Joly de Fleury:

> I respect and I submit myself to its [the council's] decrees. *But as a good citizen I cannot keep silent* on the effects of the exportation of grain abroad [further along in the letter he makes it clear that he means "extraordinary removals" regardless of the ultimate destination] which it was believed necessary to permit in order to encourage agriculture. But, Monseigneur, if this good results, we see that there is born in my opinion a terrible evil for the public in general.[28]

For certain officials the moral and political failure of liberalization was ultimately more compelling ground for objection than pragmatic arguments bearing on social control and public interest. In some way or another they acknowledged that the people had rights and claims vis-à-vis the government and vis-à-vis property owners, and that the

28. "Réflexions sur l'édit du mois de juillet 1764," ca. October 1770, C. 6690, AD Nord; Bertinière to procurator general, 29 September 1767, BN, Joly 1136, fols. 124–25; royal procurator at Meulan to same, 1 October 1766, Joly 1134, fols. 11–12 (my italics).

liberal laws had transgressed those rights and ignored those claims. From our perspective their stand might seem remarkably bold or aberrant, for we are not accustomed to uncovering what appear to be the harbingers of sans-culottic ideology or the remnants of archaic communal solidarity in the lowest echelons of provincial administration in old-regime, backwater France. But to the officials who espoused it this position was a commonplace perfectly in harmony with their world. Like many other towns in the late 1760s, Chartres suffered from exorbitantly high prices, grain shortage, and proliferating "misery," which the municipal officials blamed on the license for "monopoly" granted by the Declaration of May 1763. Even as the partisans of liberty had looked to nature for laws capable of freeing them from the constraints of the positive laws of traditional monarchy, so the police of Chartres invoked a higher law to justify their dissent. Though the Declaration of May 1763 rendered internal trade totally free, they argued that there were explicit bonds and obligations from which no piece of legislation could free citizens, highborn or low. Whatever the law stipulated, the liberty of May must "always remain subject to the *rules of justice,* subordinated to the *rights of humanity.*"[29] Abstract and threadbare to our eyes, this formula nevertheless comes closest to capturing the outraged mood of the consumers at the marketplaces. Put into operational terms by the Chartres police, it meant that they had the responsibility, and by logical extension the authority, to combat the abuses of an unchecked liberty that led to monopoly and then to misery.

In accounting for popular disturbances, officials everywhere insisted on the loathing consumers felt to see "the grain [that was] naturally destined for their subsistence" slip out of their hands. In the view of the subdelegate of Quimper in Brittany, the people had "rights" over "commodities of first necessity," at least in times when scarcity threatened to deprive them of their sustenance. "I would dare to say," he continued in a language that is maladroit yet plain in meaning, "that whatever the functions that have regulated property might be, each individual is in the right to say that what is necessary to make up his subsistence cannot be renounced for him by someone else when he cannot procure it by dint of his own work alone." An astute

29. 2 September 1768, B. 3953, fol. 82, AD Eure-et-Loire (my italics).

observer, the subdelegate was alert to the implications of this credo, which invested the propertyless with rights and fastened restrictions on the rights of property and the propertied. "These maxims would be dangerous if they were spread among the people," he allowed, "but they are salutary and sacred in the studies of Princes and of the persons who govern."[30] That is to say, it was not up to the people themselves to take consciousness of their rights and lay claim to them. In order to preserve the social order, it was the vocation of the police to enforce these rights for the people, preemptively and without fanfare. Riots were proof of police dereliction, for if the public officials discharged their responsibilities properly, the citizenry would never find it necessary to mutiny. Though crudely fashioned, this subdelegate's thesis anticipated the analysis of Necker and other proponents of government intervention in provisioning affairs. On the local level, it meant that the police had frequently to act, in the phrase of a subdelegate from Champagne, as the "representative" of the people.[31]

A burgeoning number of officials passed beyond utterances of bewilderment, admonition, and expostulation to direct action. In addition to price fixing, the police in places widely dispersed throughout the realm intervened by intercepting supplies on the road or preventing their departure from the town or village, constraining all exchanges to take place exclusively on the marketplace under the public gaze, levying supply quotas on merchants or obliging them to appear regularly at the local market in return for permission to trade in the area, requiring dealers to register with authorities, inspecting granaries and private homes suspected of containing hoards, and taking inventories of all grain held in storage. Of the officials who stopped to reflect on the significance of their actions, most appear, like Masson of Arcis-sur-Aube, to have suffered a jarring emotional strain and to have ulcerated about their disobedience even when they were sure that what they were doing was necessary and right. Yet the mass of interventions were remarkably unspectacular, and it may very well be that the bulk of the police who undertook them acted unselfconsciously and instinctively, as they always had in times of stress "from

30. Durun to intendant of Brittany, 11 February 1772, C. 1725, AD Ille-et-Vilaine.

31. Gehier (Bar-sur-Aube) to intendant of Champagne, 10 January 1775, C. 299, AD Aube.

time immemorial," oblivious or indifferent to the new laws, like the commissaire of Nogent-le-Rotrou, the syndic of Montrésor, or the judge of Pompiez. Many of them simply did not apprehend or acknowledge an incongruity between their conception of their duties and their coercive options, on the one hand, and the imperatives of liberalization on the other. Certainly many of these officials were astonished the first time they received a rebuke from their superiors or notification that one of their sentences had been overturned by a higher jurisdiction.[32]

The failure of the police to implement the liberal policy with staunchness elicited angry protests, first from traders and factors directly aggrieved by their conduct, and later from *économistes* and other liberal partisans who accused them frankly of sabotaging the new regime. Sieur Montgolfier, an enterprising Brie grain and flour trader who also ran his own mill, expressed the irritation and sense of insecurity of many merchants. During the summer and fall of 1767 at Rebais, Coulommiers, and nearby markets, mobs looted his wagon convoys, attacked his emissaries, and harassed him in his day-to-day enterprises. The royal constabulary remained "a tranquil spectator of events that it should foresee and prevent." In chorus with Laverdy the merchant warned that the "continued inaction" of the police served to "authorize" and incite "the perturbers of commerce."[33]

The physiocrats fervently and doggedly denounced the treachery of the field police. "The inferior police required to maintain the execution of the Declaration of 1763 and the Edict of 1764," wrote Roubaud, "seem to ignore them, and for the sake of the well-being of the people, they aggravate public fears, the price spiral, and the dearth by destroying liberty, despite the solemn dispositions of the law." Every judge and officer has "erected himself into interpreter and arbiter of the law" and every day they violate the law "drawing on the Old Regulations expressly revoked by the same law." "One of the most disastrous effects of the regulations," noted the liberal Parlement of Grenoble in an address to the monarch, was to "have habituated the

32. Masson to intendant of Champagne, 29 May 1770, C. 299, AD Aube; B. 2376, AD Eure-et-Loire; Haberty to intendant (?), 4 September 1765, C. 94, AD Indre-et-Loire; Bouget to intendant of Bordelais, 28 June 1770, C. 1431, AD Gironde.

33. November 1767, BN, Joly 1135, fol. 80.

people to hold the government responsible for high prices or dearth."
The police, Roubaud complained, intervened in response to popular
cues that they themselves inculcated, while the people perceive such
interloping as a model and sanction for riot, plunder, and popular
price fixing. Turgot deplored the inclination of the police in his own
jurisdiction to emulate "the people" in their "reasoning" on liberty
and the grain question.[34]

The critics blamed the police fronde variously on ingenuous dolt-
ishness, rank venality, corporate narcissism, demagogic self-indulgence or manipulation, and reactionary ideology. Laverdy toiled ar-
duously to bring the police into line. He railed at officials who
showed laxity in dealing with breaches of the liberal laws or with
disruptions of public order. Authorities who "welcomed . . . the
complaints of the people" or betrayed "overblown anxieties" in applying the liberal laws were upbraided, suspended, and occasionally
dismissed.[35] Though his will never flagged, the controller general's
campaign to discipline the police was at best only a limited success.
He failed to anticipate both the depth and the breadth of official dis-
affection. He underestimated not so much police attachment to habit
as the extent to which this attachment was selective and derived from
a rational and empirical approach to their work. He misunderstood
not their particularism but the conditions—structural and circum-
stantial—which made the officials helpless as well as unwilling to abjure that particularism. Laverdy lacked the means and the information
to deal with this resistance effectively and discreetly. Chronic but
only spasmodically manifest, often unreported or brought to light
long after the fact, characteristically sober and elliptical rather than

34. Pierre-J.-A. Roubaud, *Représentations aux magistrats, contenant l'exposition rai-
sonné des faits relatifs à la liberté du commerce des grains, et les résultats respectifs des règlemens
et de la liberté* (London, April 1769), 39, 80, 93; "Avis du Parlement de Dauphiné . . .
au Roi," 26 April 1769, in *Ephémérides du Citoyen* 7 (1769):156; Turgot, "Lettre circulaire aux officiers de police dans les lieux où il y a des marchés de grains," 15 February
1766, C. 479, AD Haute-Vienne; *Journal économique* (April 1770):173.

35. Laverdy to Flesselles, 25 September 1765, AN, F^{12*} 150; Laverdy to procurator
general, 20 June 1766, BN, Joly 1133, fols. 94–95; Laverdy to intendant of Champagne, 5 June 1767, C. 1908, AD Aube; Laverdy to procurator general, 5 October
1766, Joly 1134, fol. 30; Laverdy to Ducluzel, intendant of Touraine, 20 July 1768,
C. 96, AD Indre-et-Loire; Laverdy to municipality of Châlons, 11 January 1768,
C. 413, AD Marne.

shrill and defiant, and scattered in scores of tiny cavities throughout the realm, each of which had its own peculiarities, this opposition could not be quashed in a single stroke.

Contested by the crowd of police from below, Laverdy also had to face defections from the elite of the grand police. Some intendants, such as Lebret of Brittany, Montyon of Auvergne, and Turgot of the Limousin, officially underwrote the ministry's hard line by enjoining local officials to implement the liberal laws zealously, repress popular disturbances, and protect commerce, or face "severe" punishment for "negligence." Yet not even Lebret could swallow the controller general's assertion that the *cherté* in the first years after liberalization was the fruit of "a lack of liberty." On the contrary, the intendant of Brittany squarely attributed the dearth and "uprisings of the people" to "the liberty that has been accorded for the export of grain." Rouillé d'Orfeuil, intendant of Champagne, felt acutely the tension between the imperatives of liberty and the exigencies of everyday public administration. Despite the explicit contraindications of the liberal laws, De la Corée, intendant of Franche-Comté, remained certain that it was "the sacred obligation" of merchants "to supply grain at a just and moderate price." De Gourgues of Montauban, La Galaizière of Lorraine, and Taboureau des Réaux of Hainaut were among the other royal commissioners who claimed to have voiced sharp warnings about the perils of the new system.[36]

The story of Cypierre, intendant of the Orléanais, is instructive, for he was politically and ideologically sympathetic to the liberal cause and had been among the first within the higher levels of public administration to call for exportation. Publicly he remained a faithful servant of royal policy. "I parade the advantages of complete liberty," he reassured the ministry; "I censure all the [police] orders that might contradict it." Privately, however, Cypierre acerbically criticized

36. Lebret to subdelegates, 29 September 1765, and Lebret draft, 18 September 1765, C. 1670, AD Ille-et-Vilaine; Laverdy to intendant of Bordelais, 28 September 1766, C. 1425, AD Gironde; Turgot, "Lettre circulaire," 15 February 1766, C. 479, AD Haute-Vienne; Montyon to police officials of Mauriac, 20 March 1770, C. 907, and to municipality of Giat, 10 April 1770, C. 910, AD Puy-de-Dôme; Rouillé to Bertin, 25 July 1768, C. 413, AD Marne; De la Corée to Terray, September 1770, C. 844, AD Doubs; De Gourgues to Terray, 16 December 1771, AN, F¹¹ 223; de la Galaizière to Terray, 30 December 1771, F¹¹ 223; Taboureau to Laverdy, November 1767, C. 6690, AD Nord.

the policy that "tied my hands" and reduced him to serving, along-side lesser officials, as one of the helpless "spectators of the different monopolies." It was an untenable position, for him as well as for his subordinates, for it undermined their authority and their credi-bility. The "people" of this circumscription, "victims" of the mo-nopolies, Cypierre complained, "see in *me* the author of their misery because they compare my silence with the firmness that my prede-cessor M. Barentin showed in similar circumstances, without wish-ing to understand that the law is no longer the same." The intendant scoffed at Laverdy's contention that the "evil" was in the "mind"—Cypierre's no less than the people's—rather than in the facts. Mo-nopoly was no less real than the poverty, unemployment, and dis-array that one noticed wherever one gazed. Nor could all the philosophy in the salons change the way the consumers/people felt about subsistence: "The people will never calmly stand by as their markets are stripped, as grain wagons traverse the marketplace en route to faraway destinations, not as long as they do not have bread."[37]

Ultimately dissidence emanating from the corps of intendants con-stituted a far less serious menace to the liberal system than hostility from the other claimants to the grand police, the magistrates of the parlements. They could not remain indifferent to the joint litany of agonistic protest voiced by police and people. The parlements were responsible, each in its region, for the maintenance of public order and for the execution of the laws of the land by the local authorities. Indeed, most local police officials were directly a part of the juridico-administrative hierarchy that led from the humblest jurisdiction of a royal procurator to the olympian summit occupied by the procurator general of the parlement. By means of this apparatus, the parlements were closer to the field police and better informed about local condi-tions than the royal ministry. Through the exercise of the grande po-lice, the parlements also competed with the king for the title of "father

37. Cypierre to Trudaine de Montigny, 16 October 1768, in Bloch, *Commerce des grains*, 134; Cypierre to bishop of Orléans, 23 September 1768, in ibid., 81; Cypierre to Trudaine, 1 and 7 September 1768 and to Laverdy, 24 September 1768, in ibid., 51, 62, 101; Cypierre to Sartine, October 1768, in ibid., 113; Cypierre to St.-Florentin, 2 September 1768, in ibid., 55–56; Cypierre to Laverdy, 15 August 1768 and mémoire, November 1768, in ibid., 48–49, 155–59.

of the people." Mordant critics of royal policy in many domains throughout the first half of the eighteenth century, the parlements did everything they could to foster their grass-roots popularity in portraying themselves as protectors of the people against the rapacity, arbitrariness, and torpor of the central government.

From the beginning the parlements were deeply involved in the experience of liberalization. Initially, all of them endorsed the reforms, albeit with widely varying degrees of enthusiasm or trepidation. Once the kingdom was plunged into disarray, the parlements spoke up with increasing vehemence. But the striking fact is that they did not cry out with a single voice, as they are generally presumed to have done on all the major issues of the time. (They did not act like Mario Einaudi's—or Robert R. Palmer's—unitary "Parliament.")[38] Quite on the contrary, they were sharply divided on the question of the liberty of the grain trade and its wide-ranging political implications. Paris and Rouen led the opposition to liberalization, while the "southern" courts of Toulouse, Aix, and Grenoble championed the reforms. The other parlements tended to gravitate from a more or less sympathetic to a negative posture as the crisis deepened. The divisions among the magistrates sprang not from differences in individual material interests (in terms of investments, *pace* Beard, magistrates in all the courts resembled one another strikingly), but from divergent ideologies and conceptions of the relation between state and society, and perhaps from differences in regional economic structure.[39] Particularly critical here was the position of the Paris sovereign court, which became the leading critic of royal policy. These magistrates believed that they faced not only a grave subsistence crisis but also a crisis in the nature of kingship.

Beginning in December 1767 the Paris Parlement appealed to the monarch to "take measures to facilitate the subsistence of the poor people." The king rebuffed this overture and several others undertaken by the court during the spring and early fall of the next year. Even as the government insisted that "the causes of the dearth are physical and do not depend on the will of those who govern," so the

38. Einaudi, *Physiocratic Doctrine*, 50–51; Robert R. Palmer, *The Age of the Democratic Revolution: A Political History of Europe and America, 1760–1800* (Princeton: Princeton University Press, 1959), 1:41–44, 86–99, 448–58.

39. On the parlements, see Kaplan, *Bread, Politics, and Political Economy*, 1:166–86, 2:408–90.

Parlement asked the king to consider "if these bread shortages, these public alarms, these popular riots do not have their hidden principle in some defect of the new system." In November 1768 the king replied that if problems had indeed arisen, it was not, as a number of sovereign courts contended, because of too much liberty, but because there was too little—that is, the reform legislation had "not been executed in its entirety in several provinces . . . as a result of the fears that swelled in the minds of a large part of our subjects and principally of those who were specifically charged with its execution."[40]

While the king reproved the volatility of the people, exacerbated by the spinelessness of the police, the Paris Parlement reminded the sovereign that in matters of subsistence the "voice of the people is the voice of God," and resolved not to permit the ministry to "tie the hands" and "shut the mouths" of the officials. Liberty was "legitimate," contended the Parlement, to the extent that it was "compatible with the public interest"; it lost legitimacy the moment it clearly began to ravage that interest. By instituting the new system, the king showed that he misconceived the public interest. By maintaining it, Louis placed the kingdom in jeopardy and failed in his primary responsibility to his subjects: to make it possible for them to find bread sufficient to meet their needs and commensurate with their means. Ultimately the question concerned the legitimacy of the king as much as that of his liberal policy. Would the monarch who had, in a sense, desacralized bread by abandoning the stewardship of subsistence recognize the voice of God?[41]

The king sought to discredit the Parlement by explaining its opposition to liberalization in terms of its notorious record of resistance to the will of the government on a host of important matters. (Certainly the courts were much more successful in paralyzing the crown during the eighteenth century than Mario Einaudi believed.)[42] On the

40. Paris Parlement, Conseil secret, 28 March, 18 April, and 4 May 1768, AN, X¹ᴮ 8955; *Recueil des principales lois relatives au commerce des grains avec les arrêts, arrêtés et remontrances du Parlement sur cet objet et le procès-verbal de l'assemblée générale de police, 28 novembre 1768* (Paris, 1769), 65–70, 77–83; St.-Florentin to procurator general, 16, 20 October 1768, AN, O¹* 410, and BN, Joly 1139, fol. 98.

41. *Recueil*, 252–54, 260; Paris Parlement, Conseil secret, 13 December 1768, X¹ᴮ 8957; Roubaud, *Représentation aux magistrats*, 385–86.

42. Einaudi, *Physiocratic Doctrine*, 47–48, 50–51, 90. On the behavior of the parlements, see Kaplan, *Bread, Politics, and Political Economy*, passim; Franklin Ford, *Robe and Sword: the Regrouping of the French Aristocracy after Louis XIV* (Cambridge: Harvard

liberty issue as well as on others, the king implied, the motive of the sovereign court was political self-aggrandizement and its goal was to undermine the power of the throne.[43] Whether or not this charge was generally true across the century is a question that merits reexamination; in this instance at least, it was patently spurious. Far from seeking to circumscribe the authority of kingship, the Parlement sought to prevent its erosion. If the magistrates offered to serve as fathers to the famished people it was because the people had been brusquely orphaned. In reference to the grain riots of the 1770s, Condorcet wrote contemptuously of the people who "removed wheat by force, paid for it the price they desired, and believed their expedition legitimate because they had the *Right to Live*."[44] To be sure, the Parlement did not condone collective consumer extortion any more than it did extortion by individual grain dealers. But, implicitly, it recognized that the people had a right to existence—not Morelly's sociopolitical right to a portion of the commonwealth but Montesquieu's moral right to a reasonable chance for survival. The right to existence was not a meal ticket but the right to compete for subsistence in a situation in which there was a rough proportion between the means and the elementary needs of most of the people. The vast majority of consumers were poorly armed for this struggle. The government's task was to assure their competitiveness by protecting them against the avarice and spoliations of the owners and traders. The government itself was to be victualer only in the last resort; indirectly, however, to prevent catastrophes, it had to play an active distributing role by managing scarcity and regulating the allocation of supplies.

The government guaranteed the right to existence in return for the

---

University Press, 1953); J. H. Shennan, *The Parlement of Paris* (Ithaca: Cornell University Press, 1968); William Doyle, *The Parlement of Bordeaux and the End of the Old Regime, 1771–90* (New York: St. Martin's 1974); Bailey Stone, *The Parlement of Paris, 1774–89* (Chapel Hill: University of North Carolina Press, 1981), and *The French Parlements and the Crisis of the Old Regime* (Chapel Hill: University of North Carolina Press, 1986).

43. Paris Parlement, Conseil secret, 23 January 1769, AN, X^{1B} 8957; Hardy's Journal, 24 January 1769, BN, ms. fr. 6680, fol. 209; arrêt du Conseil, 22 January 1769, BN, Joly 1111, fol. 25.

44. J.-A.-N. de Caritat, marquis de Condorcet, *Lettre d'un laboureur de Picardie à M.N. ★★★, auteur prohibitif* (Paris, 1775), in Daire and de Molinari, *Collection des principaux économistes*, 14:487.

submission of the citizenry. The government had an obligation to honor this right not only for the sake of justice but to assure the survival of the society as a whole. In the Parlement's conception, social life was not founded on an underlying harmony of interests but on a delicate balance of conflicting and contradictory interests, needs, and ambitions which could be kept in uneasy equilibrium only by the mediation of an agency hostage to no single party. Harmony was neither natural nor ineluctable; the government had to arrange it. In the Parlement's view, the public interest could not be defined and realized through the concourse of a multitude of private interests. It was the function of the (trustees of the) public interest to channel the private interests in a direction that was generally useful. The Parlement believed that the highest public interest was subsistence because it was the precondition for social cohesion. The experience of the 1760s seemed to be a graphic illustration of this lesson. In other matters, the court vigorously defended the sovereign claims of private property, especially against the aggrandizement of the state. (Mario Einaudi shrewdly pointed to areas of common commitment that bound parlements and physiocrats, notably "the belief in certain immutable laws which had to be protected against sudden and ill-considered alterations.")[45] The Paris Parlement refused, however, to accept an unqualified and absolute idea of property when that idea clashed with the exigencies of provisioning. It tacitly rejected the notion that property was a natural right anterior to all forms of social organization and superior to the claims of society as a whole. It stood as the defender of what we have called the police tradition. Nor did it stand there alone. The Paris Parlement's analysis, if not all its specific recommendations, could have served as a platform for the whole antiliberal movement of the sixties and seventies (and perhaps even for the resurgent corporatist ideology of the nineteenth century).

The Rouen Parlement, which had eagerly demanded freedom to export in 1763–64, pressed the critique with even more effrontery. A violent uprising in March 1768 was the catalyst in the court's about-face: it was as if the rebellious citizenry delivered the magistrates from their reform contract. Even as the controller general sent the army to restore order, so the Parlement issued an arrêt that implicitly held the

45. Einaudi, *Physiocratic Doctrine*, 52.

government responsible for the disorders. The magistrates brazenly recalled the king to his duty: "The most powerful tie of obedience and affection of the subjects is the attention the prince pays to their needs." The "theory of liberty," the court contended, "has been contradicted in practice." The fact that liberalization had "hurled an entire people into the most horrible misery and upset the whole commercial economy" was ample proof of its erroneousness. "The system called *economic*," the Rouennais charged, was another version of "the republic of Plato, an imaginary speculation." It was flawed in its assumptions about human nature, social organization, and public administration. Obsessed with their concept of the perfect *évidence* and infallibility of natural law, the *économistes* had forgotten human nature: "The passions will always resist this evidence." Private interest, the motor force on which the physiocrats constructed their system, the Rouen magistrates maintained, will "perpetually violate" the natural order that it is supposed to guarantee. To establish "self-interest, this violent passion," as "the general law" would be "to cast us into the pure state of nature."

Grain liberty conjured for the Rouennais an apocalyptical vision whose horrors went beyond famines and uprisings to social and political disintegration, the logical product of unchecked liberty: "Suppress all the Regulations, leaving only an unlimited liberty [and] the balance spring of society will be destroyed; the Peoples will be [indiscriminately] blended; the sovereign will be nothing more than a magnate distinguished by some sort of mark but without any power to be useful; thus, this system, which appears to lay the foundation for everything, tends in fact to shake and destroy everything." "Unlimited liberty" is not only "contrary to the happiness of your subjects," the Parlement lectured the monarch, but it is also "an alteration of the French Constitution."[46]

Lofting a trial balloon for the liberalization of the grain trade in

46. Rouen Parlement, Conseil secret, 23 March–15 April 1768, AD Seine-Maritime; Laverdy to Miromesnil, 23 March 1768, and Laverdy to de Crosne, 10 April 1768, C. 107, AD Seine-Maritime; Laverdy to Miromesnil, 27 March and 4 April 1768, in *Correspondance Miromesnil*, 5:135, 142–44; Amable-Pierre Floquet, *Histoire du parlement de Normandie* (Rouen, 1840–42), 6:424–25; remonstrances of 5 May and 19 August 1768, and "Lettres Suppliques," Rouen Parlement, Conseil secret, 15 and 29 October 1768, AD Seine-Maritime.

1755, a reviewer in the *Journal de Trévoux* had written: "It is not incompatible, this liberty, with the monarchical government." Fifteen years later Galiani told his friend Suard: "In every government, the grain legislation gives the tone of the spirit of the government . . . if you tamper too much with the administration of grain in France, if you succeed, you alter the form and the constitution of the government."[47] Unlike their Rouen colleagues, the Paris magistrates did not perceive liberalization as a threat to the form or constitution of the government, at least not in the short run. But they did believe that liberalization fundamentally changed the relationship between state and society, estranging the one from the other and placing them both in jeopardy. In the Parlement's view, state and society were interdependent and intertwined. In the liberal conception, the state functioned on the margin of society, abandoning it largely to its own devices. By instituting liberalization, the Parlement alleged, the state renounced its responsibilities to society. Liberalization upset the balance of society and at the same time announced that it was no longer the duty of the government to maintain this balance. The Parlement decried the advent of the spectator state because the magistrates believed that it would lead to chaos and social disintegration. By abrogating all the rules of conduct, the government lost view of its very purpose; laissez-faire, the court argued, was ultimately an antisocial policy. Although it had heatedly combated the bloated king of the administrative monarchy, the Parlement rejected the lean king of liberalism. For years and years it had relentlessly tried to limit the power of the king. Now it exhorted the monarch to exercise his authority with vigor.

"In these moments of crisis," the physiocrat Du Pont remarked disdainfully, "the Magistrates . . . become *people* themselves."[48] Denounced thusly for their ignorance and obscurantism, the parlementaires regarded their detractors as genuinely dangerous enemies of the

---

47. *Journal de Trévoux* (October 1755):2601–2; Galiani to Suard, 8 September 1770, in Eugène Asse, ed., *Lettres de l'abbé Galiani à Madame d'Epinay* (Paris, 1882), 1:138–39.

48. Du Pont to Prince Carl Ludwig (1773), in Carl Knies, ed., *Carl Friedrichs von Baden Brieflicher Verkher mit Mirabeau und Dupont* (Heidelberg, 1892), 2:146. Cf. Joly de Fleury's remark: "Everyone is *people* when they lack bread" (speech of 5 July 1763, in *Recueil*, 48).

commonweal. The new political economy was not merely erroneous; venturing into the realm of everyday material life, it became a public menace. Private interest, the dynamic to which the physiocrats entrusted their system, would "perpetually violate" the natural order it was supposed to guarantee. Preaching the seditious and "inhuman" dogma of constant *cherté*, the physiocrats propelled everyone into a chaotic state of nature in which strife replaced structure. The magistrates anticipated Galiani's view that physiocracy was a real peril, "a Mississippi, a Jansenism, a Fronde, a crusade, even one of those epidemic diseases of the spirit by which the French nation is sometimes attacked and which causes cruel ravages until the calm of reason returns."[49]

In the midst of the onslaught against liberalization, when the government felt besieged and the *économistes* betrayed a hint of demoralization, several parlements publicly and effusively thanked the prince for his embrace of reform and implored him "to cede to none of the [antiliberal] demands." In an *avis* ghost-written by Bigot de Sainte-Croix, a renegade Rouen magistrate intimately associated with Quesnay's circle, the Parlement of Grenoble angrily assailed its reactionary sister courts. Liberty was not merely a matter of convenience. Both social and political organization derived from the laws of nature. "There is a law, Sire," the Parlement affirmed, "anterior to the civil laws, a law founded immediately by Nature, whose maintenance must be the single end of all social institutions, a law by which and for which you reign, it is the sacred law of property." Since property was a barren prerogative unless owners had the freedom to utilize it as they pleased, it was the duty of the state to guarantee "the liberty" as well as "the security of property." The magistrates reasoned that it was the function of the prince to "judge" positive laws "by their conformity to the natural order and to the essential laws of justice" rather than "by confronting . . . positive laws with the facts [of daily life]." A wise prince would not be deterred by the crisis. Pledged to govern according to nature's laws, he would support the liberal legislation because it approximated the laws of nature. The empty stomachs of the people did not entitle the state, as Linguet later argued, to infringe

---

49. Galiani, "Mémoire to Sartine" (1770), in Asse, *Lettres*, 1:412; Galiani to Sartine, 27 April 1770, in ibid., 1:63. Galiani also referred to the physiocrats as "bloodsuckers of hemorrhoidal veins" (Galiani to Suard, 8 September 1770, in ibid., 1:142).

on the property rights of grain holders. For grain was the same as any other property, undistinguished by the fact that it was universally needed. While the Paris and Rouen Parlements censured the king for failing to fulfill his fundamental duties, the Grenoble magistrates riposted that those so-called duties were in fact abuses of power, "arbitrary institutions." Such a conception of kingship was "impossible," "unjust," and "ruinous."[50]

Despite the spirited defense mounted by the liberals, the combined opposition of people, police, and the majority of the parlements, along with the continuing streak of crop shortfalls, the violent dislocation of the market system, and the intensely disruptive recession, forced the government to abjure the physiocratic faith before the end of 1770. Old-style kingship resurfaced as Louis XV reaffirmed the dual vocation of paternalism and absolutism in his waning years. By the end of 1770, the physiocrats were in total disarray, vanquished in the arena of public policy even as they had been derided in the salons and stoned and insulted in the marketplaces.

In his study Mario Einaudi rightly points to the fears that physiocratic theory aroused concerning the potential for abuse of power by an ostensibly untrammeled executive. In the context of the 1760s, however, during the halcyon years of physiocratic practice, the reformers provoked the contrary anxiety. By rendering princely power hostage to nature's irrefragable law, they fashioned a conception of kingship so limited in its political and social prerogatives as to reduce the executive to passivity. By lodging the principle of legitimacy outside kingship itself, the physiocrats manacled the monarch as no other constitutional doctrine had ever dared. Far from begetting despotism, the *coup de nature* spawned central impotence. In the sixties the peril of radical disengagement loomed as far more ominous than the risks of overgovernment.

Physiocracy has enjoyed a very mixed reception over the years. Though advocates and opponents stressed different aspects of its system, the most salient line of cleavage can properly be called political.

---

50. The *avis* took the form of a letter addressed to Louis XV dated 26 April 1769. The manuscript copy is in B. 2314, AD Isère. It was also published in the *Ephémérides du Citoyen* 7 (1769):109–256.

In one sense or another, physiocracy was about the exercise of power and the relation of state to society. The quarrel began with the publication of Quesnay's first essays, and it gradually engulfed the *beau monde* as well as the *menu peuple*, "civil society" as well as the "political classes" (to use today's stilted euphemisms), the producers as well as the consumers, the technocrats as well as the sheriffs. It did not end with the crushing defeat of the physiocrats in 1770.[51] One of the most astonishing qualities of physiocracy—proof of its validity in the eyes of true believers—was its uncanny resiliency. It revived with unwonted celerity four years later. Discredited and disgraced a second time, it was reborn yet again in the eighties, and it furnished a discourse and a program that found great favor beginning in 1789. The Rolands of the Revolution, who were legion at all levels of public life, owed far more to Turgot's version of Quesnay-*cum*-Gournay than to Rousseau, or to anyone else for that matter. In the nineteenth century positions became even more acutely crystallized. Stripped of its archaisms, physiocracy metamorphosed into the "liberalism" (European-style) which competed with (or compromised with) various brands of authoritarianism for control of the French Right. With some notable exceptions, historians and political economists on the Right hailed in physiocracy the founding vulgate of the modern capitalist order, while those on the Left reproached physiocracy for its class bias, its Social Darwinism, and its myriad rigidities. The debate was habitually venomous.

While twentieth-century scholarship has attempted a more dispassionate assessment based on an appreciation both of physiocracy's impressive theoretical insights and of the "developmental" conditions in which it emerged, the polemical inflection is rarely overcome. It made little difference that Colberto-Jacobinism had became a national tradition, residing in the one camp as much as in the other. Even as the Socialists ascended to power in 1981, so the partisans of a purified (and rejuvenated) liberalism began to make the case for the "minimum state."[52] And in a nation where politicians are not ashamed of intellectual prowess, they began to write and speak about the physi-

---

51. On this rout, see my introduction to Galiani's *La Bagarre*. Galiani along with Linguet, Necker, Diderot, and Mably constituted the front line of antiphysiocracy.

52. See, e.g., Guy Sorman, *La Solution libérale* (Paris: Fayard, 1984), dedicated "aux liberaux de tous les partis," and his *L'Etat minimum* (Paris: Plon, 1985).

ocrats, Turgot, and the once irretrievably obscure Bastiat as the ideological forbears of the Hayeks and the Friedmans, the Margaret
Thatchers and the Ronald Reagans.

Viewed in this context, Mario Einaudi's study is relatively chaste
and prudent. Focused on a single important theme, the essay avoids
unnecessary diversions. With exemplary discipline, Einaudi plays the
lean prince or the legal despot, constrained from encroaching or
straying by the natural law of his sharply etched *problématique*. A
friendly interlocutor who ventures to impute to him views that
may contravene Einaudi's mandate or his mind is secure in the
knowledge that both he and his protagonist are protected by the
academy's version of judicial review. Clearly the physiocrats fasci-
nated Einaudi, despite their preciosity, their *suffisance*, their dogmatism. One can more easily envision Einaudi, in so many ways an
eighteenth-century man, *chez* Madame d'Epinay or Madame Geoffrin
or Madame Necker than at Quesnay's rather confessional *entresol* or
Mirabeau's weekly seminar–pep rally.

Yet for all their hyperbole and narcissism, the physiocratic community, extending from Quesnay through Condorcet, went farther
than any other thinkers in the task of establishing the grounds for a
science of society, of economics, and (more cumbersomely) of politics. In this pioneering enterprise—the invention of new ways to understand relations between individuals and the community, between
society and state, between moral truths and the physical universe,
between economic development and sociopolitical organization—
Einaudi recognized their originality, their audacity, and the abiding
significance of their ambitions. They were not satisfied with irony or
ricanement or *scandale*, rhetorical neutron bombs that slew the enemy
but left their structures intact. Nor were they consoled or daunted
by their pathetic evanescence and pettiness in the Great Scheme of
Things. They were builders even as they eradicated. At the heinous
intellectual risk of system making, they mapped out the complex connections that constituted social life. This was not the quasi-consensual
High Enlightenment that right-minded texts now distill for us. This
was a more parlous undertaking both in its theoretical moorings and
its pragmatic engagements. This was a long way from Tocqueville's
disdainful literarification of politics: how could Einaudi ever forgive
him for this facile, myopic, and supercilious reading?

The physiocrats came to the forefront when, as their adversary Linguet put it, a metamorphosis transformed the "philosophical insect" into an "economic insect."[53] Their allure for Mario Einaudi seems to have been transmitted by his father, Luigi, illustrious statesman, great scholar of political economy, and collector of physiocratic writing, to whom *The Physiocratic Doctrine of Judicial Control* is dedicated. For Luigi Einaudi, it was an incalculable merit in itself for the physiocrats to have fashioned so precociously—well before Smith— "a systematic theory of Economic science."[54] *De père en fils*, the Einaudis took comfort in the physiocratic effort to articulate realities with theories (one of the grounds on which both men remain most vulnerable to criticism in their turn). Luigi Einaudi believed passionately that "economic science is subordinated to moral law."[55] His son seems stubbornly to have read this axiom into physiocratic discourse, which more commonly gave expression to an ostensibly antithetical formulation: that everything in the moral order derives from the physical world, nature's peculiar domain.[56]

One part of the physiocratic legacy, embraced by the Americans and very much on Mario Einaudi's mind in the 1930s, was the conviction of the need for "a higher order to be preserved against the inroads of legislators." The physiocrats interested him because of the enduring pertinence of their quest to "achieve a stable political order through a constant adherence to a fundamental law." That fundamental law was "the higher order of the laws of nature," at once physical in its Newtonian analogy and moral in its divine provenance.[57] Whether the higher law is written down as a constitution or reified or sanctified over time in other ways, it can best be shielded by some manner of judicial review—such was the lesson history had taught to

53. Simon N.-H. Linguet, *Réponse aux docteurs modernes* (London, 1771), cited by Georges Weulersse, *Le Mouvement physiocratique en France de 1756 à 1770* (Paris: F. Alcan, 1910), 2:683.

54. Mario Einaudi acknowledged Mirabeau's advantage over Smith (*Physiocratic Doctrine*, 25).

55. I owe the references from and about Luigi Einaudi to Roger Chartier, "Luigi Einaudi: Between Politics and History," the inaugural lecture of the Luigi Einaudi Chair in European Studies at Cornell University, Ithaca, Cornell Western Societies Program, 1989.

56. Kaplan, *Bread, Politics, and Political Economy*, 1:115.

57. Einaudi, *Physiocratic Doctrine*, 88, 58, 20–23.

kings as well as to presidents. And in this light it is not hard to imagine Mario Einaudi in the 1930s closing his eyes for an instant and glimpsing a crowned and bilious Roosevelt administering the stinging *séance de flagellation* to the chief magistrates of the nation in the unseasonable manner of Louis XV in 1766.[58]

Though it is not Einaudi's major concern, he addresses the question of the relationship between a commitment to a higher law as a guarantee of stability and the practical burden of instituting nature's imperatives. For even if he did not venture to explore the *historical* problem of the physiocratic flirtation with power, he understood a critical point that has eluded innumerable commentators: that the physiocratic enterprise was a compound of drastic innovations, a sweeping repudiation of much that underpinned the old regime. Yet Mario Einaudi's formulation is curious and revealing—in some ways consonant with the irenic (one dares not blurt out the epithet "conservative") mood of François Furet's Enlightenment-Revolution revisionism.[59] Thus Einaudi depicts physiocracy as "a doctrine rooted in the necessity of bringing *radical reforms* to France in order to *save her from revolution.*"[60] Is one to extrapolate that Quesnay's zigzag might have obviated the *Contrat social* (let us not even think about the *journées* of the Terror or the gulags of a more distant future)?

Of course *The Physiocratic Doctrine of Judicial Control* authorizes no such peregrinations. Yet let us note that, in contradistinction to many other interpreters, Einaudi refuses to administer the standard retrospective sedative, a massive and patronizing dose of philosophical Valium that preserves physiocratic honor while disqualifying their ideation as manic-depressive millenarianism. Indeed, he may have gone too far in portraying them as hard-nosed realists, men a bit like his father: "What matters is that the physiocrats did not waste their energies in contrasting an ideal system of natural law with the existing

58. 3 March 1766, in Jules Flammermont, ed., *Remontrances du Parlement de Paris au dix-huitième siècle* (Paris, 1888–98), 2:559.

59. See François Furet, *Penser la Révolution Française* (Paris: Gallimard, 1978); Furet, *Marx et la Révolution Française* (Paris, Gallimard, 1986); Furet's volume in the Hachette "Histoire de France," *La Révolution de Turgot à Jules Ferry, 1770–1880* (Paris: Hachette, 1988); and the interview with Furet in Pierre Lepage, "La Révolution Française est terminée," *Le Monde*, 26 August 1988.

60. Einaudi, *Physiocratic Doctrine*, 28 (my italics).

system of positive law. They undertook to discover the causes which favor or hamper social progress." But Mario Einaudi recognized that theory and zeal engender a certain faith without which outsiders cannot sustain their cause. What powered the physiocrats was their knowledge that history—the truth?—was on their side: "It was the physiocrats' belief that in the long run the physiocratic order would inevitably assert itself even upon an unwilling world."[61]

Einaudi's message to us in this frugal essay is rich, ambiguous both heuristically and involuntarily ("isn't it?"), and stimulating. It is a partial rehabilitation of the physiocrats as political thinkers. It is about the genesis of constitutionalism and its practice. It is about the connections between politics and economics, but it does not merely invite the now fashionable consignment of *économisme primaire* to world-historical limbo. For Einaudi tells us that if politics has "primacy over economics" (Sidney Tarrow's phrase) in some ontological way, then there is no political theory that is not grounded in political economy—political economy being, in its eighteenth-century avatar, the study of moral philosophy. Present in the interstices of this monograph, the connections between freedom and regulation, between individual and community, between liberty and equality, are the veritable leitmotifs of Mario Einaudi's career. Here he does not venture to confront realities and theories, surely because such a task would have required a very different enterprise. But he does remind us forcefully about the problem of interpretation. Even as his father loathed the scholarly shorthand that smothered and nullified complexity and originality by hasty and unyielding classification (thus opposing, for instance, in a depleting and reductive manner, mercantilism and liberalism),[62] so Mario Einaudi bequeathed to us not one eighteenth century, not a homogeneous Enlightenment, not a single party of humanity, but a diverse, motley heritage, effervescent with debate and contradiction, febrile, agitated, frightened, hopeful, backward-looking, and progressive—all at once. That is not to say that certain voices did not dominate, that certain currents were not more significant than others, that certain analyses were not more truthful or more

61. Ibid., 26.
62. "In what way is it important to know whether Ferdinando Galiani was a mercantilist or a liberal?" asked Luigi Einaudi. "In no way" (cited by Chartier, "Luigi Einaudi").

useful or more beautiful. But to name and thus domesticate them all under the same label is a betrayal of everything that Einaudi, father and son, stood for.

Still there are some fundamental issues that are begged. Everything in his career suggests that Mario Einaudi refused the Tocquevillean bifurcation, and affirmed, following his father, the necessary union and collaboration between the two liberties, political and economic. In what way did physiocratic theory nurture or determine this perspective? Did Einaudi begin with the premise that the right of property, and the absolute freedom to dispose of it, were anterior to any form of social or political organization? Implicitly, then, did political liberty follow from and depend on a laissez-faire system? Did a political economy engendered by and in its turn guaranteed by the two liberties preclude a moral economy recognizing the rights and entertaining the claims of the dispossessed?[63] In the same vein, does it follow that the legal despot (the state) could not act opportunistically in response to serious threats without incurring the vengeful and didactic wrath of the judicial Argus? What did Einaudi-Lemercier think of his countryman Galiani's rather disabused view of nature as "too great a Lady" to have to bother with our tattered bodies: "Let's leave her the care of great movements, the great revolutions of empires, the long run [even] as she has that of the stars and the elements." Our business, reckoned Galiani's Chevalier, was "politics [which] is nothing other than the science of preventing or parrying short-run movements set in motion by extraordinary causes," a different conception of science than the one expounded in *L'Ordre naturel* or *L'Intérêt général*.[64] If Ei-

63. For a recent *populiste* discussion of the moral economy in the French context, see the essays by the editors in Florence Gauthier and Guy-Robert Ikni, eds., *La Guerre du blé au XVIIIe siècle* (Paris: Les Editions de la Passion, 1988), esp. 7–30, 111–44. These essays manifest an authentic compassion for "popular" political culture and political economy. But they are deeply flawed by their rhetorical self-indulgence, lack of intellectual rigor and clarity, scholarly parochialism, and telic purview.

64. See Ferdinando Galiani, *Dialogues sur le commerce des bleds* (1770), ed. Fausto Nicolini (Milan, n.d.), 221–23. See also Galiani's letter to d'Epinay in which he wrote contemptuously of the physiocrats, who have "so often said that nature left to herself was so beautiful, worked so well, put things in balance, etc.," 23 June 1770, in Asse, *Lettres*, 1:92. For a similar perspective, see Jacques Necker, *Sur la législation et le commerce des grains* (Paris, 1775), 393–94. For Lemercier de la Rivière's texts, see n. 2, above, and *L'Ordre naturel et essentiel des sociétés politiques* (1767), in E. Depitre, ed., *Collection des économistes et des réformateurs sociaux de la France* (Paris: P. Guethner, 1910).

naudi's keen interest in regulation belies the implication that he underwrote the physiocratic apothegm that the government that governed least governed best, his desire to keep power in check remained
a gnawing anxiety.

So is it in the last analysis "Einaudi–Montesquieu: *même combat?*"
Montesquieu is a more or less brooding absent presence in *The Physiocratic Doctrine of Judicial Control*. If Einaudi has no sympathy for
Louis Althusser's rendition of the baron de la Brède, he finds congenial the Americanized version of Montesquieu. He never squarely
confronts the bitter physiocratic critique of Montesquieu's conceptions of political power, with the attendant glosses on "division" and
"separation" for which the philosophe was not always responsible;
and this despite Diderot's emphatic proclamation that Lemercier superseded Montesquieu in everything that the science of politics sub-
sumed. Einaudi invokes rapidly Du Pont's harsh denunciation of a
system that is far too mercurial in conception. Perhaps too graciously,
he apologizes for Letrosne's rejection of "counterforces" as superflu-
ous in his design of vigilant judicial control. Yet he concedes that
merciless physiocratic deprecation of the notion of checks and bal-
ances undermined their own case for judicial control and raised
doubts about the sincerity and reliability of a political structure
erected around "this very fiction of legal despotism."[65] In the late
thirties did Einaudi regard Montesquieu's relativism as insufficiently
comforting?

Physiocratic allergy to Montesquieu invites attention to a final
point hinted at by Einaudi regarding the problem of exercising power
which echoes his admonitions against procrustean taxonomies and
linear theories. On the one hand, physiocratic liberalism meant spectator kingship—minimal government. On the other hand, in his
curmudgeonly diatribe against American mimesis of English institutions, Turgot, perhaps the old regime's fiercest critic of monarchical hubris, reaffirmed "the very core of the physiocratic doctrine,
namely, centralization of all functions of the state in the hands of the
sovereign."[66] For all of his appetite to reduce the range of stately
power, Turgot (as a former minister and field administrator) fully

65. Einaudi, *Physiocratic Doctrine*, 43, 36, 52.
66. Ibid., 78.

understood the ambiguities surrounding the birth of liberalism—no immaculate conception, this rough *accouchement*. In order to be in a position to do little, the state had to do very much. It had to do it sweepingly, vigorously, even brutally. Nor was it clear (theoretically or empirically) at what point, if any, muscular liberalism could give way to a gentler disposition. Controller General Laverdy had to force grain to be free and to bludgeon the unschooled and the skeptics to see what was *évident*. Turgot's own instructions to the Paris police chief in 1775 epitomize the deep tensions between the ambitions of lean and bloated government: do nothing to interfere with the freedom of the provisioning trade, but make sure to keep the peace in the streets and the marketplaces.[67] The warning of the Six Great Guilds that Turgot would need "archers, gallows and executioners" in order to realize his brand of liberty was a cruel polemical jibe.[68] Yet it underlined the point that the exercise of power defied stringent classifications and boundaries, that its practice was inherently anomalous, transgressive, inconsistent. In his elliptical way, this seems to be the caution that Einaudi wishes to convey.

67. Lenoir papers, Bibliothèque Municipale, Orléans.
68. "Réflexions des six corps," BN, Joly 462, fols. 155–56.

>>>>>>>>>>>>>>>>>>>> <<<<<<<<<<<<<<<<<<<<

2

Rousseau and Women:
An Alternative Reading

ISAAC KRAMNICK

Twenty years ago Mario Einaudi wrote a book about the first twenty years in the career of Jean-Jacques Rousseau. Einaudi's *Early Rousseau* entered an academic marketplace in 1967 in which the reading of Rousseau was still dominated by the postwar paradigms found in Jacob Talmon's *Origins of Totalitarian Democracy* (1952). Now, from the hindsight of twenty years, we can discern at least four major contributions that Einaudi's splendid book made to Rousseau scholarship. Perhaps most important, it depoliticized Rousseau, clearing the air of cold war and general partisan indictments of Rousseau as a harbinger of an authoritarian or closed society. (This would be but a brief depoliticization, however, for Rousseau was soon to be enlisted by the Students for a Democratic Society as well as by Marshall Berman's politics of authenticity.)[1] Einaudi's second contribution was to show the continuity in Rousseau's thought. While others emphasized contradiction and confusion, Einaudi depicted, quite rightly, a developmental logic in Rousseau's writings.

The book also made the then novel claim that Rousseau's life and thought had particular meaning and relevance for men and women in

1. Marshall Berman, *The Politics of Authenticity* (New York: Atheneum, 1972).

the second half of the twentieth century. Einaudi's Rousseau is an existential hero confronting "disintegration, loneliness, and chaos." Out of his confrontation with the "paradoxes and absurdities of modernity" emerged a "pattern of action and belief which modern man finds understandable and valuable in sorting out the issues he faces."[2]

Einaudi's fourth and most enduring contribution to Rousseau studies was to give Rousseau's early and lesser-known writings the prominence and status they now enjoy. After Einaudi no student of political theory reads only Rousseau's *Social Contract* and *Emile*. The *Discourse on Arts and Sciences*, the *Discourse on the Origin of Inequality*, and *A Discourse on Political Economy* are now essential reading due, to a great extent, to Einaudi's seminal study of the early Rousseau. Today, in fact, it seems almost inconceivable that the young Rousseau was conventionally overlooked until Einaudi convinced us otherwise. Had not Rousseau himself, after all, told posterity in his *Confessions* that it was an incident at age eight in which he was falsely accused and punished for a petty wrongdoing that forever set before him the quest for justice?[3] The theme of this chapter is prompted by Einaudi's *Early Rousseau* and its injunction that one must look at the young man Rousseau, the author of those profound early works.

ROUSSEAU THE MISOGYNIST

The subject of Rousseau and women has ostensibly produced little disagreement among scholars. Two decades of primarily feminist scholarship has concluded that Rousseau stands as the quintessential modern spokesman for a view of women that demeans and subordinates them. He is for many, along with Aristotle and Saint Paul, a major touchstone in the cultural lineage of patriarchy. What makes this all the more difficult to understand, let alone excuse, is, as many have noted since Wollstonecraft, that Rousseau is the first great egalitarian theorist to be found in the canon of Western political theory—but only where men are concerned. Rousseau's views on women,

2. Mario Einaudi, *The Early Rousseau* (Ithaca: Cornell University Press, 1967), 7.

3. Jean-Jacques Rousseau, *The Confessions*, trans. J. M. Cohen (Harmondsworth: Penguin Books, 1952), 29–30.

although scattered through most of his writings, are particularly focused in his *Emile*. They make up, as is self-evident, the traditional
litany of what we now recognize as cultural sexism.

> Consult the woman's opinions in bodily matters, in all that concerns
> the senses; consult the men in matters of morality and all that concerns
> the understanding.
>
> The man should be strong and active; the woman should be weak
> and passive; the one must have both the power and the will; it is
> enough that the other should offer little resistance. . . . It follows that
> woman is specially made for man's delight . . . his virtue is in his
> strength, he pleases because he is strong . . . it is the law of nature. . . .
> If woman is made to please and to be in subjection to man, she ought
> to make herself pleasing in his eyes . . . her strength is in her charms,
> by their means she should compel him to discover and use his strength.
> The surest way of arousing this strength is to make it necessary by
> resistance.
>
> To be pleasing in his sight, to win his respect and love, to train him
> in childhood, to tend him in manhood, to counsel and console, to
> make his life pleasant and happy, these are the duties of woman for all
> time, and this is what she should be taught while she is young.
>
> This habitual restraint produces a docility which woman requires all
> her life long, for she will always be in subjection to a man, or to man's
> judgment, and she will never be free to set her own opinion above his.
> What is most wanted in a woman is gentleness; formed to obey a crea-
> ture so imperfect as man, a creature often vicious and always faulty,
> she should early learn to submit to injustice and to suffer the wrongs
> inflicted on her by her husband without complaint.[4]

Rousseau was a sexist, clearly. He was, in fact, one of the most
influential purveyors of such views through his enormous influence
on the romantic movement in the nineteenth century. I have no wish
to deny or vindicate this reading of Rousseau. But there is an alternative possible reading of Rousseau and women which suggests that
it is an issue by no means as clear-cut as conventionally depicted.
Rousseau's attitude toward women *and* their place in his political
thinking are much more complicated than a simple verdict of sexism.
He cannot be acquitted of the charges, but a case can be made for a
good deal more ambivalence about women in his public creed and his
private life than is usually acknowledged.

4. Jean-Jacques Rousseau, *Emile*, trans. Barbara Foxley (London: J. M. Dent &
Sons, 1961), 306, 329, 328, 333.

ROUSSEAU AND REPUBLICAN
MOTHERHOOD

The corpus of Rousseau's writings on politics produces a developmental model characterized by three stages. There is the state of nature, civil society, and the true community forged by the social contract. The first is inhabited by natural men and women; the second by artificial men, primarily; and the third by citizens, men and women. In the state of nature human beings are amoral; in civil society, immoral; and in the community, moral. Another way to put that development is from *amour soi* to *amour propre* to *amour general*. Natural society is characterized by intuitive compassion and pity, civil society by calculation and competition, and community by a politicized compassion known as the General Will. The state of nature for Rousseau is an anthropological metaphor; civil society is the existent reality of emergent liberal, bourgeois society that was eighteenth century Europe. True community was both the democratic ideal of antiquity and a future potential for bourgeois Europe. Finally, and most important for my argument, each of these stages privileges the particular qualities of a triadic member of the family. The state of nature privileges the characteristics of the child, civil society privileges the father, and true community privileges the mother. In fact, Rousseau's ideal may well be labeled the maternal state.[5] Some details may help to fill in this schematization of Rousseau's politics.

In his version of the state of nature, Rousseau renders all human beings Robinson Crusoes. (It was, after all, the only book he would have Emile read.)[6] They are abstracted from history, tradition, community, and family. The metaphor of natural men and women as found in part 1 of the *Discourse on the Origin of Inequality* has no family, no love, no property. Autonomous and independent men and women care only for self-preservation. They have no moral relations and no fixed property. They couple and move on "and even the offspring was nothing to its mother as soon as it could do without her." They were "strangers to vanity, deference, esteem and contempt." They had self-respect, but not the selfishness that comes

5. Berman, *Politics of Authenticity*, 203–6.
6. Rousseau, *Emile*, 149.

from comparing and preferring oneself in relation to others. Along
with this self-respect, natural men and women were prompted by the
"natural feeling" of pity and compassion from which would later
flow "all the social virtues." It is the "gentle voice" of compassion
that takes noble savages outside themselves and hurries them to the
aid of others in distress as they pass them in their self-absorbed quest
for preservation.[7]

His *Emile* makes clear that for Rousseau childhood is the analog of
the state of nature. The child is free and absorbed in self. Before the
age of reason the child knows no moral teachings, "knows the essential relations between men and things, but nothing of the moral relations between man and man." The child is naturally compassionate,
"capable of tenderness" and "the joys of pity."[8]

Civil society, depicted and deplored in part 2 of the *Origin of Inequality*, ensues with the advent of agriculture and metallurgy. Families
and private property, Rousseau's famous *meum* and *teum*, emerge in
civil society and the inherent equality of men and women found in
natural society is ended with the sexual division of labor that assigns
women the task of child rearing. *Amour soi* gives way to *amour propre*
as self-respect becomes selfishness. The serpent responsible for the
fall from grace is the urge to make comparisons, which accompanies
social life, for "the first feeling excited by this comparison is the desire to be first."[9] Compassion is lost in the restless quest for esteem
and preference. Civil society is the habitat of immoral men.

> Man must now, therefore, have been perpetually employed in getting
> others to interest themselves in his lot, and in making them, apparently
> at least, if not really, find their advantage in promoting his own. Thus
> he must have been sly and artful in his behavior to some, and imperious
> and cruel to others . . . insatiable ambition, the thirst of raising their
> respective fortunes, not so much from real want as from the desire to
> surpass others, inspired all men with a vile propensity to injure one
> another. . . . In a word, there arose rivalry and competition on the one
> hand, and conflicting interests on the other, together with a secret de-
> sire on both of profiting at the expense of others.[10]

7. Jean-Jacques Rousseau, *Discourse on a Subject Proposed by the Academy of Dijon:
What Is the Origin of Inequality among Men, and Is It Authorized by Natural Law*, trans.
G.D.H. Cole (New York: Dutton, 1950), 235, 227, 226–29.
8. Rousseau, *Emile*, 170, 51; see also 28, 35, 49, 53, 174.
9. Ibid., 197.
10. Rousseau, *Origin of Inequality*, 248.

Rousseau provides a cynical parody of Hobbes and Locke as the "suppressed cries of natural compassion . . . filled men with avarice, ambition and vice," which culminates in "perpetual conflicts" and "a horrible state of war." The solution is the consensual act of establishing government, a common arbitrator that renders "secure to every man the possession of what belongs to him." Rousseau offers a ruthless critique of the egoism of competitive market society. His indictment of liberal values anticipates Marx in its bitterness. Naturalness is replaced by artificiality. "Society offers to us only an assembly of artificial men." Men are alienated from their real selves. It became their interest "to appear what they really were not. To be and to seem became two totally different things."[11]

Natural man was authentic man who lived for and within himself. Social—read modern market—man lives "outside himself" and "only knows how to live in the opinion of others." The market determines identity and sense of self, for men are "always asking others what we are, and never daring to ask ourselves." Few critics of modernity and competitive egoism have surpassed Rousseau in his scathing indictment of civilized—read market—man. "Civilized man, on the other hand, is always moving, sweating, toiling, and racking his brains to find still more laborious occupations, he goes on in drudgery to his last moment, and even seeks death to put himself in a position to live, or renounces life to acquire immortality."[12]

For our purposes, it is important to realize that Rousseau is here, in fact, talking about *men*, not humanity. Civil society, as deplorable as it is, is the domain of fathers and enshrines the values of fathers. "Ambition, avarice, and tyranny" are the values of fathers, Rousseau notes in *Emile*. The laws are "more concerned about property than people," more interested in peace than virtue, and that is because "the laws give too little authority to the mother."[13] It is the father who works ceaselessly and ruthlessly to increase the property of the family's holdings. It is he who "enjoys not a moment's relaxation." Only when this egoism of the father is transcended by compassion and love for others can true moral community be found.[14]

11. Ibid., 249, 251, 247.
12. Ibid., 270.
13. Rousseau, *Emile*, 7.
14. Rousseau, *Origin of Inequality*, 275.

This triumph of the General Will introduces the third stage in Rousseau's developmental model—the true community forged by the social contract. The principal agency for transcending egoism is the hegemony of mothers. In them the "gentle voice" of compassion and pity has survived civilization and modernity; it flows through their milk, assuming, of course, that they are active and hardworking and have not succumbed to the aristocratic temptations of idleness, reading, fancy clothes, and, alas, baby farming. For Rousseau there is a dialectic with "the violence of self-love" confronting the "natural feeling" of "compassion." The former is dominant in men, the latter in women. When there is a street brawl, he tells us in *Origin of Inequality*, men prudently retreat, lest they become hurt. It is "the market-women who part the combatants, and hinder gentlefolk from cutting one another's throats."[15] The General Will is politicized compassion and pity for others and its teachers are mothers. Rousseau's utopian vision of true community is, in fact, a maternal state.

Before I turn to that maternal ideal more specifically, it is important to note how significant Einaudi's reading of Rousseau is as a foundation for the argument I am making. Twenty years ago it was he who most vividly drew attention to the organic relationship between Rousseau's texts (to be sure, not in gender terms as offered here). He described the earlier works of Rousseau "as descriptions of what Rousseau did not want to accept as a way of life." Einaudi was not deceived, as were many, into misreading Rousseau as an apologist for primitivism and the noble savage. He saw quite correctly that *The Social Contract* was by no means a contradiction of Rousseau's earlier writings but a logical development out of them: "The contrast between the *Discourses* and *The Social Contract* is that between analysis and prescription. In the former, Rousseau tells us what is wrong with the world as it exists and tries to give us the criteria by which we can evaluate ourselves. In the latter, he provides the norms that ought to be followed in a free democratic state."[16]

To return to my argument and to that third stage of analysis, the prescriptive utopian ideal of a free democratic state or true community: in this new order egoistic liberalism would be transcended, human nature transformed. Humanity would realize its species poten-

15. Ibid., 226.
16. Einaudi, *Early Rousseau*, 157.

tial. "Each individual, who is by himself a complete and solitary whole," will recognize himself as "part of a greater whole" from which he receives "life and being."[17] Acknowledging that "each citizen is nothing and can do nothing without the rest" produces a moral polity. The triumph of the General Will over particular wills is, then, the triumphant return of compassion and pity, for when citizens "respect the sacred bonds of their respective communities, they will love their fellow citizens."[18] *The Social Contract* represents a profound realignment of priorities. The public realm is privileged over the private sphere. It is beautifully put in Rousseau's resounding repudiation of representation found in chapter 15.

> The better the Constitution of a State is, the more do public affairs encroach on private in the minds of the citizens. Private affairs are even of much less importance, because the aggregate of the common happiness furnishes a greater proportion of that of each individual, so that there is less for him to seek in particular cares. In a well-ordered city every man flies to the assemblies. Under a bad government no one cares to stir a step to get to them, because no one is interested in what happens there because it is foreseen that the General Will will not prevail, and lastly because domestic cares are all absorbing.[19]

How does Rousseau propose that states actually enter this utopian moral third stage where the General Will prevails and egoism is overcome? Rousseau, we must remember, offered various practical suggestions. Nationalism and "a purely civil profession of faith" would both turn individuals from preoccupation with self to love of community. These strategies to which he would return time and again in his writings would be of profound influence on the great democratic nationalists of the next century, such as Mazzini. Reducing the size of states was another practical suggestion Rousseau offered. A face-to-face society, "one in which every member may be known by every other," is much more likely to evoke concern for the public good.[20] One of the most powerful tools Rousseau envisioned encouraging love of community over love of self was education—state-controlled education. This advocacy is a benchmark of Rousseau's rejection of

17. Jean-Jacques Rousseau, *The Social Contract*, trans. G.D.H. Cole (New York: Dutton, 1950), 38.
18. Rousseau, *Origin of Inequality*, 282.
19. Rousseau, *Social Contract*, 93.
20. Ibid., 139, 49.

the individual-centered ideals of the liberal tradition for which state control of education is anathema to this very day. "To form citizens," Rousseau tells us, "is not the work of a day." It requires states "to educate them when they are children." The state must teach its citizens "to regard their individuality only in its relation to the body of the state, and to be aware, so to speak, of their own existence merely as a part of that of the state. They might at length come to identify themselves in some degree with this greater whole, to feel themselves members of their country, and to love it with that exquisite feeling which no isolated person has save for himself."[21]

Central to Rousseau's strategy for transcending the private and privileging the public is also an undermining of the authority of fathers. Education for public spirit specifically requires that "government ought the less indiscriminately to abandon to the intelligence and prejudices of fathers the education of their children, as that education is of still greater importance to the state than to the fathers." The prejudices of fathers, we remember, foster egoism, ambition, avarice, and tyranny. "Public authority by taking the place of the father" brings into being a maternalized state. Rousseau's language in describing the impact of "public education . . . under magistrates established by the sovereign" renders the state as mother:

> If children are brought up in common in the bosom of equality; if they are imbued with the laws of the state and the precepts of the General Will; if they are taught to respect these above all things; if they are surrounded by examples and objects which constantly remind them of the tender mother who nourishes them, of the love she bears them . . . we cannot doubt they will learn to cherish one another mutually as brothers, to will nothing contrary to the will of society.[22]

We now better understand the metaphorical importance of Rousseau's preoccupation with breast-feeding in *Emile*. Breast-feeding is symbolic of the politicized maternal state. If mothers abandon their babies to "hired nurses" egoism reigns unchecked. "How should they love one another? Each thinks of himself first." But when mothers "deign to nurse their own children, there will be a reform in morals." Most important, there will be, Rousseau adds, "no lack of citizens

21. Jean-Jacques Rousseau, *A Discourse on Political Economy*, trans. G.D.H. Cole (New York: Dutton, 1950), 307–8.
22. Ibid., 308–9.

for the state." By nursing their children mothers perform the crucial function of passing on to children the compassion that in the General Will is the politicized love for others. If women suckle their own children "natural feeling will revive in every heart."[23]

We have here the source of the powerful nineteenth-century ideal, the cult of the republican mother, which insists that the cultivation of public-spirited citizens takes place in the home by the example of nurturing, self-denying, loving mothers. Because of its use by later opponents of women's suffrage, this ideal of the republican mother has been justly criticized by feminist activists and scholars. To dwell on its forward-looking inadequacies neglects, however, its backward-looking progressive aspects. The cult of republican motherhood was an intrinsic expression of the general intellectual repudiation of the monarchical and aristocratic principles in favor of the republican ideal of self-government. This republican ideal placed tremendous stress, much too much we know in retrospect, on personal virtue and morality. It insisted that one great failing of the old order was its sinful, vice-ridden, corrupt, luxurious, and wasteful immorality. People governing themselves would introduce a new virtue and morality in public life, expressing writ large on the public stage the private morality of the virtuous middle-class bearers of the ideology of self-government. Rousseau's idyllic contrast of the peasant family with the sinfulness of Parisian high life, and Jefferson's of yeomen farmers with vice-ridden city dwellers (high or low), both capture the flavor of this vision.

At work here is the persistence of the humanist conviction (with its roots in antiquity as well as the Renaissance) that the moral tone of society and the public sphere is dependent on the personal morality of governors, whether they are kings and dukes or artisans and farmers. Structural variables of class and the economy are irrelevant before the controlling influence of personality. Moral persons produce moral societies, thus the importance of the family in the great transition from monarchic/aristocratic rule to self-government. Here were shaped the personal qualities that produced the new more moral public order. In this great shift of regime principles, private virtues were seen as the key to a good society and thus the crucial political

23. Rousseau, *Emile*, 12–14.

and civic role of the mother, albeit all the while she was being denied the public trappings of citizenship.

What I am suggesting is that the republican mother cannot be dismissed out of hand as demeaning to women simply because she would later be used to fight suffrage. She deserves credit for embodying a specific progressive moment in modern history in general and in women's history in particular. Wollstonecraft bears witness to this more balanced assessment. She shares the basic humanist assumption that I have suggested informs the ideal of republican motherhood. "Private virtue," she writes, is "the only security of public freedom and universal happiness." Elsewhere she notes that "public spirit must be nurtured by private virtue." Wollstonecraft demands that both men and women pay closer attention to the cultivation of personal and private virtues such as modesty and chastity. But she, too, like Rousseau, sees the family and motherhood as the crucible for forging the private virtues required for a republican order of self-government. "If you wish to make good citizens," she writes, "you must first exercise the affections of a son and a brother. This is the only way to expand the heart; for public affections, as well as public virtues, must ever grow out of the private character." She is convinced that "affection for mankind" is produced only by the first affections of familiar love.[24]

Wollstonecraft's assumptions are very close to Rousseau's. She insists that "few . . . have had much affection for mankind, who did not first love their parents, their brothers, sisters and even the domestic brutes whom they first played with."[25] In *Emile* Rousseau asks: "Can devotion to the state exist apart from the love of those near and dear to us? Is it not the good son, the good husband, the good father, who makes the good citizen?"[26]

Running Wollstonecraft's familial nursery for citizenship is the mother. "If children are to be educated to understand the true principles of patriotism," she writes in the dedication to her *Vindication of the Rights of Women*, "their mother must be a patriot." Wollstonecraft suggests, in fact, that the most important task of woman as an active citizen is "to educate her children." To be sure, unlike Rousseau,

24. Mary Wollstonecraft, *A Vindication of the Rights of Women*, ed. Miriam Brody Kramnick (Harmondsworth: Penguin Books, 1972), 88, 251, 279.

25. Ibid., 279.

26. Rousseau, *Emile*, 326.

Wollstonecraft does not see this citizenly responsibility as simply breast-feeding and other natural expressions of maternal love, nurture, and care. Wollstonecraft's republican mother educates citizens not only through her power of example but also by cultivating the rational faculties of her children. Not only, then, does Wollstonecraft depart from Rousseau in seeing women doing much more than merely being republican mothers—being shopkeepers and professionals, for example; she also sees the republican mother as herself a rational mentor. If she is to develop in her children "the love of mankind," she must study and master "the moral and civic interests of mankind; but the education and situation of women at present shuts her out from such investigations."[27] It is the language of Wollstonecraft's feminism, but expressed, still, in terms of Rousseau's discourse of republican motherhood.

ROUSSEAU AND SEXUALITY

Having argued that in his political theory women played a more redemptive role than Rousseau scholarship usually concedes, I now turn to the theme of his general chauvinism, which begins with marriage. One cannot read *La Nouvelle Héloise* without sensing Rousseau's bitter indictment of marriage as a commercial transaction. Julie asks herself if her father has sold her. "Yes, he has made his daughter into a piece of goods . . . and profited at my expense. He has paid for his life with mine!" Rousseau envisions marriage as a choice made "more on their hearts." Sophy and Emile fall in love at first sight.[28] In place of marriages arranged for family profit, Rousseau proposes in his *Letter to d'Alembert* that public festivals be held where youth of marriageable age "have occasion to get a taste for one another and to see one another . . . which better permits them to show themselves off, with the charms and the faults which they might possess, to the people whose interest it is to know them well."[29] On the other hand, like Wollstonecraft, Rousseau can be read as also pleading for mar-

27. Wollstonecraft, *Vindication*, 87, 259, 87.
28. Jean-Jacques Rousseau, *Julie ou La Nouvelle Héloise*, in *Oeuvres complètes* (Paris: Gallimard, 1959), 1:28, 94; *Emile*, 378.
29. Jean-Jacques Rousseau, *Politics and the Arts: Letter to d'Alembert on the Theater*, trans. A. Bloom (Ithaca: Cornell University Press, 1960), 128.

riage based not only on physical and sexual attraction but on a friendship that would survive the couple's growing old. Many years after
they had come together Saint-Preux tells Julie, "When age had
calmed the first fires of our love, the habit of thinking and feeling
together would generate a friendship no less tender to succeed our
transports."[30]

On the question of sexuality itself, it is possible also to discern a
different Rousseau. Convention has it that Rousseau regards women
as passive objects, devoid of sexual interest, and designed by nature
for male gratification. There is ample evidence of this in his novels,
his *Letter to d'Alembert*, and most self-consciously in his treatment of
Sophy in *Emile*. Yet a careful reading of Rousseau reveals that he had
a much more ambivalent appreciation of female sexuality. In his *Letter
to d'Alembert* Rousseau describes sexual desire and passion as "equal
on both sides." Why then, he asks, must "the order of attack and
defense" have man "the maker" and woman "the receiver" of "advances"? His answer is "nature wanted it so." Man must be auda-
cious; "someone has to declare."[31] But it is not simply nature that
would have it so; it is also Rousseau. He is, in fact, preoccupied with
what he sees as the limitless nature of female sexuality. Sophy has
"sexual power" that "is or appears to be boundless." In contrast to
this Rousseau laments "the limited power of the male, and the moderation of his desires." Sophy's nature is "inflammable." She herself
worries about her desires; "she doubts her control of herself." Rousseau, in turn, worries about the possibility of women's domination of
men resulting from the insatiable quality of their desires. He fears that
"men tyrannized over by the women, would at last become their victims, and would be dragged to their death."[32]

How, then, do you prevent this inevitable outcome of women's
natural inclination "to carry everything to extremes"? Rousseau re-
plies that "this enthusiasm must be kept in check." "Do not leave
them for a moment without restraint," he advises in book 5 of *Emile*.[33] But the restraint is, of course, not physical but ideological. And
so Rousseau offers the ideal of woman as timid, modest, and chaste,

30. *La Nouvelle Héloise*, 1:23, 83–84.
31. Rousseau, *Letter to d'Alembert*, 83–84.
32. Rousseau, *Emile*, 393, 391, 322.
33. Ibid., 333.

her desires "veiled by shame."[34] We are left with this, then. Rousseau's ideal of female sexual passivity is an artifice designed to repress an otherwise uncontrollable female sexual assertiveness. He seems to personify the often made feminist claim that fear of female sexuality is the source of male domination.

There is one very important respect, however, in which Rousseau departs from this feminist formulaic linkage of domination to fear, and that is in Rousseau's own sexual life. Nature and his own writings may have destined women "to let themselves be vanquished" and to be always the "submitting" partner,[35] but in his own bedroom Rousseau was the passive and submissive male to dominant, assertive females. His "tastes and desires, . . . passions" throughout his life, he writes in his *Confessions*, were "diametrically opposed" to what "should normally have developed." His "peculiarity," as he described it, was to experience sexual pleasure only if he were "to fall on my knees before a powerful mistress, to obey her commands, to beg for her forgiveness." Involved also was "the one favor" necessary for ultimate gratification, being beaten by his lover. One should not minimize the significance Rousseau gives to these predilections in his characterization of self. It is revealed in all its candor in the course of retelling the traumatic episode of his childhood when he was falsely accused of stealing a comb. The exquisite pleasure of being beaten by the hands of his beloved Mlle. Lambercier is inextricably linked in his psyche to his commitment to root out (male) injustice whether perpetrated by "fierce tyrants" or "rascally priests."[36]

ROUSSEAU REVISITED

Some reassessment of Rousseau's views on women is in order, then. His attitudes, as we have seen, are more complex than is generally acknowledged. To be sure, he writes in hierarchical imagery, confining women always to the lower ranks of status and privileging men with the higher. Yet in his political theory the highest stage of ethical politics is rendered in terms of the transvaluation of male and

34. Rousseau, *Letter to d'Alembert*, 84.
35. Ibid., 86.
36. Rousseau, *Confessions*, 26–27, 28, 30.

female, father and mother. In his writings he ridicules women "when
they take on the masculine and firm assurance of the man." He be-
rates Emile, who "cringes and grovels before" Sophy.[37] Yet in his
own life Rousseau, far from, as Eva Figes put it, "shudder[ing] at the
very notion of women making sexual advances," preferred masterful
women.[38]

This analysis may seem to have strayed far from my original
charge, which was to offer some reflections prompted by Einaudi's
Rousseau. Yet one of the most original contributions of Einaudi's
Early Rousseau was its depiction of Rousseau as a "modern man"
whose life and thought had particular meaning for people in the twentieth century dealing with the issues of "disintegration, loneliness,
and chaos" they face. It was a brilliant insight in 1967, and in these
reflections on gender and sexuality in Rousseau we see its protean
relevance to our lives today, so preoccupied with these very concerns.

I offer no explanatory scheme to help clear up these confusions in
Rousseau. All I can do is point to certain avenues one might want to
explore, avenues that, in fact, just as Einaudi would have it, apply as
much to our contemporary concerns as to Rousseau's. The ambivalence over gender in his public creed and over sexuality in his private
needs must surely in some way be linked to the death of his mother
in giving birth to him. It marks his life and thought with the dual
themes of a constant quest for maternal love and an agonizing sense
of guilt.

A second potential path to pursue is not psychological but intellectual. It is a quest for correctives to the overly simplistic and fixed
ways we tend to characterize ideas and preferences in the language of
hierarchy and privilege. It is as inherent in the way we read Rousseau's
texts and life as we do any other. If nothing else, however, poststruc-
turalist scholarship commends to us a more complicated understanding of binary hierarchies of privilege and status. The relationship between the subordinated low and the privileged high is by no means
static and determined. As Peter Stallybrass and Allon White note in
their *Politics and Poetics of Transgression*, the "lower strata . . . are both
reviled and desired." Along with revulsion (note Rousseau's preoc-

37. Rousseau, *Letter to d'Alembert*, 88; *Emile*, 394.
38. Eva Figes, *Patriarchal Attitudes* (Greenwich, Conn.: Fawcett, 1971), 104.

cupation with Sophy's cleanliness) goes attraction and desire. Their formulation seems particularly apt when applied to Rousseau and gender. There develops, they note, a dependence on precisely those others who are being rigorously opposed and excluded at the social level. It is for this reason that "what is socially peripheral is so symbolically central."[39]

Women may be socially peripheral for Rousseau, but they are also symbolically central. Sorting out how and why that was the case will, as Einaudi noted twenty years ago about Rousseau in general, render him crucial in our coming to terms with "the paradoxes and absurdities of modernity."[40]

39. Peter Stallybrass and Allon White, *Politics and Poetics of Transgression* (Ithaca: Cornell University Press, 1986), 4–5.
40. Einaudi, *Early Rousseau*, 7.

3

The Liberal Agenda of the French-Italian Inquiry

ROY PIERCE

THIS CHAPTER is a retrospective review of the four books that appeared in the French-Italian Inquiry, which was directed by Mario Einaudi at Cornell University between 1949 and 1955.[1] At that time, the fate of postwar Western Europe was a crucial issue in comparative government studies. By 1949 Mario Einaudi had already contributed a substantial section on constitutional government in postwar France and Italy to a textbook on comparative government.[2] In those years the flow of developments in Western Europe produced a degree of intellectual excitement in Boardman Hall[3] similar to what students of the Soviet Union or China must feel today as they read about each

1. Mario Einaudi, Jean-Marie Domenach, and Aldo Garosci, *Communism in Western Europe* (Ithaca: Cornell University Press, 1951); Mario Einaudi and François Goguel, *Christian Democracy in Italy and France* (Notre Dame, Ind.: University of Notre Dame Press, 1952); François Goguel, *France under the Fourth Republic* (Ithaca: Cornell University Press, 1952); Mario Einaudi, Maurice Byé, and Ernesto Rossi, *Nationalization in France and Italy* (Ithaca: Cornell University Press, 1955).

2. Mario Einaudi, "Constitutional Government: France and Italy," in Fritz Morstein Marx, ed., *Foreign Governments: The Dynamics of Politics Abroad* (New York: Prentice-Hall, 1949), pt. 3.

3. Boardman Hall housed the Government Department and the History Department, as well as classrooms. It was razed in 1954 to make way for Olin Library.

new turn of events in a part of the world to which they are in the process of acquiring what will almost surely be a lifelong professional commitment.

THE MAJOR THEMES OF THE INQUIRY

The volumes of the French-Italian Inquiry, as their titles clearly indicate, are about communism, Christian Democracy, the French Fourth Republic, and the nationalization of industry. In the pages that follow I say very little directly about these subjects, but instead discuss several central themes that run throughout Mario Einaudi's contributions to the books of the inquiry that together may be called the inquiry's agenda. By this I mean something akin to the existentialist notion of a "project." It refers both to acts performed, or—more appropriately in this case—to subjects discussed *and* to the underlying orientations that led to their being placed on the table in the first place. But if the element of intention is essential to my meaning, it does not exhaust it, because I mean something that is not only intended but also achieved. In speaking of the inquiry's agenda, I refer to central themes raised because of conviction about their long-term importance and treated with such rigor and clarity that their message cannot fail to be understood.

There are four such major themes:

1. the direction of scholarly attention to Italy within a democratic context;
2. recognition of the importance of European economic cooperation within the framework of an Atlantic community;
3. separation of religion from politics; and
4. focusing of responsibility for political success or failure on political elites.

These themes constitute elements of the best of European liberalism, a current of thought that was, at the time, only thinly represented in continental Europe, as expressed by a scholar with a special degree of familiarity and a special bond of sympathy with Italy.

ITALY AS A DEMOCRATIC NATION

It may appear odd to single out as a distinctive theme of something called the French–Italian Inquiry that this inquiry directed people's attention toward Italy. But just as Mark Twain said that Wagner's music wasn't as bad as it sounded, my point is not as tautological as it seems. For I have said nothing about the books in this series focusing attention on France. They did that, of course, but scholarly attention in the Anglo–Saxon world would have turned toward France in the early postwar period even in the absence of the volumes under discussion here. The consequent scholarship would, of course, have been much poorer as a result, but scholarship there would have been, and it would have been organized around concepts appropriate to democracy. Lines of continuity and discontinuity with the Third Republic would have been emphasized. The unspoken assumption would have been that French politics reflected a deeply rooted democratic tradition. The ways in which that tradition was expressed concretely would have been conventionally described. Only departures from that democratic tradition would have required investigation and explanation.

It is less certain that Italy would have been perceived in the same democratic perspective if the French–Italian Inquiry had not been undertaken. Italy might well have been regarded with suspicion in the early postwar years, through filters calibrated more to the Fascist past than to the democratic future, if the inquiry had not turned scholarly attention toward Italy as a democracy grappling with difficult social problems and struggling against a powerful, antidemocratic, domestic challenge in the form of the Communist party. Italy is presented not only as a budding democracy but also as a beleaguered one.

This perspective on Italy would have been promoted even if the inquiry had dealt with Italy alone, but it was reinforced by the linkage of Italy with France. For the pairing with France meant that Italy was not a unique case. It shared common problems with France, a country with an impressive democratic heritage. Italy's problems could not be traced exclusively to distinct national experience. Italy was a modern democracy and should be considered in that light by scholars and statespersons.

The world would have been compelled to regard Italy in that democratic perspective soon enough in any case. After all, Italy is one of the great success stories of the postwar era. If one takes the underground economy into account and combines it with the statistically visible evidence of economic performance, Italy may have recently surpassed Great Britain in gross national product rankings.[4] But the books of the inquiry accelerated that inevitable recognition, and to our considerable enrichment. The inquiry not only enlightened us about Italy in a uniquely authoritative fashion; it also made possible the series of major contributions that followed: by Samuel H. Barnes, Joseph LaPalombara, Giacomo Sani, and Sidney Tarrow, among others. It may well be the reason why Italy was selected as one of the sites for the studies reported in Gabriel Almond and Sidney Verba's *Civic Culture*.[5]

Before World War II, scholars interested in democracy in Europe concentrated on British politics. By focusing on France and Italy, the inquiry altered the balance of attention between Great Britain and the continent. By treating France and Italy in parallel fashion, it also shifted the direction and the nature of scholarly investigation on the continent itself. Thanks to the inquiry, there was no lag between the restoration of Italy as a democratic nation and the scholarly perception of Italy as a democratic nation.

EUROPEAN INTEGRATION AND THE ATLANTIC COMMUNITY

A second theme that emerges in sharp relief from the inquiry is early recognition of the potential significance of European integration and the crucial importance of linkage between Western Europe and the United States. There is nothing short of a prophetic quality to the occasional, but always inspired, comments that are made on these subjects.

4. *The Economist*, "A Survey of the Italian Economy: The Flawed Renaissance," 27 February 1988 (supplement to vol. 306), 4–9.
5. Gabriel A. Almond and Sidney Verba, *The Civic Culture* (Princeton: Princeton University Press, 1963).

We are, remember, in the early postwar years. The only major expression of European unity at the time was the European Coal and Steel Community, referred to from its origin as the Schuman Plan.[6] The North Atlantic Treaty Organization receives only fleeting mention in the inquiry volumes. The Marshall Plan, however, is given a central and commanding role.

In part, the role of the Marshall Plan was viewed as defensive. Speaking of the Italian elections of 1948, Einaudi had this to say:

> The championship of political freedom, however notable in itself, would not have been enough to carry the day for Christian Democracy had it not been accompanied by the more concrete hope offered by the Marshall Plan. Without the Plan there would have been no alternative to the setting up of a dictatorship to carry the country through a period of economic readjustment and of even lower standards of living. The only party in a position to do that would have been the Communist Party. The Marshall Plan, by holding out the hope of the reintegration of the country within the Western economic system and of a slow improvement of the standard of living of the people, instead of restricting Italy's freedom of choice, introduced that freedom for the first time, and made the Italian elections free in the substantial meaning that a ballot could be cast in more than one way.[7]

If the circumstances of the period led to this kind of emphasis on the defensive role of the Marshall Plan, as the financial expression of the protective role of the United States vis-à-vis an economically weakened and militarily defenseless continent,[8] the inquiry nevertheless also projects the vision of a vibrant, attainable future. The historic context is defined by the cold war and its transposition onto the domestic political scenes of France and Italy, the two Western European countries with large Communist parties. Democratic institutions and practices are under direct and immediate threat in both countries. The Marshall Plan and—in less clear-cut fashion—the Schuman Plan are barriers against imminent attack. But they are also the foundations of

6. A favorable view of the even less embracing French-Italian Customs Union of 1948 appears in Einaudi, "Constitutional Government," in Morstein Marx, ed., *Foreign Governments.*

7. Einaudi and Goguel, *Christian Democracy in Italy and France,* 52–53.

8. The magnitude of the contribution was barely acknowledged in France, even in Jean Monnet's 1952 report on the first French modernization plan. See Alfred Grosser, *Les Occidentaux: Les pays d'Europe et les Etats-Unis depuis la guerre* (Paris: Fayard, 1978), 105.

an enduring, good society expressive of liberal principles. Such a society has its own inner strength and provides its own defenses. "While the aims of the Marshall and Schuman Plans are primarily economic at this stage, they are bound to bring about far-reaching social and political changes that will create the conditions under which communism will not be able to survive."[9]

By the time of the publication in 1955 of the book on nationalization of industry, some of the inquiry's earlier enthusiasm for the European Coal and Steel Community has subsided and, perhaps in part because of the deflating experience of the French rejection of the European Defense Community Treaty, the outlook for the future is stated in muted tones. "There are at present no indications that any such expansion [of the supranational approach] will be forthcoming in the near future, at least not without the amendment of the terms provided by the Schuman Treaty."[10]

This moment of caution not long before the Messina conference and the Rome treaties created the European Economic Community is insignificant compared to the clarity with which the implications of the European Coal and Steel Community were viewed while it was still little more than a document. The Schuman Plan, we were told, provides for "the combination of an invigorated economic system and a faster circulation of goods and men" which "denies the basic premises of communism, which are those of the inflexible allocation of men to the performance of fixed tasks in a society from which the experimental approach and the free trade of ideas have been banned."[11]

SEPARATION OF CHURCH AND STATE

The third basic theme of the French-Italian Inquiry is the separation of church and state. The inquiry is at once an explanation of how and why religion became intertwined with politics in France and Italy and a plea for a genuine, and not simply formal, separation of religion from politics.

9. Einaudi, Domenach, and Garosci, *Communism in Western Europe*, 41.
10. Einaudi, Byé, and Rossi, *Nationalization in France and Italy*, 61.
11. Einaudi, Domenach, and Garosci, *Communism in Western Europe*, 44.

The role of religion in politics in the European countries of the Mediterranean basin and the Iberian peninsula is difficult for young Americans to grasp. When students today learn that the electoral choices of voters in any of those countries can be predicted more accurately on the basis of their religion and, for those professing to be Catholic, the frequency of their church attendance than on the basis of any other demographic characteristic—including age, sex, class, or region—their responses range from puzzlement to disbelief. The inquiry volume on communism pointed out long ago that the words *laicism* and *clericalism*, which had been "fighting words in Europe" since the eighteenth century, were "unknown to the Anglo-Saxon world."[12] And better than any other works I know the inquiry volumes both describe the contemporary relevance of religion for politics and explain how the admixture of religion and politics originated and developed.

This is done mainly in the book on Christian Democracy, in the historical sections in particular.[13] The description and explanation also appear, in a gem of encapsulation, in the fifth chapter of François Goguel's *France under the Fourth Republic* (1952). In that chapter, Goguel—who was already an outstanding young French scholar, and who was eventually to succeed André Siegfried as the dean of French political scientists—not only traced the origins and development of the historic association of the Catholic church with the French Right but also argued that the persisting antagonism of many French democrats to the exercise even of legitimate authority was the expression of a sort of secular faith that mirrored the intensity and dogmatism of the faith of their clerical enemies:

> The existence of this [Catholic] opposition has greatly contributed to give to the idea of democracy, in the minds of those who were attached to it—one is tempted to say of its believers—a very special content: their fear of deviations, their desire for orthodoxy, their defensive attitude, their suspicious reaction to the acceptance of democracy by its former opponents—all flow from it. If democracy, in the minds of its advocates, has frequently appeared to be an idea, a value in itself,

12. Ibid., 11.
13. Einaudi and Goguel, *Christian Democracy in Italy and France*, esp. pt. I, chap. 1, and pt. II, chap. 1.

the practical application of which mattered less than its doctrinal purity, this also derives partially from the fact that political struggles in France during a considerable period took on the aspect of philosophic or religious controversies.[14]

But the inquiry is not content to describe and explain; it also advocates. The intervention of the Catholic church in political affairs has been an obstacle to the growth and development of those liberal values on the basis of which communal fraternity and economic modernization can thrive. The ambiguous position of the Italian Christian Democrats in the postwar years concerning the distinction between religion and politics generally, and the independence of the Christian Democratic party from the church in particular, is a source of great political danger. The danger is the advance of communism. Particularly in Italy, but not only there, the strength of communism "is in part due to the presence of historical traditions which have linked freedom and democracy to the battle against ecclesiastical interference in temporal life."[15] "Today European communism appears as the strongest supporter of a materialistic approach which vindicates for the community rights which the church is charged with trying to take away."[16] The message could hardly be any clearer. Communism in Western Europe thrives on the persistent promotion of ecclesiastical interests by secular political institutions; it is a matter of the highest urgency that church and state be separated on terms roughly analogous to those arrived at in the Anglo-Saxon democracies.

Rather than trace all the ramifications of the church–state question in France and Italy since the inquiry volumes were produced, or extend consideration of the question to other countries, it is enough to recall here that religion-related issues such as education, divorce, birth control, and abortion have periodically brought the larger, central question to the fore; that—at least in France—the educational issue can bring hundreds of thousands of people into the streets, on one side of the issue or the other; and that it required almost twenty years of negotiations between the Italian government and the Vatican to produce a new concordat, which was soon followed by a dispute

14. Goguel, *France under the Fourth Republic*, 152.
15. Einaudi and Goguel, *Christian Democracy in Italy and France*, 88.
16. Einaudi, Domenach, and Garosci, *Communism in Western Europe*, 12.

over how to implement its provisions relating to voluntary religious instruction in the public schools.[17]

In these days when national conferences of Catholic bishops in different countries consider similar questions of war and peace but arrive at different conclusions,[18] and when the president of the United States advocates prayer in the public schools, we are constantly reminded that the frontiers of church and state are imprecise. Students seeking guidance about how to approach these and related issues can use all the help they can get. The inquiry volumes were among the first to introduce English-speaking students to the broad question of church-state relations without cant, vindictiveness, or sanctimoniousness.[19]

RESPONSIBILITIES OF POLITICAL ELITES

The fourth and final main characteristic of the French-Italian Inquiry is that it is conducted almost exclusively at the elite level.[20] The Inquiry laments the dearth of worthy princes, dispenses advice across a wide range of subjects to those princes who are at hand, and sternly holds them to their responsibilities.

The inquiry does not regard social forces, economic foundations, and constitutional structures as irrelevant to political outcomes. The appeal of the Western European Communist parties is attributed in large part to "social rigidities and class distinctions."[21] The Marshall

17. The 1929 concordat was replaced by a new one in February 1984, following negotiations between the Italian government and the Vatican which had been formally opened in 1967. The dispute over its implementation occurred in the fall of 1987.

18. The French bishops are less categorically opposed to nuclear weapons than are the bishops of the United States. See *The Challenge of Peace: God's Promise and Our Response: A Pastoral Letter on War and Peace*, 3 May 1983, issued by the National Conference of Catholic Bishops (Washington, D.C.: Office of Publishing Services, U.S. Catholic Conference, 1983); and *Winning the Peace: Joint Pastoral Letter of the French Bishops* (San Francisco: Ignatius, 1984).

19. Religion as a factor in mass electoral behavior was not studied empirically in France before 1965 because it was believed that the subject was so emotion laden that the public would not answer questions about it.

20. The only portion of the inquiry that lingers at any length on the mass level is the discussion by Goguel of the 1951 French election (*France under the Fourth Republic*, 90–120).

21. Einaudi, Domenach, and Garosci, *Communism in Western Europe*, 55.

Plan furnished Western Europe with the vital economic margin that guaranteed survival and held open the promise of a brighter future. Constitutional issues are closely analyzed in the treatment of the early postwar Italian Christian Democratic party.[22]

It is men and women, however, who are the agents of political change, and it is on whether they meet their responsibilities well or ill that the decisive political outcomes depend. The rise and consolidation of Italian Fascism was the result of the "failure and crisis of the Italian political classes."[23] Fascism and the decadence of post–World War I Italy reflected simultaneously "a constitutional, political, administrative, and economic crisis," yet it is not the severity and complexity of the crisis that bear responsibility for the depressing outcome. The fault, rather, rests with those Italian political leaders who held a majority in Parliament and the country but who failed to overcome the crisis. In this view of political responsibility, conditions are not actors, they are not unchangeable, and they may not serve as excuses. It is the responsibility of political leaders to change or overcome conditions, not to yield to them.

The inquiry is not exactly indulgent toward the early postwar French and Italian political elites. Neither France nor Italy "has succeeded in developing a political class conscious of its responsibilities and an administrative machinery fully able to perform the tasks of a modern state." The two continental countries fare badly on this score in a comparison with the Anglo-Saxon democracies. "Both countries are still far removed from the developments which in England have, within the last century, brought to a position of command a political class substantially independent of private interests and in the United States have led to the New Deal, that is, to the rebirth of the concept of the common welfare."[24] There is in this comparison virtually an invitation to Robert Putnam to spell out in more detail how English politicians differ from Italian ones on the dimensions that shape their political values and orientations.[25]

The inquiry offers a good deal of advice to the somewhat dubious

22. Einaudi and Goguel, *Christian Democracy in Italy and France*, pt. 1, chap. 3.
23. Ibid., 21.
24. Einaudi, Domenach, and Garosci, *Communism in Western Europe*, 12, 15.
25. Robert Putnam, *The Beliefs of Politicians: Ideology, Conflict, and Democracy in Britain and Italy* (New Haven: Yale University Press, 1973).

leaderships of postwar France and Italy. This advice covers a wide range of matters, including the organization of the press, the administration of nationalized industries, and constitutional organization on all levels. I do not dwell on any of these issues. There is one political prescription in the inquiry, however, that I do deal with in more than summary fashion, because it occupies a commanding position with regard to much else that is contained in the volumes under discussion. This prescription has to do with the role of political parties and, in particular, with the relationship between what one may call the outside party organizations, on the one hand, and the parliamentary party and (for governing parties) the cabinet, on the other hand.

The Role of Parties

The discussion of "what must be done" to stem the advance of communism in France and Italy includes this admonition:

> The ideas of constitutionalism implied in the new French and Italian constitutions should be permitted to assert themselves fully, in order to give dignity and power to the state acting in the interest of the common good. *First of all*, the excessive claims of parties over constitutional life must be abandoned. From 1945 to 1951 parties have acted as if the sum total of wisdom were entrusted to their hands and as if they alone could speak for the national interest. . . . Unless satisfactory boundaries are established between the jurisdiction of parties and the jurisdiction of constitutional organs, crisis and paralysis will rule.[26]

The theme also appears with exclusive reference to France in an article that appeared in 1951, and it reappears in the Italian context in Einaudi and Goguel.[27]

The position that is argued throughout all of these passages is that party organizations, whether in the form of party members, local leaders, or national directorates, should confine themselves to the discussion of national issues, mainly in association with election campaigns, and allow the party in Parliament and the cabinet to carry out their legislative and executive responsibilities independently.

This position reflects a broad theory of how parliamentary democ-

26. Einaudi, Domenach, and Garosci, *Communism in Western Europe*, 52; italics added.

27. See Mario Einaudi, "The Crisis of Politics and Government in France," *World Politics* 4 (1951):64–84; and Einaudi and Goguel, *Christian Democracy in Italy and France*, 72–74.

racy should operate which is similar to the model presented in Ernest Barker's *Reflections on Government*.[28] Barker—as Einaudi's students all familiarly referred to the book—was required reading in the courses in comparative government at Cornell in the late 1940s. It was the only book on the theory of parliamentary government then and it remains the only book on the theory of parliamentary government today. But unlike the great work on the theory of the separation of powers—*The Federalist*—which tries to demonstrate how certain institutional arrangements will automatically bring about good results (or at least prevent bad results), Barker presents an idealized version of a set of institutional relationships that requires great efforts of self-restraint on the part of politicians if it is to be realized in practice.

Barker believed that parties are essential for democracy, but he also believed that the greatest internal difficulty of democracy in the twentieth century had perhaps been "the exaltation of party, and of the disciplines and loyalties of party." His position was that party organizations have the indispensable role of clarifying broad national issues for choice by the electorate, but that party organizations should not seek to supplant legislatures, which have their own proper sphere in the structure of decision making. And similarly, the legislature should not usurp the proper powers of the executive, which must be allowed to operate from its own special vantage point in the construction of public policy.[29] This is the same theoretical perspective from which the volumes of the inquiry approach the overall political process. There is no question of doing away with parties. Parties have "vital roles in political life as the vehicles and regulators of discussion."[30] But party leaders should understand that "a distinction must be made between party interests and government responsibilities";[31] there must be a "moderation of party egoism" and an "improvement of the constitutional balance [between the legislature and the executive]";[32] parties must "accept a self-denying attitude and . . . recognize the limits that must be established to their activities."[33]

28. Ernest Barker, *Reflections on Government* (Oxford: Oxford University Press, 1945).

29. Ibid., 85 and chap. 2.

30. Einaudi, Domenach, and Garosci, *Communism in Western Europe*, 52.

31. Einaudi, "Crisis of Politics and Government," 75.

32. Einaudi, Domenach, and Garosci, *Communism in Western Europe*, 53.

33. Einaudi and Goguel, *Christian Democracy in Italy and France*, 73.

The Influence of Rousseau

The theoretical basis for the emphasis in the inquiry on partisan restraint almost surely comes from Rousseau. *The Early Rousseau* did not appear until 1967, but Einaudi's special interest in the political theory of Rousseau was evident well before that date. Einaudi taught political theory as well as comparative government, and the students who took his courses or seminars in political theory during the late 1940s could not fail to recognize the particular importance he attributed to Rousseau.

The central Rousseauean idea that underlies the inquiry's insistence on a self-denying ordinance for party leaders is the distinction between the part and the whole. Rousseau distinguished sharply between particular wills, which expressed only partial interests, and the General Will, which expressed the common interest of the entire community. In the inquiry, Einaudi urges that party leaders limit their claims and allow other institutions to play their proper roles in the overall political process.

Parties are by definition partial, in that they express their particular views about what is right, but this is not the objection raised in the inquiry. The objection, rather, is that parties may seek to substitute themselves for other essential institutions—the Parliament and the executive—whose perspectives on what is right do not necessarily coincide with those of party leaders who do not have parliamentary or executive responsibilities. The formulation of national policy requires the participation of all of these major institutions. It is in this sense that parties are partial and representative of particular wills. They are parts of a larger framework of institutions which, if properly constructed, will produce better results than any of its institutional parts could produce without the contributions of the others. The inquiry does not equate the output of such a balanced system with the expression of the General Will. It makes no such grandiose claim. But the inquiry does speak unabashedly of the purpose of government as being the promotion of the "common good," or the "common welfare," both terms that have already been cited in this chapter.

This application of Rousseauean principles to modern politics is highly distinctive. It is based on Rousseau's differentiation between the whole and its parts, but unlike other works that draw inspiration from Rousseau, the inquiry does not conceive of the whole in terms of mass political participation but rather as an ensemble of complementary institutions. Restraint and self-discipline at the elite level are required if those institutions are to function properly. Responsibility for the quality of government rests squarely with the political leadership. In this context, as in others, the inquiry focuses on the behavior of French and Italian political elites.

This approach to democratic government is quite at variance from that expressed, say, in *The Civic Culture*, which presumes to locate the foundations of democratic government in the configuration of mass attitudes, at a given moment, on a range of matters, many if not most of which the great majority of the population have not considered before that moment. In this latter approach, which focuses on the broad populace, the notion of responsibility hardly appears at all. It is difficult to see how it could, without being applied in such a diffuse and abstract way as to become virtually meaningless.

The French–Italian Inquiry does not lose its way in some maze of public opinion, in which lines of causality are unclear and responsibilities are diluted. It is, instead, directed at political elites, from lower-level party members to what Michel Debré called "these princes who govern us."[34] When democracies fail it is the fault of the political leaders. If those leaders meet their responsibilities, democracies will not only survive but also prosper.

CONCLUDING COMMENTS

Having discussed the underlying themes of the French–Italian Inquiry, I have now only to add a few words about its tone. Two qualities are of special note: the measured, practical way in which points are presented, and the sense of commitment with which they are argued.

The first tonal quality is what one might call its pragmatic approach; this appears most clearly in the volume on nationalization. Nationalization of industry is the only concrete expression of what

34. Michel Debré, *Ces princes qui nous gouvernent* . . . (Paris: Plon, 1957).

Socialists mean by socialism, but the inquiry volume does not approach the issue within the context of political theory; it considers
it as a problem of administrative management. We have here an
operating illustration of what, in a broader, polemical context, was
called "the end of ideology"—the refusal to debate abstractions and
the insistence on dealing with real economic or social or political
phenomena.

The second quality of the inquiry is the sense of conviction with
which its central themes are expressed. Prepared at a time of political
reconstruction in Western Europe, when decisive choices were being
made on both sides of the Atlantic about the basic contours of the
postwar world, the inquiry resonates with concern about what the
outcome of the great adventure will be. There is no contradiction
here between the emphasis on advocacy and the levelheaded, practical
approach just mentioned. The inquiry operates on a plane of common
understanding, accessible to all, but it does so with passionate concern about how it will all turn out.[35]

I have tried to identify the underlying themes that generated that
sense of urgency and sustained that power of conviction. I selected
four central themes: the fervent wish that Italy take its place among
the Western democracies; the instant grasp of the potentialities of
the enlargement of economic freedom in Europe; the separation of
church and state; and insistence on the responsibilities of political
elites.

These themes are not simply a near handful of perhaps interesting,
but nevertheless accidental, topics touched on in the course of more
extensive treatments of larger issues such as communism, Christian
Democracy, constitutional practices, and economic organization in
France and Italy. The order of priority is, rather, the other way
around. The basic themes I have discussed, which are interrelated intellectually and historically, are among the finest and most enduring
tenets of European liberalism. Communism, Christian Democracy,
constitutional issues, and the nationalization of industry were subjects
of great and even vital importance when the books of the French-

35. It may be added that these arguments are presented with a rare degree of elo-
quence, a characteristic of portions of the inquiry which carried over into the classrooms of Boardman Hall. It was not unusual for Einaudi's classes to be followed by
spontaneous student applause.

Italian Inquiry were written. In long-term perspective, however, it is those subjects that are contingent, while the basic liberal themes from which they are unflinchingly approached in the inquiry are the permanent bedrock.

In the flow of political life through time, the saliency of particular issues varies, our models of political rectitude change, and the scale of the political stage itself may be greatly altered. Young scholars concerned with the fate of Western Europe today peer out on a scene that is very different from the one that was the backdrop to the French-Italian Inquiry.

While the Soviet Union struggles to overcome the consequences of a system that Einaudi aptly described almost forty years ago in terms of inflexibility, immobility, lack of experimentation, and the absence of free trade in ideas, communism in Western Europe is well on the way to becoming a historical curiosity. Christian Democracy never became a major political force in France, and while the Italian Christian Democratic party continues to display some of the infirmities that were diagnosed in the inquiry, it does so in conditions that are far less likely to prove fatal than those of some forty years ago.

A scholar today, considering Western Europe on the basis of the same liberal agenda that informed the French-Italian Inquiry, would be less likely to turn to England or the United States for models of political leadership.[36] The dominance of the outside party organization, against which the inquiry inveighed, is as characteristic of the British Labour party as of any major non-Communist party in France or Italy. And one may wonder what happened to the sense of the common good within the political class of the United States, which oscillates between the practice of single-issue politics and (as in Great Britain) the application of a primitive free-market ideology without regard to its human consequences. In the domestic economies of Western Europe, it is no longer nationalization of industry, but privatization, that requires critical analysis.

Within the terms of reference of the French-Italian Inquiry, the greatest changes that have taken place in Western Europe are the altered relationship between Western Europe and the United States and

36. For a similar overall perspective on Great Britain, although different in approach, see Leon D. Epstein, "What Happened to the British Party Model?" *American Political Science Review* 74 (March 1980):9–22.

the enlarged scope of European economic cooperation. The United States still provides Western Europe with its military shield, but economic relationships have been dramatically transformed, as prosperous Europeans (along with Japanese and others) now invest in the United States much as Americans earlier invested in Europe. The last volume of the inquiry appeared just before the formation of the Common Market and referred to the movement toward economic unification of Western Europe in subdued fashion. The movement itself, however, progressed inexorably to the point where now the year 1992—when the Commission of the European Communities hopes to inaugurate a genuinely frontier-free European market—is simultaneously an inspirational symbol for Europeans and a signal to the rest of the world that Western European energies and ambitions are directed toward greater economic cooperation and increased political harmony. It is also the anchoring date for a huge effort, as the European nations try to get their legal, commercial, and economic houses in order. As this colossal task proceeds, within and between the Western European nations, and indeed between Europe and the United States, there will be a multitude of problems and conflicts. There will be great need for people who, whatever their formal political affiliations, understand and apply the kind of liberal agenda that underlies the French-Italian Inquiry.

4

Exclusionary Democracies:
The Postauthoritarian Experience

T. J. PEMPEL

Assessing politics in 1951 must have been a fearsome task. How to account for the dual forces of authoritarianism and war that had wreaked horrible devastation over Europe and Asia? How to muster a personal sense of optimism for the future of individual liberties and democratic politics in countries that only recently had so systematically trampled the civil, economic, and political rights of large segments of their citizenry? The military victory by the Allies and the postwar grafting of democratic political institutions onto the former Axis powers surely gave one some room for hope. But in none of the defeated countries were the appeals of authoritarian politics truly eliminated. Indeed, the economic and social chaos that followed immediately after the war saw authoritarian forces of the Left and Right holding strong positions and offering ominously appealing alternatives to the uncertainties and ambiguities of parliamentary democracy. These extremist visions had widespread appeal among various socioeconomic groups, appeals potentially far more attractive for many than the never-tested ephemera of pluralism and democratic

In revising this chapter, I have benefited greatly from the written comments of Peter J. Katzenstein, Martin Schain, and Sidney Tarrow.

institutions. A dilemma was posed then within the former authoritarian regimes: to opt for genuine political pluralism and to allow all manner of ideologically diverse organizations to compete for popular and electoral support was to run the risk of legitimating and empowering the very forces determined to undermine pluralism and reimpose authoritarianism. But to reject such free and open competition and to restrict the political rights of "nondemocrats" was in itself to guarantee at best a stunted pseudodemocracy, in which particular doctrines and ideologies would be forbidden even to compete for support in the political marketplace.

Underlying this political dilemma was a more pressing moral problem that also arose out of the failed regimes of the past: how to structure a political system that could fuse together diverse subnational, class, and ideological forces to create a single polity, one that would pursue the interests of the nation-state as a whole while not undermining the personal freedoms and rights of society's individual members—that is, how to cope with the classical dilemma of collective versus individual rights and improvements.

Mario Einaudi and François Goguel confronted these problems in their book *Christian Democracy in Italy and France*.[1] From the vantage point of the immediate postwar chaos they analyzed the problems that had led to the emergence of authoritarian regimes in both countries and offered one potential answer to both the structural and moral problems posed for the two countries at the end of the war: Christian Democracy.

As Einaudi sketched the major goals of the Democrazia Cristiana (DC) in Italy, his political and moral attraction to party as solution is readily apparent. So too are the broad outlines of the problems and remedies as he saw them. The party would, he noted, seek to achieve three principal goals. First, it would retain for the individual the freedom and autonomy due to a divinely created being. Second, it would create economic security for the individual, while carrying out for economic society as a whole those collective policies required by the complexity and solidarity of economic life. And third, it would reassert and revitalize the link between moral principles and the direction

---

1. Mario Einaudi and François Goguel, *Christian Democracy in Italy and France* (Notre Dame, Ind.: University of Notre Dame Press, 1952).

of political life, reintroducing in modern times the values of the group and of the common good that are part of the Christian tradition.[2]

In this chapter I argue, first, that Einaudi and Goguel's analysis of Italy and France in many respects is also applicable to Austria, Germany, and Japan. The Einaudi-Goguel treatment of the prewar experiences of Italy and France is in large measure fruitful to an understanding of the authoritarian regimes that arose in the other countries as well. I also argue that their hopes for democratization in Italy and France have largely been realized. More important, they were fundamentally correct in their emphasis on the contribution that could be made by political parties to the institutionalization of pluralistic democracy in all five postauthoritarian regimes.

Contrary to many more recent analyses downplaying the significance of political parties within industrialized democracies, in the postwar regimes of Austria, Germany, France, Italy, and Japan political parties have been vital political institutions. They have been the main shapers of public choices. They have been the principal vehicles for political recruitment. They have been important rallying points for diverse socioeconomic groups. And most important, they have been vital contributors to the legitimation of the current political regimes. In this regard, political parties have played a very positive role in these five postauthoritarian regimes, much in keeping with at least a portion of Einaudi's hopes.[3]

At the same time, this success is in some ways ironic or paradoxical. Parties have gained strength in these countries, monopolizing control of governmental office and thereby legitimating the once embryonic systems of pluralism and democracy. Indeed, in several cases parties assumed such powers that alternative social, political, and economic organizations were frequently dwarfed by comparison, as Sidney Tarrow suggests in Chapter 6 of this volume. In many such cases, political parties became the inefficient and intrusive albatrosses of political life, rather than the knights on white chargers warding off the political evils of the past.

2. Ibid., 82.

3. Though Einaudi looks positively on parties, in this work he is also skeptical of making them excessively influential. He argues that if parties are permitted to extend a decisive influence over government and to carry out a continuous control over administration, parties will continue to be purely private associations.

Even more important and paradoxical, the increased strength of the centrist party or parties—precisely what was lacking in the prewar regimes—came about by the rather systematic exclusion, especially in the immediate postwar years, of parties at the ideological extremes, and most of their proposed political agendas. As these political centers became dominant, they increased the legitimacy of the regime as a whole, but in doing so they reduced the availability of meaningful political alternatives to that very center. Stated differently, centrist exclusionism led eventually to widespread acceptance of the centrist political agenda and to constitutionalization of political extremes. In short, democracy has flourished in these countries precisely because of its early exclusionism.

PREWAR AUTHORITARIANISM AND
POSTWAR PLURALISM

As Einaudi and Goguel saw it in 1951, the central problems that Italy and France had faced in the prewar period revolved around the inability of liberals and Socialists to coalesce into a cohesive political coalition able to monopolize the political center and negate the authoritarian appeals of communism on the Left and fascism on the Right. In France and Italy, the church was often at the heart of both problem and solution. Einaudi notes in particular the inability in Italy in 1924 to forge an alliance between the emerging Socialist movement and the more moderate Popolari. This was due in large part to the unwillingness of the bourgeoisie to accept the new social changes, but it was the result as well of the Catholic church's opposition to such an alliance. Mussolini, his black-shirted Squadristi, and the Lateran treaties were the more acceptable result, even though, as Einaudi notes, Catholic Action remained one of the few autonomous social organizations that Mussolini could not destroy during his reign.

Similar class tensions had prevailed in France. Openly Fascist parties confronted Communists and Socialists, again leaving a vacuum at the center, although France's parliamentary institutions were far more strongly entrenched and politically relevant into 1940 than they were in Italy. But no government could be formed to create an effective defense against fascism, and by the time of the invasion and surrender, it was obvious that party government had become peripheral to real power. Again, Catholicism proved to be largely antidemocratic, and extraparliamentary forces were strong. Yet unlike Italy, France had a strong Resistance that included many Catholics in its ranks.

Given this analysis of the history of the two countries, for Einaudi and Goguel the Christian Democratic movements, and the Christian Democratic parties they gave rise to, offered the best hope for both Italy and France. The DC in Italy and the Mouvement Républicain Populaire (MRP) in France held out the promise of a political democracy built around an ideological center capable of countering the contrastive appeals of communism and fascism. They would do this by carrying forward economic and social policies that balanced collective needs with respect for individual liberties. At least by implication, capitalism and the rights of private property, so central to conservatives and the business community at large, would be preserved, while at the same time capitalism's individualistic extremes and class biases would be counterbalanced by increased equality of opportunity and by components of state-guaranteed social welfare.

Italy and France provided the specific focus of the Einaudi-Goguel analysis, yet the problems these two countries faced were not dramatically different from those in Germany, Austria, and Japan. During the late nineteenth and early twentieth century all five were beset by strong class tensions, usually pitting strong right-wing and left-wing tendencies against each other. Along with disagreements about desirable outcomes, all five also experienced widespread disagreements over what constituted legitimate political processes. Parliamentary politics, constantly under attack, enjoyed only limited legitimacy. Consequently, all the countries witnessed the erosion of centrist tendencies, an inability of political parties to form effective governments, and the rise of nonparty forces that promised effective, though explicitly antidemocratic, solutions to the various nations' problems.

Though the church was far less relevant in Japan, Germany, and Austria than in Italy or France, in all three the Left-Right cleavages were similarly strong. Indeed, in Austria two hostile camps had emerged by the 1930s, the Socialists and the Christian Socialists, each with its own well-armed paramilitary units. Although in Japan the

Right was less institutionalized into a specific political party and
the threat from the Left was objectively less serious than in any of the
other countries, Left-Right cleavages were central to the ability of
the military to take power following a succession of coups and assas-
sinations. In Austria, too, it was fear of the Left that enabled the Right
to invite Hitler to invade and unite the two countries. Right-wing
terrorist groups and military cliques again made a charade out of any
notion of parliamentary governance in Germany, although, as it is
always mandatory to note, Hitler did come to power through constitutional processes, even though he trampled them once in office.

Thus all five countries, to differing extents, embraced authoritarianism primarily as a right-wing alternative to the real or imagined
strengths of the Left. At one extreme were the Third Reich's geno-
cidal efforts to superimpose a master race on the entire world. At
another pole, in Vichy France, though the authoritarian Right had
been domestically strong since at least the Dreyfus affair, and the
French Right applauded Hitler's armies, authoritarianism emerged
primarily as a consequence of external conquest and was somewhat
mitigated by the vigor with which the Resistance forces struggled
against the German army and the Vichy regime. In between, Austria,
Japan, and Italy revealed varying degrees of domestic suppression
mixed, at least for Italy and Japan, with reluctant or enthusiastic expansion abroad. But all five were similar in the nexus of political conditions that had led them to authoritarianism in the 1930s or 1940s,
and also in the consequent problems they confronted as they emerged
from the war.

In short, at the end of the war the dominant historical legacy in all
five countries was a weak political center, a major Left-Right cleavage, and strong nonparty centers of power. All were deeply divided
over the principles by which to organize the economy and the major
directions to pursue in foreign security and economic policy. Although constitutions were rewritten to create or strengthen parliamentary government, there was no historical reason to assume that
these would survive or that the governments would be formed by
forces committed to, or capable of achieving, the maintenance of social pluralism or parliamentary democracy.

Nor, given the massive political, social, and economic problems
that each of the five countries faced, was there any reason to anticipate
that any of these governments could institute policies that would ef-

fectively unite the countries and make radical improvements in economic and social conditions. In summary, the five shared three common traits.

First, all five lacked a tradition of strong parties and parliamentary rule. Parties had exerted varying degrees of power and influence in each of the five, with France's undoubtedly being the strongest. But even there, the church, the bureaucracy, and the army remained major alternative centers of power. This situation was mirrored in the other countries, usually with weaker parliaments and parties and other, different, and often stronger power contenders, including right-wing thug groups, well-entrenched oligarchic vestiges, the navy, and miscellaneous emperors, chancellors, and kings. New constitutions established formal parliamentarism in all five countries, but as traditionless creations they needed to take root if they were ever to grow.

Second, all five lacked an established political center. Social and economic tensions had been rife in the prewar period leading to ideological and organizational extremism that eventually polarized the prewar regimes. These were reduced at the end of the war in ways that ranged from land reform in Japan and Italy and the territorial removal of the Junkers to East Germany, to the purge or execution of certain prewar rightists and the elimination or radical circumscription of the military in Austria, Japan, and Germany. Nonetheless, in ideology and sociopolitical organization, all five countries still had strong centrifugal pulls in the early years after the war.

Third, all five faced major socioeconomic problems of recovery as a result of the war's devastation. The hows of solving these exacerbated tensions between Left and Right. In its most extreme forms, the debate was over capitalism versus socialism or communism and over alliances in the emerging bipolar cold war.

It was the first and second conditions that had been most important in leading to the creation of authoritarian regimes in the prewar periods. As Gregory Luebbert has convincingly argued, the prewar industrialized countries faced essentially four political choices: liberal democracy, societal corporatism, traditional dictatorship, and authoritarianism.[4] Those that went in the last direction were almost always characterized by weak parties and parliaments, and by strong

4. Gregory Luebbert, "Social Foundations of Political Order in Interwar Europe," *World Politics* 39 (July 1987):449–78.

socioeconomic divisions, usually emerging most prominently out of cleavages between labor and capital. The end result was that the state stood master of society; those controlling the state were themselves devoid of controls; the guardians guarded themselves.

Given the prewar history of these countries and, more important, the scale of the problems they continued to confront in the postwar years, there was little to suggest that parties and parliaments could establish their political supremacy, that politics could become centrist, or that socioeconomic problems could be resolved. Yet from the vantage point of the late 1980s, all five would appear to have done rather well. Only France could be said to have undergone a true regime change, from the Fourth to the Fifth Republic, and few would argue that France is the worse off as a result. France certainly remained a parliamentary and party-dominated democracy throughout. Centrist tendencies would appear to be far stronger in all five countries than ever before in their modern histories, even though in Italy, France, and Japan well-organized and serious challenges to this center remain. Parliamentary supremacy and respect for the democratic rights of citizens have become well established. Political parties and the party system have become institutionalized as the sole legitimate route to governmental control. Socially and economically all five could more readily be included in a box marked "success" than in one marked "failure." And more fundamental, to differing degrees all five political systems seem well legitimated, relatively flexible, resistant to authoritarianism, and likely to remain so in the near future. The relevance of political parties to such successes seems undeniable.

PARTIES AND DEMOCRACY

In the years following World War II, the moral and political superiority of democracy and pluralism was a virtual article of faith among large segments of the Western scholarly community, not to mention among the political and general public. So too was the centrality of political parties and elections as a means of ensuring "good" policies and "good" politics. Among the industrialized countries, the key concerns were the relative merits or demerits of particular expressions of political democracy. Most American and British authors took it for granted that the Anglo-American model was most advantageous in providing choice for voters mixed with stability in governance. Adherents of the continental model stressed the greater range of options offered to citizens by a multiparty system, and the greater capacity for including ideological minorities in the system. The relative advantages of presidential versus parliamentary forms of governance were debated, as were the significance of fixed versus flexible dates for electoral competition, and the strengths or weaknesses of different types of electoral and party systems. Yet amid these vigorous debates there were few voices challenging the merits and importance of elections, parties, party systems, or parliaments per se. Whatever their particular expression, pluralism and electoral democracy were taken as desirable goals.

This bias was translated into studies of the emerging nations of Asia, Africa, and the Middle East. Modernization studies, sensitive as many of them were to charges of cultural bias, and sympathetic as many of them were to "modernizing oligarchies," "democratizing armies," and "tutelary democracies," almost invariably took Western forms of political democracy as the most desirable end points and the logical strategic goals of political modernization.[5]

Valuable as the specifics of the Einaudi-Goguel analysis might have been therefore, their overall adherence to democratic ideals was by no means a stunning departure from orthodox goals at the time it was written. Nor was their faith in the potential power of parties and party systems, and in particular of the Christian Democratic parties, to be the main engines in the series of political, social, and economic transformations that would lead from authoritarianism to pluralism, and that would institutionalize democratic processes.

By the middle of the 1980s, there was far less consensus on such points. Among the later industrializers, a number of countries such

5. The quantity of literature on this subject is immense. Consider only the seven volumes published during the late 1960s by the Social Science Research Council in a series titled *Studies on Political Development*. Some of the bias for democratizing oligarchies is evident in Edward Shils, "Political Development in the New States," *Comparative Studies in Society and History* 11 (July 1960): 382–406. It is also explicit in Samuel Huntington, *Political Order in Changing Societies* (New Haven: Yale University Press, 1968).

as the four Asian newly industrializing countries (NICs)—Taiwan, South Korea, Hong Kong, and Singapore—attracted incredibly positive evaluations despite the absence of competitive political parties and meaningful political democracy in any of them.[6] Meanwhile, one-time models of party democracy in the so-called Third World such as Lebanon, Chile, Nigeria, Uruguay, Colombia, and even India fell prey to fissiparous internal tensions, military coups, dominance by narcotics dealers, or total collapse.

In the industrialized world there was also disenchantment with the once unchallenged virtues of electoral and party-based democracy. At least three different types of challenges arose. First, there were challenges based on the fact that elections and parties offered at best limited policy options. Otto Kirchheimer highlighted this as the simultaneous "waning of opposition" and the rise of the "catch all-party."[7] Others pointed to the choices between Tweedledum and Tweedledee, the slide into Butskellism, the emergence of various Grand Coalitions, and the end of ideology.[8]

Still others challenged the virtues of parliamentary democracy by pointing to the alleged policy failures that resulted. In the late 1970s the economic crises of stagflation and unemployment left electoral democracies open to charges of ungovernability.[9] Low strike rates and high productivity gains led many to tout corporatism as a more politically desirable arrangement than pluralism.[10] In societally fragmented countries such as the Netherlands, Belgium, and Switzerland, consociationalism was seen as a desirable substitute for freewheeling

6. See, among others, Roy Hofheinz and Kent Calder, *The Eastasia Edge* (New York: Basic, 1982); and Frederic C. Deyo, ed., *The Political Economy of the New Asian Industrialism* (Ithaca: Cornell University Press, 1987).

7. Otto Kirchheimer, "The Transformation of the Western European Party System," in Joseph LaPalombara and Myron Weiner, eds., *Political Parties and Political Development* (Princeton: Princeton University Press, 1966), 177–200. See also Kirchheimer's "Germany: The Vanishing Opposition," in Robert Dahl, ed., *Political Oppositions in Western Democracies* (New Haven: Yale University Press, 1966).

8. The literature on this topic, too, is voluminous. One classic work is Daniel Bell, *The End of Ideology* (Glencoe, Ill.: Free Press, 1960).

9. See, among others, Anthony King, "Overload: Problems of Governing in the 1970s," *Political Studies* 23 (1975):284–96.

10. Philippe Schmitter, "Interest Intermediation and Regime Governability in Contemporary Western Europe and North America," in Suzanne Berger, ed., *Organizing Interests in Western Europe* (Cambridge: Cambridge University Press, 1981), 287–330.

but potentially destabilizing party competition.[11] State-led planning drew others to admire the alleged merits of strong bureaucracies capable of bypassing the inconveniences of parties, elected officials, and public and interest group demands.[12] For still others, some specific objective—such as the development of the social welfare state or the assurance of sound defense or internationally competitive economic policies—took precedence over the means whereby it was achieved.

Finally, a third challenge to pluralist democracy came as many other political power centers revealed themselves capable of circumscribing parties and elections. Multinational corporations, interest groups, national bureaucracies, and single-issue movements were but a few of the major candidates offered up as alternative power centers among the advanced industrialized countries. To many, their powers undermined any claims to the primacy of electoral competition, party government, and democratic pluralism.

This is by no means the place to attempt even a superficial analysis of such studies. Suffice to say that if pluralistic democracy based on competitive parties, elections, and parliamentarism looked like a consensual goal in the 1950s, it did not in the 1980s; if political parties and party systems looked like the major agreed-upon linkages between society and state when Einaudi and Goguel were analyzing the prospects for war-torn Italy and France, there were many other contenders for that role thirty-five years later. Yet an examination of these two countries, along with the other three major authoritarian powers, over the period since Einaudi and Goguel were writing reveals the tremendous insight of their book, and in addition serves as a reaffirmation of the significant role of political parties in structuring regimes, along with an implicit testimonial to the normative merits of pluralist democracy.

11. The classic statements include Arendt Lijphart, *The Politics of Accommodation* (Berkeley: University of California Press, 1968); Kenneth D. McRae, ed., *Consociational Democracy: Political Accommodation in Segmented Societies* (New York: McClelland and Stuart, 1974); and Hans Daalder, "On Building Consociational Nations: The Case of the Netherlands and Switzerland," *International Social Science Journal* 23 (1971):355–70.

12. See Mancur Olson, *The Rise and Decline of Nations* (New Haven: Yale University Press, 1982). See also Chalmers Johnson, *MITI and the Japanese Miracle* (Stanford: Stanford University Press, 1982); and Andrew Shonfield, *Modern Capitalism* (Oxford: Oxford University Press, 1965).

PARTIES IN THE
POSTAUTHORITARIAN PERIOD

What is striking from today's vantage point is that all five countries entered the immediate postwar years with strong ideological cleavages dividing the societies and structuring the party system. Their party systems had at best limited traditions of moderating these social tensions and establishing widely legitimate governments. Residues of the old Right were especially strong and electorally autonomous in Italy and France. In Japan, Germany, and Austria war crimes trials, political restrictions, and purges eliminated the most visible members of the old Right, although the less publicly incriminated were able to find succor in more mainstream conservative parties such as the Hatoyama Liberals in Japan, the Christian Democratic Union (CDU) in Germany, and the VdU/FPO in Austria.

The Marxist Left in all five countries posed an even more vigorous threat. Well-organized and electorally appealing Communist parties existed in France, Italy, and Japan; though Austria's Communist party (KPO) ultimately proved less significant, it appeared potentially strong in 1945. Only in the German Federal Republic was there no active Communist party—largely because of the cold war and reactions to the Communist dominance in the East German sector. The ideological Left was enhanced in the first four countries by robust Socialist parties deeply rooted in Marxian ideology. And within Germany, the pre-Bad Godesberg Social Democratic party (SPD) also adhered to a program heavily committed to Marxism.

The extremes also did well in most of the elections immediately following the war. The case was most dramatic in Italy; there the Communists drew 19 percent of the vote and the Socialists an additional 21 percent, while on the Right the monarchists and qualunquists drew 8 percent between them. In France, the Communists gained 26 percent and the Socialists 24 percent of the first vote after the war. In Germany, the Left-Right division pitted the Christian Democrats (CDU) and their Bavarian affiliate, the Christian Social Union (CSU) against the SPD, with each drawing just about one-third of the vote. Japan's early elections were also fragmented affairs, with the country's electorate divided into two camps, Left and Right, and the center almost a total vacuum. A strong Socialist party gained the largest number of votes in the 1947 election, enabling it to form

Japan's first left-of-center government, while the Japan Communist party (JCP) drew nearly 10 percent of the vote in 1949. The Austrian case was more complicated. Before the elections of 1945 the seemingly strong Communists indicated to the Soviet Union that they anticipated gaining between 25 and 30 percent of the vote, but the Austrian People's party (OVP) drew just below 50 percent and the Socialist party of Austria (SPO) drew an additional 45 percent, leaving the Communists (KPO) with just over 5 percent and only 4 seats in Parliament. The Left-Right division in Austria, like that in Germany, was undeniable, but largely without the extreme pulls of independent party organizations representing overt authoritarians such as ex-Fascists and Communists.

Yet by the late 1980s the extremes in all five countries were drastically more feeble: parties of the Left had become less popular, less ideologically vitriolic, or both; most of the militant right-wing parties had become all but irrelevant; political parties with strong centrist orientations monopolized the preponderance of ideological space and the lion's share of popular votes.

The five countries had institutionalized political democracy by the 1980s, and the parties gravitating toward the center had come to set the nation's political agenda, largely without major input from the parties of the extreme. To the extent that the parties that appeared "extremist" in the 1940s were viable in the 1980s, they had come to accept the basic premises of parliamentary democracy, the importance of individualism and personal freedoms, some form or another of capitalist economics, and the broad foreign policy outlines that kept their countries allied militarily and economically with the United States and its allies. Until they did they were systematically shut out from the corridors of national governmental power.

From the perspective of the Einaudi-Goguel book this would appear to be a happy, albeit somewhat surprising, consequence. On the most superficial level of predictive evaluation, the book could only be called half right. Christian Democracy in Italy has proven to be the strongest electoral force in the country for the entire postwar period, very much fulfilling the role Einaudi hoped it would perform.[13] Until

13. It should be noted, however, that Einaudi was somewhat skeptical about the ability of the DC to remain organizationally unified, given its own internal tensions (Einaudi and Goguel, *Christian Democracy*, 69).

1980, the DC provided all of Italy's prime ministers and by far the vast proportion of its cabinet members. Even in coalitions, the DC has always been the major partner. And while its critics are many, both in and out of the country, few would challenge the party's basic role in moving Italy away from authoritarianism and toward pluralistic democracy, alliance with the United States, and many of the Christian ideals that were contained in the party's original programs and promises as analyzed by Einaudi.

By way of contrast, the MRP, although it was the strongest party in the Fourth French Republic, went into electoral decline and ceased to function officially in 1967. Goguel's fear was realized. It was, he suggested, a party doomed to doctrinal isolation in French politics, "squeezed between the individualists on its right who reject the intermediacy of the secondary communities between the citizens and the state, and the collectivists on its left who think that every right conducive to the emancipation of the individual must be transferred to the state."[14]

At a much deeper level, however, reading Einaudi and Goguel's book in the late 1980s sensitizes one to significantly broader issues involving the transition from authoritarianism to democracy, the role of political parties in making that transition, and the ability of particular parties to carry out public policies that bring about national integration and social cohesion, on the one hand, and yet respect individual rights, on the other. The predominant conclusion one arrives at is that in all five countries, despite the tremendous handicaps presented by historical tradition, socioeconomic divisions, and the massive problems confronted, and despite the challenge posed from antisystem, authoritarian forces, it has been political parties committed to varying degrees of social pluralism and pluralistic democratic institutions which have structured politics over the postwar period. In effect, the parties have proven to be effective, semiautonomous organizational links between pluralistic society and the democratic state. And they have used these powers to restructure the politics of each of the five countries in ways that have made these countries fundamentally different in the 1980s than they were at the end of the Second World War.

14. Ibid., 131.

The specific forms that this has taken varies widely across the five countries. All five are common, however, in the preeminence of a political center, shaded variously to the center-Left as in Austria or the center-Right as in Japan or Italy. In Italy, as noted, this has taken the form of long-term single-party dominance by the DC. The Japanese case is similar. From its formation in 1955, the conservative Liberal Democratic party has outdrawn its nearest electoral rivals by a margin of two to one, and has monopolized virtually all cabinet positions.

In both Germany and Austria the number of parties, and their ideological range, is smaller than in Italy or Japan. In Germany, it has been the comparative right-of-center CDU/CSU that has predominated over the postwar period, although it has shared power with, and on several occasions in the past two decades surrendered power to, the SPD. Austria is the only one of the postauthoritarian cases in which the more left-of-center party (the SPO) has been the unquestionably preeminent party of late (ruling alone from 1970 until 1983). But until 1966, the Proporzsystem saw a de facto coalition between the two largest parties, the SPO and the OVP, which monopolized the center-Left.

France occupies something of an odder position, with a more diffuse set of parties sharing power over time and with no single party or ideological tendency predominating over the entire period. The Christian Democratic MRP was first among equals for several elections immediately after the war; the Gaullists were the predominant "party" in the early part of the Fifth Republic; and now, the long-term presidency of Mitterrand suggests that France may have perhaps the least centripetal "center" of the five.

Particularly striking from the perspective of the late 1980s is the extent to which, in all five countries, the divisive ideological tendencies of the 1940s and 1950s have been modulated.[15] The authoritarian extremes of both Left and Right which appeared so problematic immediately after the war have either been drastically moderated or completely peripheralized.

15. The general centrism in these five countries presents an intriguing contrast to the recent party-driven anticentrism of the United States and Britain under Ronald Reagan and Margaret Thatcher. See Joel Krieger, *Reagan, Thatcher, and the Politics of Decline* (Oxford: Oxford University Press, 1986).

This is most striking in Austria, where the KPO was marginalized very early and the SPO has increasingly moderated its ideological stance. Today the SPO is essentially a pragmatic, reform-minded, and anti-Communist party that has refused to compromise with the Communists at home and has been sharply critical of the Soviet Union in foreign policy. Democratic corporatism and cross-party compromise are well-established principles in Austria.

The ideological transition of the German SPD at Bad Godesberg has been well chronicled and is part of the political folklore surrounding deradicalization in industrialized societies.[16] West Germany is broadly accepted as a *parteienstaat* (party state), and the major challenge to German centrism today clearly comes from the Greens, not from either of the two major parties.

The PCI was long committed to the primacy of parties and elections for Italy. But its views have become even more democratic following the moderation imposed by Palmiro Togliatti's *svolta di Salerno* and long-term governance in many local regions. Both the PCI and the Socialists are committed to parliamentary democracy and to the broad outlines of economic and foreign policy that came to be well established under the Christian Democrats.

Japan's JCP has gone through great ideological transformations to become "lovable" (to use its own phrase), and even so its voter appeal rarely goes above 10 percent. On many issues it is more conservative than Japan's Socialists, who belatedly, in 1985, following years of decreasing electoral appeal, also went through an ideological transformation, renouncing the party's longstanding adherence to the "dictatorship of the proletariat" and selecting a woman as its party leader, both moves designed to display a new and more moderate image.

In France, too, the pull toward the center can be seen, even as the four major parties have crystallized into two de facto blocs, one on the Left (Communists and Socialists) and one on the Right (Gaullists and the Union pour la Démocratie Française (UDF)). Michael Lewis-Beck has argued that "any declaration of an end to ideology among the French electorate is premature. On the contrary, the distribution and impact of ideological thinking appears remarkably stable throughout the post–World War II period."[17] This may be somewhat true at

16. Kirchheimer, "Transformation of the Western European Party System."
17. Michael S. Lewis-Beck, "France: The Stalled Electorate," in Russell J. Dalton

the level of heritage and verbiage. But it is hard to deny the fact that the Communist party has diminished greatly in strength, that France was recently governed by an unusual Left-Right "cohabitation," and that the Socialists under Mitterrand in the 1980s were hardly committed to a Marxian program.[18] They certainly proved to be far more tolerant of capitalism and a pro-Western foreign policy than they were three decades earlier. With the exception of right-winger Jean-Marie Le Pen, perhaps, what is striking is that many adherents of parties of the Left and of the Right identify themselves as "centrist" even if the parties they support do not.

EXCLUSIONARY DEMOCRACY: THE SOLUTION AND THE PROBLEM

What explains the fact that in these postauthoritarian regimes there has been such a move away from the ideological extremes and toward the center? And in the same vein, what explains the variations in such tendencies among the five postauthoritarian regimes? The answer to this question goes back to the dilemma posed at the beginning of this chapter—how to make the transition from authoritarianism to democracy when not all of the legitimate contenders are themselves committed to pluralist or democratic principles.

Political parties and elections are the necessary first solution to the problems of authoritarianism. Authoritarianism is a system of exclusionary politics; it attempts to deny the legitimacy of social divisions and of electoral politics. For pluralistic democracy to function, institutions must be created that can allow for social conflict without tearing the system apart, and without trampling minority rights. Democracy involves common acceptance of a set of rules about politics and governmental change, one that uses the vote as the common currency by which power is demonstrated. Socioeconomic groups must develop loyalty to such a democratic system, and to pluralistic tolerance for one another's demands and quirks, if democracy is to func-

---

et al., *Electoral Change in Advanced Industrial Democracies: Realignment or Dealignment?* (Princeton: Princeton University Press, 1984), 440.

18. An excellent discussion appears in Peter Hall, *Governing the Economy* (Oxford: Oxford University Press, 1986), chap. 8.

tion.[19] At the same time, as noted above, such loyalties can be counterproductive to democracy when the beneficiaries of tolerance are themselves willing to eliminate it for others if and when they have the power to do so.

As Adam Przeworski has phrased it, "If a peaceful transition to democracy is to be possible, the first problem to be solved is how to institutionalize uncertainty without threatening the interests of those who can still reverse this process."[20]

It is impossible to offer a conclusive argument as to "why" the postauthoritarian regimes developed as they did—that is, with strong centrist tendencies manifested typically in a single party committed to maintenance of the pluralistic and democratic institutions, and with hitherto "extremist" parties eventually coming to accept many of the core principles of parliamentary democracy. It is possible, however, to offer a plausible interpretation that, if true, would explain the particular variations seen among Italy, Germany, Austria, Japan, and France. The core of the answer lies in what I would call the exclusionary character of the democracies formed in these countries immediately after the war. More specifically, it would seem to rest on three related propositions. First, the stronger the domestic roots of authoritarianism, the stronger the need for an exclusionary tendency among one or more centrist democratic parties (or a coalition) to wipe the historical slate clean. Second, the stronger the institutional challengers to democratic institutions that remain in the postauthoritarian period, the greater the reluctance of that same democratic party in power to surrender or to share office with such "nondemocrats." The stronger the extremes presented, the more systematically excluded they must be. And third, the stronger the challenge to parliamentary democracy, the greater the political need of the centrist party (or par-

19. This point is explored in an interesting vein by Dankwart Rustow, "Transitions to Democracy," *Comparative Politics* 2 (1970):337–63, and it also forms an important part of the argument for democratic corporatism in Peter Katzenstein, *Small States in World Markets* (Ithaca: Cornell University Press, 1985). A more skeptical version of the role of parties in the transition can be found in Guillermo O'Donnell, Philippe C. Schmitter, and Laurence Whitehead, eds., *Transitions from Authoritarian Rule: Prospects for Democracy*, 4 vols. (Baltimore: Johns Hopkins University Press, 1986).

20. In O'Donnell, Schmitter, and Whitehead, *Transitions from Authoritarian Rule*, 3:59, as quoted in Daniel H. Levine, "Paradigm Lost: Dependence to Democracy," *World Politics* 40 (April 1988):386.

ties) to "govern flexibly," that is, to adapt the politically appealing elements of the program of the more extremist parties.

In the countries where a U.S. military occupation followed the war and the United States was relatively free to rewrite constitutional provisions, it could create conditions that made it difficult for proauthoritarian forces to gain any shred of legitimacy. Thus, in Germany the new rules meant only party members can sit in Parliament; there is a 5 percent minimum in elections for a party to gain seats in Parliament; the Right was explicitly purged and so forth. Similarly, in Japan provisions of the new constitution eliminated the legal standing of the military and guaranteed government by party and Parliament. Later, the Occupation used its authority to weaken Marxian unions, purge the Left, and strengthen the conservative parties that seemed most to the Americans' liking.

In Austria the structures of democracy involved a return to the constitution of 1920, since the Allies argued that Austria had actually been illegally occupied by the German armies in 1938. But the pro-Western forces were able to stymie Soviet intentions by an occupation that meant Austrian laws would take effect unless vetoed by a *majority* of the Allied commanders. As long as a prodemocratic coalition could be formulated, as in fact was the case in 1945, the major difficulties involved keeping out the presumed opponents of democracy, and indeed this was accomplished by Proporzsystem.

It was in Italy and France that greater difficulties were faced in the creation from the top of institutions favoring specific parties identified as prodemocratic. There the authoritarian controls of an occupying force were weakest, and it was in these countries that the Communist parties and the Marxist Socialists, along with the fringe Right, posed the strongest and longest-running threat to centrist dominance. This required far more covert and less blunt manipulation by America to isolate the Left and shore up the center. (It should be noted, however, that in Japan, the Socialists, with their Marxist orientation, continued to draw nearly 30 percent of the vote and to be the second-largest party through most of the 1960s.)

The emergence of centrism and the exclusion of extremes was perhaps quickest in Germany and Austria, initially through U.S. Occupation efforts and then later by the repeated electoral defeats of the KPO in Austria, and by the ideological conversion of the SPD in Germany at Bad Godesberg. As a result these two countries wit-

nessed the earliest and least problematic shifts from governance by
one party to that by its opponents, and the shortest periods of exclusionary politics—at least for established political parties. In both of
these countries transitions among the major prodemocratic parties
were unquestionably difficult for the party in power to accept. But
they could always surrender office convinced that if the opposition's
program might hurt their supporters it would not destroy them.
They also knew that enough votes the next time around would bring
them back to power. Their opponents, distasteful as they might
seem, were at least committed to the legitimacy of free and competitive elections and to the validity of a multi-party system.

This certainly was far less the case in Japan, Italy, and France; thus
in these three countries there were much stronger efforts by the governing party to hold on to power and to do so by excluding, and
attempting to delegitimate, their ideological opponents. The Liberal
Democratic party (LDP) and the DC have been masters at this, although, as is suggested by the third proposition above, they have
succeeded only by being flexible in their programs of governance and
thereby adapting or pirating important parts of the programs of their
allegedly antidemocratic opponents. To date this has kept both in
power on a semipermanent basis. Indeed, as political parties the LDP
and the DC have monopolized institutional political life to the point
where narrow party concerns frequently take precedence over broader
national needs. But their long-term dominance has also made it difficult for their opponents to attract support through continued appeals to extremist principles. The very longevity of rule by the DC
and the LDP has served to force their more radical opponents into a
choice between moderation and permanent marginalization.[21] Increasingly, of late, they have chosen moderation.

France thus becomes something of the interesting outrider in several ways. It has had no major center party since the MRP. It continues to be bifurcated between Left and Right. It has even witnessed the
only regime change among the group. Again, it would be impossible

21. Sidney Tarrow has labeled this tendency "soft hegemony" in describing the
situation in Italy (the term would appear equally appropriate for Japan). Tarrow, "Soft
Hegemony and One-Party Dominance: The Experience of Italian Christian Democracy," in T. J. Pempel, ed., *Uncommon Democracies: One-Party Dominant Regimes*
(Ithaca: Cornell University Press, 1990).

to claim that the above analysis offers a full explanation for this difference. Yet France underwent by far the least traumatic structural changes after the war; it was only in 1958, with the Fifth Republic, that major structural changes took place. No real resolution of the Left-Right cleavages was thus imposed from outside; that from the prewar period was essentially allowed to reemerge uninterrupted. Indeed, it was the weakness of the party system under the Fourth Republic that led to the Gaullist imposition of the Fifth Republic as a highly exclusionary alternative. The strength and extremism of both Left and Right have made it more difficult to establish a political center capable of freezing out either. The commitment of the French Right to keep out the Communists has been unquestioned. Indeed, it has been a Right far more convinced of the inexorable correctness of its own historical agenda and hence far less willing to adapt the programs of the Left than has been true in Italy or Japan. At times this inflexibility has hurt French conservatives electorally. It has certainly reinforced the centrifugal tendencies of all parties concerned.

Yet the France of the late 1980s, despite the absence of a clear and definable center, and the persistence of ideological political competition, is a country marked by widespread acceptance among all of the major parties of the validity of parliamentary and electoral politics. Witness only the economic conservatism of Mitterrand, or the government of cohabitation over which he presided. Any parties not committed to these principles are truly peripheral to French politics today in ways that were untrue right after the war. Changes in governments that would have been unimaginable in the 1950s seem almost tritely polite today.

Thus, in some senses what I have labeled "exclusionary democracy" has its very definite appeals to committed pluralists and to those anxious to see the institutionalization of democratic institutions and practices. In the five cases at issue it has resulted in the strengthening of parties and the party system, and in the legitimation of a democratic alternative to past authoritarianism. Yet the narrowing of the practical ideological spectrum and the de facto reduction in the range of choices to the electorate must be recognized as the logical accompaniments to that alternative. Such an alternative is clearly hostile to the norms of democracy. At the same time, to the extent that democratic institutions do in fact become institutionalized, and former "extremists" moderate their prior programs, new challenges to the "ex-clusionists" remain a possibility, as witness the emergence of the Greens in Germany, or single-issue, nonparty movements in Japan or Italy.

From a normative point of view, however, it seems fair to conclude that Einaudi's analysis in 1951 was one compatible with that offered here for a broader selection of postauthoritarian regimes. He clearly had certain doubts about political parties and the people who ran them. Yet, it also appears, given his clear adherence to social plural-ism, his respect for the political preeminence of independent political parties, and his undoubted desire to see democratic institutions made a permanent part of modern politics, that the postwar political trajec-tories of all five countries are by and large ones he would applaud. Indeed, it is tempting to suggest that his applause would extend to even the exclusionary component, if, by such exclusion, democracy could be created in the main.

>>>>>>>>>>>>>>>>>>>> <<<<<<<<<<<<<<<<<<<<

5

The French Communist Party:
The Seeds of Its Own Decline

MARTIN A. SCHAIN

In *Communism in Western Europe*, the phenomenon of communism is presented as a problem that emerged from the division, the injustice, and the alienation of the past, a problem that could be managed and reduced "under the multiple impact of constitutionalism, the modernization of governmental and economic institutions, the breaking down of social divisions, and effective integration of economic and political areas of authority."[1] For Mario Einaudi and Jean-Marie Domenach, the existence of a Communist party in France (and Italy) with widespread electoral support, a large membership, numerous front organizations under its control, and the capability to mobilize tens of thousands of people in the streets was an index in itself of the polarization of French political life and the fragility of French (and Italian) democracy.

The idea that communism was a problem, a danger, and a challenge for democracy was generally a starting point for scholarship

I am grateful to my colleagues Christine Harrington and Ted Perlmutter for their comments on a preliminary version of this chapter.
    1. Mario Einaudi, "Communism in Western Europe," in Mario Einaudi, Jean-Marie Domenach, and Aldo Garosci, *Communism in Western Europe* (Ithaca: Cornell University Press, 1951), 57.

during the 1950s. Indeed, it was an essential aspect of the *problématique* of French and Italian politics. Nevertheless, there were important differences among scholars in the way the problem was understood. Thus, while *Communism in Western Europe* makes reference to the issue of communism as foreign subversion—the Soviet "roots" analyzed in Chapter 6 of this book by Sidney Tarrow—it tends to focus most clearly on the domestic environment that continues to nurture the foreign object. Indeed, the problem cannot be eradicated by force: "But the fact remains that the elimination of communism as a fifth column in Western Europe does not eliminate the political and social problem posed by communism. . . . It remains also a long-range political issue, to be met steadily through the successful affirmation of policies capable of creating a modern and open society where, by definition, communism cannot gain the upper hand." [2]

Recent scholarship has been both more positive about the contribution that French and Italian communism has made to democracy in both countries, and less prone to focus on the importance of the Soviet roots. Nevertheless, a rereading of Einaudi's work raises essential questions about the role and survival of communism in France which continue to be relevant for scholarship in the 1980s. Like Tarrow and Pempel, I use Einaudi's work of the 1950s to refocus attention on the two key problems of comparative politics as applied to France: the construction of democratic stability and political development. For the French Communist party (PCF) played an essential role in the construction of political stability during the period of the Fifth Republic, but in the process it helped create the conditions that led to its own decline.

Einaudi and Domenach argued convincingly that the survival of the PCF was related to conditions of economic, social, and political underdevelopment in France. The impressive expansion of the French economy, however, along with the emergence of mass consumption and the elimination of many of the most obvious manifestations of working-class separateness during the first decade of the Fifth Republic, seemed to have little impact on the level of PCF support or on the ability of the PCF to renew and expand its organizational strength. Indeed, the PCF emerged during this period as a key participant in

2. Ibid., 51–52.

the construction of political consensus around the major institutions of the Fifth Republic. Clearly the reports of the demise of the PCF were at least premature.

During the 1980s, however, the PCF has suffered a dramatic reversal of fortunes: a decline in both electoral support and organizational strength. Does this mean, therefore, that in fact the Einaudi-Domenach analysis was valid, but that the effects of economic, social, and political change were delayed by a decade? Economic, social, and political change (or development) are indeed important for understanding both the survival and the decline of the PCF. Now, in retrospect, however, we can understand a great deal more about the process through which the PCF first maintained its strength, and then declined. Indeed, an understanding of this process permits us to re-evaluate many of the assumptions and predictions elaborated by Einaudi and Domenach thirty-five years ago.

THE PCF AND THE CONSTRUCTION
OF LEGITIMACY

National Coalition Building

For Einaudi and Domenach the PCF was a problem for French politics, "a disintegrating and corrupting element within our society." What was needed to combat this danger was the acceleration of processes that tended to build more modern representative institutions, more substantial working-class integration into social and political life, and a more open society. What was not anticipated was that the PCF would be not simply a "problem" for French democracy but also part of the solution; that the Communists would be key participants in the modernization of French social and political life; that they would not be content to be the victims of social, economic, and political development, but would be actors in that process. Like the history of Italian communism that of French communism is filled with contradictions. While communism initially gave political voice to social and political alienation, it ultimately served as a vehicle of political integration.

What has differentiated the PCF from other political parties in

France during its history since 1920 has been its multifaceted orientation toward political change, and its ability to plow several fields at the same time. It has mobilized masses of people for *luttes sociales* and, sometimes at the same time, effectively engaged in electoral politics. While most forces in French politics that have engaged in the politics of oppositional mobilization have been movements that have eventually disappeared, the PCF successfully institutionalized such mobilization through its organizational capacity. This capacity of the PCF to *encadrer* large numbers of disaffected and alienated voters was periodically used to oppose policies of the Fourth and Fifth Republics. Nevertheless, Georges Lavau has argued—and I agree—that a more important effect was to make a major contribution to the legitimation of key aspects of the democratic process.[3]

The core of Lavau's analysis focuses on the Communist party's aspirations to go beyond mere opposition and share or gain governmental power at all levels. Thus, in the name of revolutionary communism, the alienated working class was integrated into the complexities of representative government. According to Lavau's analysis, the PCF in this way tended to legitimize "the political and juridical principles of democracy by its respect for electoral procedures, and the parliamentary institution, by its deference for political functions, by its attraction for the state, its aversion for disorder, its superficial criticism for law. . . . In short, the PCF legitimizes the system, while constantly crying about its illegitimacy."[4]

The integrative capacity of the PCF has been expressed both directly and indirectly, and both at the national level and at the local level of the French political system. Lavau's thesis has been questioned by other scholars (especially Annie Kreigel) who have labored in the same vineyards, and he himself has analyzed what he contends may be a gap between the functions of PCF behavior and the functional impact and importance of that behavior. Nevertheless, the integrative behavior of the PCF during the post–World War II period provides

3. Georges Lavau, *A quoi sert le parti communiste français?* (Paris: Fayard, 1981), 34–44; and "The French Communist Party between State and Revolution," in Donald Blackmer and Sidney Tarrow, eds., *Communism in Italy and France* (Princeton: Princeton University Press, 1975).
4. Lavau, *A quoi sert le parti communiste français?* 36–37.

us with one key to the process through which an alienated working class has been integrated into the French political system.

There is ample evidence that economic affluence in the 1960s had little impact on the sense of alienation and injustice felt by large numbers of French workers, and that this discontent continued to be focused on political objects, although there is also evidence that these same workers were able to see the democratic process as a means of resolving discontent. Indeed, those most active politically were also those least alienated from the political process.[5]

The political process for large numbers of these workers, however (particularly those who were politically active), was defined by the Communist party, and from the earliest days of the Fifth Republic one of the party's principal aims was to maintain and expand its presence in electoral office by engaging more effectively in political coalition building at the national and local levels. Certainly the PCF was not seeking to solidify support for the Fifth Republic. Quite the opposite. What it was seeking was to protect its own position within the French state and the French electoral system, to consolidate the opposition to the Fifth Republic, and in the long run to develop a step-by-step project of Socialist change.

Nevertheless, in retrospect the party was engaged in a dialectical process of construction of legitimacy, a process through which opposition to the republic was progressively converted into opposition within the republic. Levite and Tarrow have argued that "legitimacy is not a natural or a permanent property of political objects but a *construction* of periods of crisis or transformation or both."[6] Increasingly, during the period of the Fifth Republic, the alternatives offered by the PCF were those of policy change rather than institutional or regime change, alternatives that effectively diminished the party's revolutionary vocation. The decisions involved in developing these alternatives, however, concerned not only the party itself but also other key actors within the political system. Moreover, the legitimacy

5. See Duncan Gallie, *Social Inequality and Class Radicalism in France and Britain* (Cambridge: Cambridge University Press, 1983), esp. chaps. 3 and 4.

6. Ariel Levite and Sidney Tarrow, "The Legitimation of Excluded Parties in Dominant Party Systems: A Comparison of Israel and Italy," *Comparative Politics* 15 (1983):300.

that was constructed was not only that of the party but also that of the Fifth Republic.

The first major movement in that direction was the decision by the PCF, in 1965, to support the presidential candidacy of François Mitterrand. This decision solidified the first tentative electoral bargains with the Section Française de l'Internationale Ouvrière (SFIO) in 1962 on mutual withdrawals in parliamentary elections. Mitterrand lost the election, but the campaign was regarded at the time as surprisingly effective. The effort had the salutary effect of moving the SFIO (now integrated into the Fédération de la Gauche Démocratique et Socialiste [FGDS]) away from its flirtation with a third-force centrist alliance, and it set the political agenda for the reorganization of the Left opposition for the next fifteen years. Furthermore, the presidential campaign began a process of internal reorientation and reorganization within both the Socialist party and the various formations of the center.

After 1965, largely at the initiative of Mitterrand, the PCF and the FGDS engaged in systematic negotiations intended to deepen their electoral alliance.[7] By the 1967 elections, the agreement on mutual withdrawal on the second round of the legislative elections was firmly established and became a policy that began to undermine the flexibility of the Socialists at the local level, since local Socialist organizations no longer had the option of supporting a better-laced centrist in the second round. After the elections, the federation took the initiative in forming a coordinating group with the PCF group in the National Assembly. As a result, the FGDS and the PCF voted as a bloc on all important legislation. In return, the Communists insisted on the initiation of discussions for a common program of the Left.

During this period, the PCF was firmly opposed to the constitutional arrangements of the Fifth Republic. The official position of the party was that a constituent assembly would have to meet to draft a new constitution. This position, however, did not in itself impede the growing relationship with other parties of the Left. Although the SFIO and the radicals (the major constituent parties of the federation) had supported the constitution of the Fifth Republic in 1958, Mitter-

7. This account is based on Frank L. Wilson, *The French Democratic Left, 1963–1969: Toward a Modern Party System* (Stanford: Stanford University Press, 1971), chap. 7.

rand had not, and the opposition of both parties to the constitution had grown after the end of the Algerian War and the establishment of the popularly elected presidency in 1962. The federation, in its official statements, generally referred to the Gaullist republic as "antirepublican," "totalitarian," and "Fascist," and it systematically forbade its elected officials from attending ceremonial occasions that would appear to support Gaullist institutions. After 1962 all of the parties of the Left tended to treat the Fifth Republic as a *coup d'état permanent* (Mitterrand's term), without offering any specific alternative to the regime. Indeed, through the 1970s surveys of parliamentary deputies indicated strong opposition to the regime from deputies from all political parties except the Gaullists.[8]

As negotiations between the PCF and the federation progressed, positions on the regime were clarified. In February 1968 the parties signed a "platform" of agreement—more than an electoral agreement, but less than a common program for government. The agreement called for a modification or abrogation of twenty-five of the eighty-nine articles of the constitution. For the parties of the federation, the agreement was a concrete manifestation of their opposition to the Fifth Republic constitution as it existed; for the Communists, it was the first concrete movement away from their maximalist position of 1958. Thus, during the first period of the process of Left consolidation, the Communists moved a considerable distance toward acceptance of existing institutions, in return for a recommitment of the SFIO to Socialist goals.

The student revolt of May–June 1968, together with the most massive strike in French history, had the paradoxical impact of shattering the unity of the Left and installing a Gaullist government with an unprecedented majority. Ironically, although the parties of the Left had achieved greater agreement on the goals of government, they could not agree on how to deal with the challenge of revolution (or at least rebellion). For a brief moment the Left made a bid for power (Mitterrand's press conference on 28 May 1968), but the Communists were the reluctant followers, certainly not the leaders. Indeed, the role of the PCF and the Confédération Générale du Travail (CGT) during

8. See Robert Jackson, Michael Atkinson, and Kenneth Hart, "Constitutional Conflict in France: Deputies' Attitudes toward Executive-Legislative Relations," *Comparative Politics* 9 (July 1977): 399–419.

these events was important, even crucial, in checking an expansion of the conflict, and in refocusing it on collective bargaining goals. The events of 1968 seemed to show that the PCF would no longer seriously challenge the established regime, even when outflanked on the "adventurist" Left.

Nevertheless, within a year it was evident that the Communists would survive the electoral debacle of June 1968. Jacques Duclos overwhelmed his rival on the Left, Gaston Defferre, with more than 21 percent of the vote in the 1969 presidential elections, as opposed to Defferre's 5 percent. Although the remainder of the Left was in disarray, the PCF pressed on with its united Left strategy (which it termed "advanced democracy"), expanded its organization, and rapidly built its membership strength. The Communists emerged from the crisis of 1968 as the only intact party of the Left, but also as a party of ordered, controlled, and even constitutional change.

The decade between 1968 and 1978 was an important period of change and development for the PCF. The decade began with a recommitment to a Left alliance, and a bargaining process through which it would be constructed, and ended with a split in the alliance on the eve of the key legislative elections of 1978. The decision by the PCF to continue to pursue an alliance strategy after 1968 had an important impact on the restructuring of the party system in the post-Gaullist Fifth Republic. It lent credibility to the effort of François Mitterrand to organize the Parti Socialiste (PS) in 1971. (Mitterrand became PS secretary in June 1971 by 1 percent of the vote, on the basis of a promise to the new party's Left Centre d'Etudes, de Recherches, et d'Education [CERES] that he would seek to negotiate a common program with the PCF.)[9] The Common Program then became the basis for massive party recruitment by both the PCF and the PS (as will be discussed below). The reorganization of the Left, in turn, provoked a parallel reorganization of parties of the Right. Most important, however, the process begun with the PCF decision ultimately turned questions of regime into questions of policy. The Common Program did call for some constitutional change, but most of the changes elaborated in this long document involved legislation and

9. See R. W. Johnson, *The Long March of the French Left* (New York: St. Martin's Press, 1981), 66–67.

new goals for government.[10] The real end of the debate about the legitimacy of the Fifth Republic came with the *alternance* (the victory of the Left) in 1981.

In the end, at least in terms of the construction of regime legitimacy, it mattered very little that the PCF had broken the Common Program alliance in 1977. What mattered was that the party was integrated into the Mauroy government after the legislative election in June 1981. The Socialist-Communist government of 1981–84, for all of its trials and tribulations, finally moved the Left—both the Communists and the Socialists—away from the position of the *coup d'état permanent*, and in the process the last vestiges of the challenge to democratic stability (at least from the Left) have virtually disappeared. If, as Mario Einaudi argues, the modernization of French democracy is the development of a modern party system that provides viable choices within a democratic framework, the PCF has been a key participant in the process through which this system has developed. If, as Einaudi argues, modernization involves the construction of regime legitimacy and the political reconciliation of conflicting groups, then the PCF has been an important actor in the process through which a political settlement has emerged.[11]

Local Government

The Communist contribution to the modernization of French democracy has also been evident at the local level, where Communists have held political office (except for the Vichy period) since 1925. Because they have been a force in local government for so long, it is perhaps appropriate to analyze at this level to understand what they would do if they held government power. Of course local government is limited, constrained, and in many ways has been dominated by central administration. But it is realistic to assume that at whatever

10. The Common Program of 1972 called for some revision of the Fifth Republic constitution, including the abolition of emergency power (article 16), the establishment of a supreme court, the limitation of the presidential term to five years, the limitation of the *vote bloqué*, and the establishment of an obligatory vote of confidence for the prime minister and his program for government. None of these revisions has been put into effect.

11. Einaudi, Domenach, and Garosci, *Communism in Western Europe*, 51–56.

level Communists governed in a country like France, they would be constrained and limited. What is most interesting about the PCF experience with local government over the years has been the extent to which Communist local authorities have become integrated into the network of center-periphery relations, and how effective these authorities have been in gaining benefits within this system.

My own work supports many of Sidney Tarrow's conclusions about the administrative integration of French Communist local officials. Tarrow found that although Communist mayors were party members, their organizational involvement was surprisingly low. Fewer than half of his sample of French mayors scored "high" on his index of party involvement. While this was three times higher than the scores of center-Right mayors, it was far lower than the 76 percent of their Italian counterparts. Moreover:

> The French Communist mayors had much less experience in the party organization than their Italian comrades. More than 40 percent had never held party office higher than that of secretary of a cell or a section, and almost 30 percent reported holding no party offices at all. In their comments during interviews PCF mayors were vigorous in their denials that they were deeply involved in the party organization. . . . It is not that organization was *un*important to the PCF mayors. . . . But the PCF mayors were less integrated into the party organization than their Italian comrades.[12]

On the other hand, in order to accomplish their policy objectives, Communist mayors have, over the years, become deeply involved with an extended administrative network, a virtual prerequisite for an active and creative urban government regardless of the political orientation of the town. For Communist mayors the problem has been that, although administrative contacts have been necessary in order to achieve policy goals, such contacts were constrained by the political isolation of the PCF prior to 1981.

As a result, Communist mayors emphasized in interviews in 1978–81 that when they applied for state subsidies, the quality of their dossiers had to be more "solid, well-prepared, straight and clear" than

---

12. Sidney Tarrow, "Party Activists in Public Office: Comparisons at the Local Level in Italy and France," in Blackmer and Tarrow, *Communism in Italy and France*, 147.

those of other municipalities closer to the center-Right majority.[13] On
the other hand, critics of PCF municipalities have also emphasized the
skill with which these officials have manipulated the administration.
They have exploited the same interdependence between administration and local officials exploited by other mayors, but perhaps with
more determination and for different policy objectives.

> As for nonpolitical administrators, the PC uses its power to influence
> them: it shimmers before them advantages ("certain administrators see
> in us the means to release their career talents"); it impresses them with
> its incessant applications. The activism of the PC can be explained by
> its will to convince those who are hesitant and those who are *attentistes*,
> if not by the cogency of its ideas then at least by its force.[14]

Not surprisingly, administrative involvement has grown as the
Communist orientation toward local government has focused more
on concrete policy achievements and relatively less on using municipal power to support working-class mobilization. Three elements
have characterized the way the Communists have explained their reasons for holding local power since 1925: defense of working-class interests against the state, mobilization of the working masses as an
instrument of change, and concrete commitments to benefits and
change at the local level. What has changed over the years has been
the balance that the party has struck among these objectives, as well
as the content that has given them meaning. As the Communist view
of the purpose of local government has changed, their broader justification for power and the nature of their public appeal has also
changed.

Prior to the Fifth Republic, the balance favored the defense of
working-class interests in the short run, in order to favor mobilization in the long run. This meant supporting immediate demands
without regard for fine points of bourgeois legality. The justification
of local power was not in the quality or the effectiveness of day-to-
day administration or even reform ("model administration"), but in
support for the day-to-day struggles of the workers. Much like other
local politicians, the Communists offered to protect the collective in-

13. See Martin A. Schain, *French Communism and Local Power: Urban Politics and
Political Change* (New York: St. Martin's Press, 1985), chap. 4.

14. Jean Montaldo, *La France communiste* (Paris: Albin Michel, 1978), 159.

terests of their constituents against the central state. They justified
their position, however, not in terms of local interests but as a part of
a general, coordinated, and centralized revolutionary strategy.

This was the focus of their energy and attention. Nevertheless,
they looked at local government on two levels—long-range revolutionary objectives and immediate accomplishments. Thus, from the
very beginning they understood that their local electoral appeal was
related to policy innovation. In the 1920s Communist local governments were self-conscious innovators in the areas of services to
schoolchildren (summer camps, for example), the establishment of
sports programs and facilities (to counter the influence of church-
sponsored programs), health facilities, and public housing. Maurice
Thorez (PCF national secretary), summarizing PCF accomplishments
after ten years in local office, wrote in 1936: "Voters have for a long
time seen the Communists at work. They have been able to appreciate
the administrative qualities of Georges Maranne, to compare the accomplishments of our local elected officials with those of the reactionary elected officials in neighboring communes. The Communists are
not content to indicate remedies; they apply them."[15]

By the 1970s the balance among objectives had clearly shifted.
Challenge, confrontation, and struggle were still there, but for (or
against) policy goals, rather than for revolution. Services, programs,
and new policy initiatives at the local level had become a way of le-
gitimizing the national party and its program, rather than simply a
means of temporarily ameliorating the conditions of an impoverished
working class. Virtually the same policy orientations that had been
emphasized before the Second World War were emphasized in the
1970s, but the way they were understood was quite different.[16] Instead
of embodying a tentative means for differentiating between Communist local governments and others, and establishing contact with
the masses for other purposes, policy was now seen as a way of demonstrating the quality and substance of Communist government,

15. Maurice Thorez, *Fils du peuple* (Paris: Editions Sociales, 1960), cited by Ray-
mond Pronier, *Les Municipalités communistes* (Paris: Balland, 1983), 216.
16. There were some important changes. Communist municipalities no longer
focused quite so much on public housing, and there was considerably more emphasis
on such concerns as careful town planning and the provision of green space.

even in a bourgeois state. The electoral appeal of the PCF, they argued, was

> a tribute to the quality of administration favorable to the people, a tribute to the Communist officials in the municipalities. But we should declare above all that the time is over when the reverse is true: that the Communist ideal rallies more votes than its men, because [their elected officials] have not yet demonstrated their administrative capabilities. This argument is now out of date, and the Communists are properly considered those who get things done, despite the obstacles imposed by the government.[17]

If we consider their accomplishments, it is clear that Communist officials at the local level have been relatively skillful, successful, and progressive, compared with local officials of other political persuasions. They have also become increasingly integrated into the politico-administrative network through which these policy accomplishments have been produced, and in this sense they have become an integral part of the center-periphery political system. Moreover, they have had an important influence on that system.

The Communist experience illustrates well the ability of local governments in France to initiate and mold policy priorities, even before the 1982–83 decentralization reforms. The Communist pattern or at least aspects of this pattern have become increasingly characteristic of local government in general in France in recent years. The kinds of services and projects initiated in the early years by Communist municipalities have become far more widespread and less unique. Moreover, as national parties have developed greater coherence and have gained greater control over local elites, local government personnel and local policy priorities have increasingly reflected the needs and the priorities of national parties.

The municipal elections in 1983 reflected what the French have termed the growing politicization of local politics in France, among the parties of the Right as well as the Left. When voters were asked in 1970 if the municipal elections would be "political" in their town, only 19 percent responded that they would. By 1977 the same ques-

17. Jean Gacon, "Géographie et sociologie électorale du P.C.F.," *Cahier de l'Institut Maurice Thorez* 7 (January–February 1973):23.

tion was answered in the affirmative by 62 percent (half of them from small rural communes); in 1982, 73 percent gave a positive response to a similar question.[18] If the Communist pattern has influenced the rest of the system, however, other aspects of the system have intruded on Communist municipalities. In the 1980s, a growing number of elections in these towns have been touched by electoral fraud.[19]

Nevertheless, at least until 1981, it appeared that the PCF had found the formula for survival and even expansion. The party had overcome the isolation of the 1950s, had maintained and even modestly increased its electoral following on the national level (3.8 million in 1958, 5.9 million in 1978), had vastly increased the number of cities with Communist mayors (twenty-five cities with thirty thousand or more population in 1959, seventy-two in 1978), had increased its membership by almost 60 percent, and had used its considerable influence to help move the Socialist party sharply to the left. The success of the 1970s, however, was based on important changes in the basis of support of the party, as well as changes in expectations from PCF voters and militants, changes that I believe hold the key to PCF decline in the 1980s.

SUCCESS AND TRANSFORMATION

The Electorate: Geographic and Structural Change

The electoral success of the PCF during the 1970s was conditioned by a strategy of social and political coalition building. The steady state of its national electoral following masked a complex pattern of increases and declines in various localities. For example, in the 1973 National Assembly elections, when the PCF generally regained its 1967 level of electoral support, the party reported that 58 percent of the towns governed by Communists (with more than ten thousand population) lost votes compared to 1967. Among the 42 percent that gained votes, the gains were greatest in the *newer*, less established

18. *Sondages*, nos. 3–4 (1977):86–87, and nos. 2–3 (1978):85; Jean-Luc Parodi, "Dans la logique des élections intermédiares," *Revue politique et parlementaire* 85 (March–April 1983):46.
19. See Schain, *French Communism and Local Power*, chap. 6.

municipalities. Similarly, in 1978 the PCF vote remained stable nationally. There were gains in forty-four departments compared with 1973, but in its traditional bastions in the Seine–St. Denis and the Val-de-Marne, the party generally declined. Once again, losses in established areas were compensated by gains in newer areas of strength.[20] This changing balance of geographic support is summarized by François Platone. He demonstrates that, since 1967, the maintenance and growth of electoral support for the PCF has been entirely in provincial France, and the gap between Paris and the provinces has been growing.[21]

Most characteristic of the newer areas of strength was the dependency of the PCF on the support of broader class coalitions, as well as political coalitions with the Socialists. We can see this in two ways: by the kinds of localities in which the party was building its electoral strength; and by the kind of coalition building that was typical in these areas in the 1970s. The success of PCF electoral efforts in the 1970s was greatest in areas outside of the Paris region, and with low working-class populations. For example, at the local level, three-quarters of the towns governed by Communist mayors were located in the Paris region in 1968, compared with less than 60 percent ten years later. In 1968 a third of the PCF-governed towns still had a majority working-class population, compared with 13 percent ten years later. Even among the Communist bastions, however (those towns in the Paris region governed by the PCF since 1947), fewer than 10 percent had majority working-class populations by 1978. In addition, a significant percentage of the remaining working-class population in these bastions was composed of immigrant workers, most of whom could not vote, thus diluting the working-class electoral strength even more.[22] If the "typical" Communist-governed town has been understood as a working-class suburb of Paris, the "typical" town that elected a Communist mayor during the Fifth Republic was a provincial town with a working-class minority.

20. *Bulletin de l'élu communiste*, nos. 45–46 (1973):2–3; and "Les Elections de mars, 1978," *Le Monde*, 76.

21. François Platone, "Parti communiste: Sombre dimanche, triste époche," in Elisabeth Dupoirier and Gérard Grunberg, *Mars 1986: La Drôle Défaite de la gauche* (Paris: PUF, 1986), 196.

22. I have elaborated on this in Schain, *French Communism and Local Power*, chap. 2.

This change in the PCF constituency was related to demographic trends, as well as changes in the French work force. It was also affected by the political coalitions with the Socialists that began to emerge early in the Fifth Republic. The expansion of Communist local government can be attributed, in large measure, to the changing balance of political forces in numerous areas, as the slow construction of Left unity placed pressure on Third Force (Socialist-center) coalitions. On the eve of the 1977 local elections, thirty of the forty-six (larger) municipalities with Socialist mayors were governed either by non-Communist Left or Third Force coalitions. The healing of the division within the Left was stimulated at first by new election laws at the national and local levels which were meant to give political advantage to the more unified Right, but that, in fact, provoked both the PCF and the Socialists into arrangements that permitted both to survive. The more detailed arrangements that followed then allowed both the Communists and the Socialists to install themselves in localities in which victories by the Left had been previously prevented by their division.

Of the seventy-two large towns governed by the Communists before the 1983 elections, only sixteen had been in their control after the 1947 Gaullist sweep. In each succeeding local election the PCF was able to increase the number of towns under its control, but most of those increases came during the period of the Fifth Republic. I have calculated that of the forty-six towns in which Communist mayors took over city halls between 1959 and 1977 (there were no losses among the larger towns), eight of the initial victories can be accounted for by the operation of the electoral law alone, and thirty-eight can be attributed to popular-front coalitions or agreements. Increased voter support was of only marginal importance for most of these initial victories, although voter support tended to increase rapidly in both local and national elections that followed.[23]

Thus, the stability of Communist electoral support during the 1970s masked a transformation of historic importance. The party had become increasingly provincial, and the bases of its support had become increasingly diverse. It had also become increasingly dependent on its relationship with the Socialists. If we look at the relative weight

23. Ibid., 36–44.

Table 5.1   Relative strength of the PS and PCF in the constituencies

Lead on Left	1967	1973	1978
PS	212	276	321
PCF	258	197	153
Total	470	473	474

Source: Gérard LeGall, "Le Nouvel Ordre électoral," in *Revue politique et parlementaire* 83 (July/August 1981):17.

of the Communist and Socialist votes on the constituency levels between 1967 and 1978, we can see a shift from PCF dominance to Socialist dominance (see Table 5.1).

The class structure of the PCF vote had also changed. As the French peasant population fell rapidly in the 1970s, the proportion of peasants among the Communist electorate also fell (from 9 to 2 percent). At the same time, the proportion of white-collar workers among the PCF electorate increased from 15 percent in 1967 to 19 percent in 1978, and the proportion of blue-collar workers fell from 52 to 49 percent.[24] Perhaps most important, however, was the emerging separation of electoral strength from organizational strength.

Organization: The Distribution of Strength

Historically, there has been a considerable correspondence between concentrations of electoral strength of the PCF and areas where the party had its greatest concentrations of organizational strength. The organizational capacity of the PCF has depended on its ability to recruit members and to support its organization with the political and economic resources of a network of local and national office holders.

Party membership reached its peak in 1946, with about 800,000 members, and then dropped precipitously (more than 60 percent) through the period of the 1950s, to a low of about 300,000 in 1960–61. The Fifth Republic provided a more favorable environment for the expansion of PCF membership, which began to rise again after 1961, and especially after 1968, when the party began to build its strength on a *union de la gauche* position. Membership reached a high of about 520,000 in 1978–79, and then began to drop sharply once

24. These estimates are taken from *Sondages*, no. 1 (1973):18, and no. 1 (1978):26.

again after 1978.[25] Thus, during the postwar period, there were two important cycles of membership rise and decline, and there is every indication that the present decline is not yet at an end.

These two cycles, however, have been quite different in terms of their structural implications. During the postwar period of growth, concentrations of party membership expanded beyond the Paris region, the eastern area of the Mediterranean coast, the Rhone valley, and the Nord-Pas-de-Calais. The cold-war contraction left most of these concentrations intact but reduced in membership levels. The most significant membership losses were outside of the PCF areas of strength.

Although membership increased by 60 percent between 1962 and 1978, its distribution was concentrated in smaller areas within the postwar areas of strength. No new important concentrations were established, and the concentrations in the Paris region and the Rhone valley (mostly in the Lyon region) were reduced, according to Philippe Buton.[26]

During the early period the party maintained its electorate in its areas of membership strength, and membership losses did not prevent the PCF from surpassing its 1946 voter level in 1956 (5.5 million votes). When the PCF lost a million and a half votes in 1958, it maintained its strength in roughly those areas where it was organizationally strong.

When the party increased its vote after 1962, and the structure of its electorate changed, it was unable to translate electoral success into organizational expansion. In the 1970s the party was actually losing votes where its membership implantation was strongest and was gaining votes where its implantation was weak. Its electoral gain can be understood as a result of *union de la gauche* cooperation, rather than the *encadrement* capability of its organization.[27]

Thus, a new factor emerged in the 1970s—the increasing inability of the PCF to maintain stable electoral support in its areas of organizational strength. This has been most obvious in the case of the city

25. These figures are derived from Philippe Buton, "Les Effectifs du parti communiste français (1920–1984)," *Communisme*, no. 7 (1985):8.

26. Ibid., 21.

27. See François Platone, "Les Adhérents de l'apogée: La Composition du PCF en 1979," *Communisme*, no. 7 (1985):36–38.

of Paris, where the PCF has electorally disappeared, but it is also evident in the Lyon and Bordeaux regions, as well as in the bastions in the Paris suburbs. In the Paris region the party lost 22 percent of its 1967 vote by 1978. In the earlier period electoral expansion (1956) was not entirely dependent on organizational resources, but electoral survival can be explained by organizational implantation. This was no longer the case.

Conditional Support: Le Vote utile

The patterns I describe suggest that by 1978 voting for the PCF was becoming increasingly related to coalition and policy considerations, and less linked to the ideological commitments traditionally associated with PCF voting. These patterns imply that the PCF could no longer count on the kind of expressive voting that had sustained it through the worst years of the cold-war siege.

There is some evidence to support these implications. Surveys of PCF voters in local elections as early as 1971, for example, indicate that what differentiated them from those intending to vote for other party lists was their commitment to active and participatory local government. Only 3 percent of PCF voters thought that "representing my political attitudes" (an expressive commitment) was their reason for voting Communist, and far fewer Communist supporters, compared to those of other parties, regarded the defense of local interests as a priority. On the other hand, more PCF voters, compared to others, gave their highest priority to the development of local services (49 percent) and to the expansion of participation by local citizens (30 percent). In addition, Communist voters were those most likely (by far) to perceive mayors as real political actors, with considerable "freedom to direct their communes." These differences were supported by other surveys through 1983.[28]

In short, more than their defensive capability, what was most attractive about PCF local government to Communist voters was their willingness and their ability to get things done. Indeed, the claims

28. See Jack Hayward and Vincent Wright, "The 37,708 Microcosms of an Indivisible Republic: The French Local Elections of March, 1971," *Parliamentary Affairs* 24 (Autumn 1971):234. See also *Sondages*, nos. 1–2 (1971):79, 82; SOFRES, *Opinion publique, enquêtes et commentaires 1984* (Paris: Gallimard, 1984), table 3, p. 118.

and actions by Communist mayors indicating that they were capable of modernizing local government were the greatest attractions for PCF voters.

The breakup of the Common Program alliance in September 1977 was a profound shock to both the electorate and the membership of the Communist party. In retrospect, it now seems that the condition of the loyalty of a large percentage of both was the hope for change engendered by the coalition at the national and the local levels.

The impact on membership was evident within a year. From 1978 to 1984 membership strength is estimated to have dropped from a high of 520,000 to 380,000.[29] It took over a decade for a similar decline during the period of the cold war. Seventy percent of the 1978 militants had joined the party during the previous decade of growth, which was conditioned by the Common Program alliance.[30] Disappointment among these militants was expressed with their feet.

The impact on the electorate was not evident until 1981, despite a small loss of PCF votes in the 1979 European elections. We should recall that after recovering from the setback of the 1958 legislative election, the PCF attracted a steady "normal vote" of 20–22 percent of the vote in all of the subsequent national elections during the Fifth Republic, until 1981. In the presidential elections of April 1981 Georges Marchais lost 25 percent of the "normal" Communist vote (with 15.3 percent of the vote), and in the legislative elections in June the party was able to regain only a small piece of what Marchais had lost (0.8 percent to be exact), confirming the 25 percent falloff. During the years of Socialist government, from 1981 to 1986, the Communist vote was reduced by another 40 percent (to 9.7 percent), and then another 30 percent (to 6.8 percent in the presidential election) during the two years of cohabitation from 1986 to 1988. The party made a surprising recovery in the legislative elections of June 1988, when it increased its percentage to 11.3. Although this was the first significant recovery since 1981, it did not seem to indicate the reversal of a trend. The real recovery amounted to a gain of 12,000 votes over 1986, and this modest increase in electoral support was concentrated

29. These figures are derived from Buton, "Effectifs du parti communiste français," 8.
30. Platone, "Adhérents de l'apogée."

in an ever smaller number of localities. From 1978 to 1988 the PCF vote declined by 54 percent, from 5.9 million to 2.7 million votes. By 1988 the party no longer had a "normal" vote and no longer seemed capable of stabilizing its electoral following.

Indeed, the structure of the lost votes seemed to leave little hope for eventual party recovery. The signs were clear that the party was suffering important electoral losses among the same sectors of the electorate that had formed its historical core vote. During the Fifth Republic, about a third of the working class normally voted Communist, which gave the PCF a percentage of the working-class vote which was higher than for any other party. This working-class support dropped off sharply in the presidential and legislative elections of 1981, again in the legislative elections of 1986 (to 20–24 percent—the surveys varied considerably), and more in the elections of 1988 (to about 12–16 percent).[31]

The loss of the historic core vote is confirmed by the declining ability of the PCF to attract younger voters. "Normally," 25 percent or more of voters under the age of twenty-four voted Communist during the Fifth Republic. The PCF losses in 1981 were reflected in a decline of the youth vote to 18 percent, but this was still above the national vote. By 1986, this percentage had been reduced to 6 percent, far below the PCF mean vote for the country.[32] The party increased its support among the youngest voters in 1988 to 9–10 percent (to about its national mean), but suffered more significant losses among those between the ages of twenty-five and fifty. Clearly, the growing inability of the party to renew its support among the youngest voters in the 1980s is now beginning to feed into the middle-age cohorts. Only among the older *fidèles* does support for the PCF remain above the mean for the country. One survey indicated that more than half

---

31. Jérôme Jaffré, "La Défaite de la gauche et les progrès du parti socialiste," *Pouvoirs*, no. 38 (1986): 52. Jaffré's figures for 1986 are somewhat lower than those of other surveys. His survey results give the PCF 15 percent of the working-class vote, compared with 20–24 percent in other surveys. See the dossier by Frédéric Bon, Eric Dupin, Gérard Grunberg, and Béatrice Roy, in *Liberation*, 18 March 1986, as well as Nona Mayer, "Pas de chrysanthèmes pour les variables sociologiques," in Dupoirier and Grunberg, *Mars 1986*. The 1988 results are from the postelectoral survey of SOFRES, *Les Elections du printemps 1988*.

32. Platone, "Parti communiste," 205.

Table 5.2   Evolution of the PC vote in 23 bastions
(% PC)

			Elections		
	1978	*1981*	*1984*	*1986*	*1988 (P)*
Average	51.29	35.30	31.21	28.15	19.67

of the PCF vote in the 1988 presidential elections, and almost half in
the legislative elections, came from retired people.[33] Thus, the party
can no longer count on surviving with its core working-class support, which has been slowly diminishing; nor can it count on the
youth vote—another traditional reservoir of support—in order to
build its future.[34]

The problem in the "bastions" became more evident in 1981, when
PCF candidates lost 25 percent of their vote nationally, but 31 percent
of their electoral support in these zones of strength (compared with
1978). The losses in the "bastions" were not quite as severe in 1986 as
they were in the rest of the country (see Table 5.2).[35] In these zones of
party strength, however, where the PCF was still attracting a majority of the vote or more only ten years ago, they were supported by
only 28 percent of the electorate in 1986, and were unable to attract a
majority in a single large town where they had been dominant since
the end of World War II. In the 1988 presidential elections, their
(mean) support in these towns fell to less than 20 percent, with losses
in every town. The PCF still retained a plurality of voters in only one
town (Ivry). The "red belt" of the Paris region is now pink (the Socialists are the predominant party), and in ten of the twenty-three
bastions the vote for the National Front exceeded the vote for the
PCF in the presidential elections in 1988.

Nevertheless, the last bastion of strength for the PCF has proven
to be the popularity of its mayors. With the exception of Georges

33. Unpublished postelectoral survey for *Le Figaro*. My thanks to Pascal Perrineau
for giving me the details of this survey.
34. For background on the youth vote, see Platone, "Parti communiste," 205–6.
The 1988 figures on the youth vote are taken from SOFRES, *Elections du printemps
1988*.
35. The "bastions" cited here are the twenty-three cities with a population of over
thirty thousand which were governed by Communist mayors from 1947 to 1983.

Marchais and André Lajoinie, all of the important party leaders were defeated in the "recovery" of 1988, but ten of the twelve new Communist deputies were mayors, most from the older bastions. Half of the twenty-four victorious PCF candidates were mayors, compared with five of the thirty-two incumbents.[36] Ever since the defection of Jacques Doriot, then mayor of St. Denis, from the PCF in 1934, the Communists have been wary of permitting their mayors to develop strong local bases of support. The resurgence of strength in the bastions appears to be related less to the last-gasp effectiveness of the PCF organization than to the attractiveness of its local elected officials, given the considerable gap in votes between the presidential and legislative elections. In the legislative elections, PCF candidates ran local campaigns based on local records, and appear to have reaped the benefits of their municipal achievements.[37]

Whatever else is motivating voter flight, there appears to be a growing policy gap between the party and its electorate. Even before the debacle of the 1981 elections, PCF voters were opposed to the party's misplaced campaign against North African immigrants; a majority opposed the PCF support of the Soviet war in Afghanistan; and a majority opposed the PCF campaign against the Socialist party.[38] Moreover, the Communist leadership seemed incapable of making decisions that would attract strong support even among its shrinking electorate. In 1986, 65 percent of PCF voters were sympathetic with the (now) expelled *rénovateur* current, and 56 percent supported the replacement of Georges Marchais as general secretary of the party. At the same time two-thirds of the voters supported Georges Fiterman as the party's candidate for president in the elections of 1988; the PCF nominated André Lajoinie, who was supported by only 16 percent.[39]

Of course, none of this would have mattered very much in the old days, when "the only party in France" could turn out a reasonably loyal electorate and could fall back on reasonably secure zones of party strength. It now seems clear that this is no longer the case, and

36. See *Le Monde*, 18 June 1988.
37. See Stephane Courtois, "Parti communiste: Les dernières cartouches?" in Philippe Habert and Colette Ysmal, *Elections legislatives 1988* (Paris: *Le Figaro*/Etude Politiques, 1988), 26.
38. See the surveys in *L'Express*, 11 April 1981, and *Le Matin*, 14 March 1981.
39. *Liberation*, 9 July 1986.

the PCF, if it is to survive at all, will have to build new strength the way it did in the 1970s, on the basis of social and political coalitions. It does not appear, however, that the party has learned the lessons of its success in the 1970s or of its failures of the 1980s.

CONCLUSION

Economic, social, and political change (or development) were indeed important for understanding both the survival and the decline of the PCF. Economic and social change reduced the available traditional demographic base for Communist recruitment, and the affluence of the 1960s deprived the party of its issues based on the failure of capitalism. These changes as such, however, did not undermine either the party's electoral support or its ability to recruit militants. In this sense, Einaudi and Domenach underestimated the positive attractions of communism in France, as well as the broad bases of alienation.

Their more subtle arguments about political change as the basis of Communist decline, however, have been more durable, though in ways that they could not have anticipated. If I am correct, the PCF avoided the trap noted by Einaudi, "of protracted and vain opposition to an order of things that is showing vitality and change," by becoming part of the process of change itself. Hoping to reap the benefits of broad coalition politics, they became one of the major architects of a more modern party system, which offered positive choices to a more broadly based electorate. The process in which they were engaged also helped build the legitimacy of the regime. In this sense, the PCF was part of the solution to the problems of the French political system elaborated by Einaudi and Domenach. At the same time, however, the PCF slowly altered the bases and the conditions of its electoral support and its membership strength.

By the time it concluded that the benefits of this process to the party would not be worth the price it was paying, it was too late to return to principled opposition. By the 1980s the PCF was not able to find an alternative to "advanced democracy" which was acceptable to a generation of Communists raised on coalition politics.

The elements of decline of the PCF were in part demographic, in part nurtured by the very process that assured its success in the 1970s. The effectiveness of the counterculture was diminishing by the early 1970s; the party organization was never able to expand much beyond these increasingly weakened bases, even when membership vastly increased; and the conditions of electoral support were changing from ideological to policy commitment. It is possible that the PCF would not have been able to avoid the consequences of these elements.

After 1978, however, the rigid nature of the party itself, a factor emphasized by Einaudi and Domenach, appears to have made a major contribution to its decline. In effect, the party could not make key decisions that would maximize its own success. An important PCF exile, Henri Fizbin, argued in 1980: "We were convinced that it was possible to compensate with political progress the consequences of demographic change, and that led us to bring up factors profoundly anchored in party practice, but which distanced us from Parisian [that is, organizational] realities." Fizbin was accused of a "lack of ideological firmness" by the PCF's political bureau.[40]

40. Fizbin's account is related in François Platone, "L'Echec électoral du parti communiste," in Alain Lancelot et al., *Les Elections de l'alternance* (Paris: PUF, 1986), 93.

6

Communism in Western Europe: Of Roots, Grafts, Growth, and Decline

SIDNEY TARROW

IN 1951 Mario Einaudi wrote in the introductory essay to *Communism in Western Europe*:

> Their [the Communist parties'] acknowledgement of the tie that binds them to the Soviet Union has been open and uninterrupted since that winter (1920–21) . . . when both the French and Italian Communist parties were founded. Upon these roots European communism has grafted a great variety of native elements appealing strongly to different social groups. It is this combination . . . that explains the notable advances of communism in postwar Europe, making of France and Italy one of the focal points of Communist influence.[1]

The thesis of this chapter can be simply stated but will be harder to demonstrate. First, like Einaudi, I believe that in 1951 the Communists' "acknowledgement of the tie that binds them to the Soviet Union" had been "open and uninterrupted" since 1921. But how this tie bound the two parties to the USSR and with what implica-

I am grateful to Stephen Hellman and Martin Schain for comments on an earlier version of this essay, and, of course, to Mario Einaudi, whose work was its inspiration.
   1. Mario Einaudi, Jean-Marie Domenach, and Aldo Garosci, *Communism in Western Europe* (Ithaca: Cornell University Press, 1951), 3.

tions for domestic policy has since been disputed by both Communist and non-Communist scholars.[2] For example, Palmiro Togliatti's "centrism"—invisible in the international arena until 1956—actually seems to have dated from much earlier and could be seen in his domestic strategy by 1944.[3]

Second, also like Einaudi, I believe it is possible to see a great number of native elements that were grafted onto the "root" of French and Italian communism as they accommodated themselves to the complexities of life in a constitutional democracy. These became ever more prominent after Einaudi wrote and especially so after the end of the "hard years" of the cold war.[4] But I am not as certain as Einaudi or his contemporaries were that the "real" root of the parties was foreign and that the graft was domestic. Nor is it entirely clear that their electoral success derived in some linear way from domestic adaptation; on the contrary, as I argue below, in the case of the PCI, its greatest difficulties resulted from the analytical gaps and contradictions in its domestic alliance strategy.

Moreover, the relationship between international root and domestic graft has turned out to be far more complex and contradictory than the simple formula: "domestic graft modifies international root to produce electoral success." The PCI's international ties were considered an early and constant liability by some. They were also a defi-

2. I refer primarily to the following works: Donald Blackmer's penetrating analysis of the PCI's reactions to trends in international communism after World War II, in his *Unity in Diversity: Italian Communism and the Communist World* (Cambridge: MIT Press, 1968); Jeffrey Frieden's analysis of events in the Comintern, "The Internal Politics of European Communism in the Stalin Era, 1934–1949," *Studies in Comparative Communism* 14 (Spring 1981):44–69; Joan Barth Urban's definitive study of the PCI's relations with Moscow since the war, *Moscow and the Italian Communist Party: From Togliatti to Berlinguer* (Ithaca: Cornell University Press, 1986); Stephen Hellman, "The Evolution of the Left in Italy, 1948–1988," paper presented at the Conference on Culture and Politics in the Italian Republic, Bellagio, 4–8 July 1988, and Hellman's recent *Italian Communism in Transition* (New York: Oxford University Press, 1988).

3. See, e.g., Giulio Ceretti, *Al'ombre des deux T: Quarante ans avec Maurice Thorez et Palmiro Togliatti* (Paris: Julliard, 1973). On the immediate postwar period, see Harold Hamrin, *Between Bolshevism and Revisionism: The Italian Communist Party, 1944–1947* (Stockholm: Scandinavian University Books, 1975).

4. These views, which are no longer novel, were first presented in Sidney Tarrow, *Peasant Communism in Southern Italy* (New Haven: Yale University Press, 1967); and in Donald Blackmer and Sidney Tarrow, eds., *Communism in Italy and France* (Princeton: Princeton University Press, 1975), especially in the chapters by Hellman, Lange, Ross, and Tarrow.

nite benefit in soldering a part of the working class to the party electorally via the revolutionary project that was associated—at least
symbolically—with the Soviet Union. And while domestic accommodation was undoubtedly useful in increasing the party's following,
it also deepened the contradictions between its revolutionary projects
and domestic strategies, eventually increasing the tensions between it
and the Soviet Union.

Let us be clear on definitions: by "international roots," I mean the
theory not only that the PCI and PCF were affiliated with the international Communist movement, but that the fundamentals of their
strategic lines had been laid down by Lenin and Stalin and were still
safeguarded by the Soviet Union. By "domestic grafts," I mean the
adaptation of the parties' strategies through the construction of a
broad coalition of social and economic groups and the design of a
reformist policy.

That there were international ties and broad domestic adaptation
in both the French and Italian parties is not in doubt. But the international ties were more complex than the simple picture of extrater-
ritorial dependency that Einaudi portrayed. What he saw as domestic
grafts were in part the result of attachments to traditional leftist subcultures and in part the outcome of a misspecification of the directions
of European capitalism—and were therefore far from salutary. At
least in the Italian case, an important explanation for the success came
neither from root nor graft, but from a third element—the party's
institutional vocation and the healthy respect that this provided its
leaders for the autonomy of the political.

Einaudi's understanding of the reasons for the success of Italian and
French communism after the war was more farsighted and more sensitive to domestic political alignments than that of many of his contemporaries.[5] For example, Gabriel Almond and his collaborators,
though finding that French and Italian communism were far less foreign to their political cultures than their British and American counterparts, nevertheless insisted on the traditional distinction in the

5. See Gabriel Almond et al., *The Appeals of Communism* (Princeton: Princeton
University Press, 1957), chap. 3. For the empirical materials that—even in the early
1950s—demonstrated that the French and Italian parties had domestic sources that
differed radically from those of the British and American ones, see part 2 of this
important book.

Communist "operational model" between the party elite and its mass following—a distinction that was fast disappearing in the PCI. Although Einaudi shared their Atlanticism and their distrust of communism, he better understood the fundamentally new character of communism in Western Europe and its sources of strength.

But Einaudi's understanding of the PCI and PCF would fail to explain the incredible durability and periodic electoral successes of both parties. If, in 1951, it could seem that communism "lived off poverty," it could therefore be argued that it would be defeated by economic modernization.[6] But it was precisely during a period of capitalist prosperity—the 1960s—that French and Italian communism not only survived, but grew in strength. If communism was the result of poverty, how could this occur as capitalism was demonstrating not only its capacity to produce prosperity, but also its ability to respond to cyclical fluctuations such as that of the mid-1970s?

Was it perhaps because the original "roots" of the PCI and PCF were not as foreign as Einaudi and others thought? Because the parties were able to graft onto themselves elements that were more compatible with capitalist democracy than he thought possible? Or was there something apart from both international root and domestic graft that explained political success in what were emerging as mature capitalist democracies? Perhaps there was less incompatibility between Communist practice and democratic institutions than either the Communists or their critics imagined.[7]

Finally, how can we understand European communism's current crisis? As the result of the delayed revenge of domestic prosperity on parties with vestigial international vocations? As the outcome of the evolution of the international environment itself and especially of the

6. Einaudi, Domenach, and Garosci, *Communism in Western Europe*, 51. But unlike the cold warriors, Einaudi did not regard communism in Europe as a police problem, "even though the police aspects of Communist activity have not escaped the attention of governments." He regarded it as the result of societies with incomplete modernization which lacked a state with a fully developed concept of the public interest.

7. I refer here not to the question of internal democracy, but to the capability of Communist parties to adapt strategically to the practice of parliamentary democracy. For an argument close to this one, and by no means sympathetic to communism, see Giuseppe Di Palma, "Establishing Party Dominance: It Ain't Easy!" in T. J. Pempel, ed., *Uncommon Democracies: One-Party Dominant Regimes* (Ithaca: Cornell University Press, 1990).

development of a "Third Way" in the Soviet Union which has outflanked even the most advanced efforts of Western communism to
adapt? Or as the ultimate consequence of the contradictions that result from the particular adaptation of each party, which left intact
little of their original revolutionary inspiration or of their capacity for
mobilization?

In Chapter 5 of this volume, Martin Schain deals with some of
these questions for French communism. A brief return to the Italy of
1951 may help us in reflecting on them as well. In this chapter, I focus
on three crucial areas: Italy's exposure to the international system; its
political conflict structure, the dominant social coalition that the
Christian Democratic party formed within it, and the opposing one
that the PCI tried to construct; and the PCI's role in the political institutions that channeled these conflicts and coalitions into political
exchange.[8] In conclusion I turn to the party's current decline.

THE POSTWAR
INTERNATIONAL SETTLEMENT

In his introductory essay in *Communism in Western Europe*, Einaudi
posits as a given what had not yet been demonstrated: that the PCI
and the PCF were directly dependent on the Soviet Union for policy
direction. But there is a basic difficulty in analyzing the impact of the
Soviet Union on the PCI's postwar reconstruction: since reconstruction occurred in what was clearly going to be an American sphere of
influence, how could Soviet control be exercised over the PCI's poli-

8. The interpretation offered here is a synthesis of several papers, articles, and a
book. For the sake of economy, I will cite all these sources here and then draw on
them without explicit reference. The major sources are "The Italian Party System
between Crisis and Transition," *American Journal of Political Science* 21 (May 1977):
193–224; the introduction to Luigi Graziano and Sidney Tarrow, eds., *La Crisi italiana* (Turin: Einaudi, 1979), vol. 1; the conclusion to Peter Lange and Sidney Tarrow,
eds., *Italy: Crisis and Consensus* (London: Frank Cass, 1981); "Three Years of Italian
Democracy," in Howard Penniman, ed., *Italy at the Polls, 1979* (Washington, D.C.:
AEI, 1981), 1–33; "The Crisis of the Late 1960's in Italy and France and the Transition
to Mature Capitalism," in Giovanni Arrighi, ed., *Semiperipheral Development: The
Political Economy of Southern Europe* (Beverly Hills: Sage, 1986); and *Democracy and
Disorder: Protest and Politics in Italy, 1965–1975* (Oxford: Oxford University Press,
1989), chap. 2.

cies outside the restricted ambit of the party's internal life without smothering its capacity for adaptation?

The ideologization of the academic debate after World War II did not help matters much. For example, strategic turning points such as Togliatti's *svolta di Salerno* could be interpreted with opposing sign depending on whether the observer saw the Italian party as charged by Stalin with mechanically implementing the Yalta agreements, or believed that it was using the postwar reconstruction to launch a strategic line of which Stalin would not have approved.

At least with the advantages of hindsight, American influence over postwar reconstruction is far easier to detect than Soviet, although Einaudi hardly mentions it. Italy entered the postwar world with the influence of the United States internally guaranteed by its major ally, the Democrazia Cristiana (DC), against whose emerging control over government the Communists were more or less helpless. The Americans financed postwar reconstruction, failed to insist on a thoroughgoing renewal of the Fascist state, and threw their influence against the PCI and its union leaders.[9] It was generally seen as no accident that both the PCI and the PSI were eased out of a share of power soon after Alcide de Gaspari's 1947 visit to Washington.

This much is clear: the presence of a strong Communist-Socialist electoral bloc, both parts of which were currently close to the Soviet model, reproduced international tensions within the Italian political system and helped to consolidate the emerging party system around Marxist and Christian Democratic poles. International polarization, however, was more important for the domestic political strategies that it permitted than for the direct ability of either foreign power to interfere in domestic politics. In the short and medium term, American hegemony and Russian threat dominated debate. But in the long run, the symbiotic domestic duopoly of the two major domestic parties was what really shaped the postwar regime.

9. A weakness of *Communism in Italy and France* is Einaudi's failure to document how this influence was exercised, for example, in the splits that were engineered in the unified trade union confederation, the Confederazione Generale del Lavoro (CGL), which had been created after liberation. American advice and support were crucial to the creation of both the Christian Democratic Confederazione Italiana Sindacati Lavoratori (CISL) and the Social Democratic Unione Italiana del Lavoro (UIL).

The USSR's influence was the first to wane. Although political strikes that served its foreign policy interests were common in both Italy and France in the late 1940s, they soon proved unpopular among the workers, were repressed with vigor by newly modernized police forces, and were rapidly abandoned. By the middle of the 1950s the Communist-Socialist Confederazione Generale Italiana del Lavoro (CGIL), reeling from losses in recent plant elections—and especially in the crucial Fiat elections of 1955—began to lay the foundations for the economic strategy that would bring it into prominence in the 1960s. Within the PCI, as Blackmer has shown, the 1956 Soviet party congress was shrewdly used to increase the party's independence from the USSR.[10]

Soviet constraints remained more mediated than direct: first, through a generation of exploited workers and ex-Resistance fighters who would not have happily supported a party that cast aside the heritage of the victors of Stalingrad; and second, through the competition of a Socialist party whose claim to sharing the banner of Marx—at least until 1956—limited the PCI's freedom of movement. For pro-Sovietism *itself* had domestic political roots among a generation of workers who had suffered under Fascism and—not without reason—identified the USSR as the main contributor to the defeat of world Fascism. Moreover, the DC's close embrace of the United States gave the PCI the opportunity to accuse it of passively complying with encroachments on Italian sovereignty.

As for American influence, it too became more mediated and less direct during the course of the cold war. Although incidents of American pressure were many—Catholic Action's *comitati civici*, the letters that American relatives "spontaneously" wrote to Italian voters warning of the loss of American aid if Italy went Communist—they were increasingly rare during the 1950s and were soon secondary to the DC's homegrown brand of *political* anticommunism. With no more than a "relative" majority of the votes, the governing party had to construct a coalition around religion, patronage, and anti-Communist ideology, rather than around the power of its American ally.

The major vector that unified membership in the American-led al-

10. Blackmer, *Unity in Diversity*, 59–66.

liance with domestic political anticommunism was the construction of a political-economic settlement based on Christian Democratic power and capitalist reconstruction. The relations between these two facets of the postwar reconstruction are easily misunderstood. It was not that the Christian Democracy was ever a "capitalist" party: had it been such, it would have exercised power too narrowly to retain it for long. In the 1950s, it was the conservative Partito Liberale Italiano (PLI) that came far closer to filling this role. Nor did the United States impose a free enterprise path on Italy (with the large role of the state sector in the economy, this would have been far from easy).

Rather than adopt market liberalism to attract bourgeois supporters to its banners, the DC, though ideologically populist, adopted an anti-Communist strategy to consolidate its hold on power and to gain a firm position in the emerging Atlantic alliance. Market liberalism was used in the service of a political strategy, rather than the other way around. But once adopted, the strategy had profound implications for the domestic political economy. Combined with the (American-engineered) divisions and weakness of the unions, and in the presence of a large rural potential industrial work force with no trade union consciousness, it justified and encouraged a managerial offensive that led Italy to a market-oriented economic reconstruction.

During the late 1940s and early 1950s the treatment of strikers became more repressive and the power that the workers had gained in the factories during the Resistance was whittled away by management as the major union confederations split along ideological lines. But we should not forget the Left's early collaboration in the restoration of managerial power, as factory committees that had been set up by the Committees of National Liberation were disbanded.

The political benefits that this system gave the DC should be obvious; but just as important were the gains to Italy's newly liberated economic managers. For the cold war and the splits in the labor movement that it produced helped to guarantee low wages and managerial control of the workplace during a period of rural exodus and expanding international trade that was highly favorable to countries at Italy's stage of development. The exclusion from power of the political representatives of the working class in 1947 was not carried out on behalf of a bourgeois coalition, for there was none that was strong enough to maintain power. But it reinforced managerial power in the workplace while reducing the political influence of the PCI and the unions.[11]

Why does this distinction make a difference? Had the DC been the representative of a victorious capitalist coalition, the economy would have entered the republican period with a far more liberal economic culture than it did, and the bourgeoisie would have entered it with a greater degree of hegemony than it possessed. That capitalist reconstruction was fueled not by triumphant market liberalism, but by political anticommunism and a managerial offensive, was a development that left the country governed by a political-economic structure with little cultural legitimacy.

The result was that, while the Left was temporarily stymied in the workplace and was isolated in the political system, the legitimacy of its political-economic vision was still strong. Though politically isolated, it remained ideologically unified until 1956, with its working-class bastions unreconciled to capitalist domination. The economic development of the 1950s—far from destroying the Left's appeals—simply increased the resources that it could muster in mobilizing its still-alienated working-class base when the opportunity for mobilization arose, as it did in the early 1960s. But by the same token, unless that mobilization potential was nurtured and developed, it could be squandered.

American hegemony was in some ways a double-edged sword. For while it enabled the DC to exclude the PCI and the PSI from the government, split the Socialists into pro-Communist and pro-American parties, and helped to isolate the CGIL, it also constrained the Catholics—despite their total lack of experience of democracy—to govern through liberal democratic practices.[12] We take for granted

11. Using Fiat as an example, Einaudi cites technological modernization and entrepreneurial dynamism as the major factors retarding Communist penetration of the workplace. While the Fiat empire was modernizing, however, it was also repressing organized labor in a far from progressive manner. Fiat used a company union to combat the CGIL's influence and "exiled" PCI militants to distant and difficult shops. For an account of this period, see Aris Accornero and Vittorio Rieser, *Il mestiere dell'avanguardia, Riedizione di "FIAT confino"* (Bari: De Donato, 1981).

12. Critics correctly point to the government's frequent use of prefectoral commissions to overturn elected left-wing local governments and to the 1951 electoral law that was intended to take votes from the Left. But no evidence has been adduced that these measures were of *American* origin—there was ample precedent for central gov-

today that the DC is a party of liberal democracy, but this was by no means guaranteed by its origins in a church that—it bears remembering—had cohabited comfortably with Fascism.

The postwar Italian system was not only *born* a republic; unlike some other creations of postwar international settlements, it stayed that way, in no small measure because its American sponsors exercised their hegemony in a liberal direction. Although the top leadership of the DC had impeccable democratic credentials, there was concern in progressive segments of the party about the rapid "conversion" of many former proponents of the corporate state to Christian Democracy after World War II. We do not know what their influence would have been had American tutelage not been present; in any event, American policy favored pluralism and the DC never had to chose between its moderate and conservative wings.[13]

The constraints imposed by American "liberal" hegemony thus helped not only to produce a capitalist process of reconstruction but also to resocialize a generation that had grown up under Fascism into believing the novel idea that you defeated your enemy at the ballot box. It also encouraged a centrist and reformist—but non-confessional and pro-capitalist—vocation for political Catholicism.[14] As early as 1949, the integralist strand of progressive Catholicism represented by Giuseppe Dossetti and his followers had been definitively defeated by the centrism of de Gaspari and his allies.

As for the Communists, it might have been expected that, once ejected from power, they would revert to Stalinist type. But despite the politically motivated strikes they organized against the Marshall Plan and the temporary influence of such Stalinists as Pietro Secchia in the party after 1947, Togliattian centrism was never fundamentally challenged, except by easily marginalized minorities. For not only did

---

ernmental interference in local matters and for electoral manipulation in Italian political history—and there is no evidence that the United States ever knowingly supported right-wing subversion in Italy, as it did in Chile.

13. In the south, for example, there was almost relief in some parts of the DC when the land reform alienated many large landowners—many of them former Fascists—from the governing party. See Tarrow, *Peasant Communism*, 306–8.

14. In the south, for example, American advisers were sympathetic to a reform of the latifundia during the early postwar years.

the centrist leadership have deep roots in the Popular Front period, but it weathered the *anni duri* of 1947–55 remarkably well.[15]

This briefest of surveys of the postwar role of the PCI raises a question that Einaudi assumed was already answered: "How important was the Soviet root in the development of a Communist presence in Italian domestic politics after 1945?" The USSR *was* important as the symbol of what the international proletariat could accomplish; but as the anti–Marshall Plan strikes demonstrated, the Soviets could do more harm than good in manipulating the internal life of a Communist party, and they had few means of influencing Italian politics. Although they could—and did—chastise Togliatti for his moderation after 1947, they could not engineer leadership changes in Western Communist parties without triggering major crises, and they could certainly not alter the effects of the cold war on their European allies.

For once submerged in the turbulent world of Italian domestic politics—a prospect, by the way, that Togliatti seems to have welcomed—the PCI could not rely on its Soviet mentors to *fare politica* except "in the final instance"—and we all know how often that appears as an operative factor in history! Togliatti knew better than to flaunt his party's independence of the Soviet Union, at least until after 1956. But this does not demonstrate in any real sense that the Soviet root determined the direction in which the branches of the PCI tree would grow.

Far more important in determining how the tree would grow was the influence of the United States. But not even this influence was direct or unidirectional. The United States supported a Christian Democratic ally that carefully preserved its populist roots, while using political anticommunism to advance its electoral chances. If managerial prerogatives became dominant as a result, this was the result of a political operation and not of the hegemony of market liberalism. The working class retained its loyalty to the PCI, while parts of the peasantry and the middle class were susceptible to a radical vision. In the absence of true capitalist hegemony, when the

15. For example, at both the 1948 and 1951 PCI congresses, Urban points out that anti-Americanism was far more prominent than pro-Sovietism, and "the canons of Marx, Lenin, and Stalin continued to receive scant attention." Urban, *Moscow and the Italian Communist Party*, 219.

unions finally gained the resources to challenge managerial prerogatives—as they did in the 1960s—the explosion was immense.

SOCIAL ALLIANCES AND DOMESTIC GRAFTS

If Soviet control of its internal life and U.S. political hegemony were important conditioning factors, it was the party's increasing symbiosis with the DC in domestic politics that determined the course of PCI strategy after 1945. Despite the changes of the postwar decades, these two parties remained the two poles of political competition. As a result of this duopoly, the domestic political balance was frozen for a generation in approximately the form in which it had emerged from the war. While the Socialists lost their early leadership of the Left to the PCI, and an extreme Right soon reappeared, the division of the vote between center-Right and Left changed little from 1948 to 1963. Each was consolidated around a closely woven fabric of party and mass organizations within which it enclosed supporters and serviced their needs; neither could begin a major strategic change without stimulating a competing move by the other.

The degree to which these party "subcultures" actually enjoyed the active participation of their supporters should not be exaggerated. In both the PCI and the DC, partisan involvement became a flexible and more-or-less open affair. This would mean that beyond the baroque drama of political rhetoric, political comedies developed behind the scenes in which the two parties learned to live with each other.

Participation in the PCI was always greater than in its opponents, but after the height of the cold war it too declined.[16] Although the PCI was the most rigid mass party in the system, it was soon clear that party cells were no longer very effective and that many party members failed to carry out even the most elementary tasks for the party. As for the DC, its long possession of power led many to affili-

16. Hellman, "The Evolution of the Left," 11. See also Adriano Ballone, "Il militante comunista torinese (1945–1955)," in Aldo Agosti, ed., *I muscoli della storia; militanti e organizzazioni operaie a Torino, 1945–1955* (Milan: Angeli, 1987), 112–13.

ate with the party whose reasons for political activism had more to do with personal advantage than with political faith. In other words, although party conflict was intense at the elite level, the division of Italy's political community into airtight political subcultures was always exaggerated.

For one thing, polarization was limited by the two parties' inter-class strategies. The DC had always had a populist vocation deriving from Catholic social doctrine and from the still-living heritage of anti-Fascism. More important than either was de Gaspari's shrewd monopolization of the political center, which was aimed both at avoiding isolation into a confessional ghetto and at denying the Communists a monopoly of the lower-class vote. Both in the working class—especially in industrializing northeastern Italy—and among the peasantry, the DC remained dominant due to a winning combination of relying on the cultural influence of the church and producing concrete benefits for a broad coalition of social forces.

This strategy made the DC both more and less than a party of business. To the outrage of its leftist factions, it worked to facilitate the projects of capitalist clients; but to the disgust of both business and the Left, it never ceased to regard itself as the protector of more vulnerable social groups. Religious mobilization and "assistance-ism" were hardly competing approaches in the social landscape of postwar Italy. The DC used both in combination with the political anticommunism that assured it a foothold on the Right. This made it a formidable electoral opponent.

As for the PCI, its strong rural base, its relative weakness in the Industrial Triangle, and its ambition to organize an interclass coalition in the south were the preconditions of a strategy of social alliances that fed into Togliatti's "Italian road to socialism." The growth of the "native graft" that Einaudi wrote about in 1951 was an almost inevitable objective outcome of the choice of an electoral strategy; but it was also dictated by the DC's corresponding appeals to some of the same social groups whose support was sought by the PCI.

Whatever its sources, the strategy of social alliances gave the PCI a claim to representing intellectuals, workers, farm laborers, and small family farmers, and a chance to appeal to the new urban middle class that mushroomed after 1945 as the traditional petite bourgeoisie declined.[17] The struggle between the DC and the PCI was thus never anything like a raw confrontation between capitalists and workers.

The existence of opposing interclass coalitions organized by each of the two major parties was both a spur to and a limitation on the possibilities of the other party. Because the DC electorate had substantial working-class and peasant components, the PCI needed to seek support from the urban middle class; but because its opponent could take advantage of such a move, the party was never free to take its traditional lower-class constituencies for granted and launch a fully fledged campaign to attract what it called the "productive middle strata."

In other words, once involved in a situation of strategic interaction with the DC, the PCI could of course talk freely of appealing to "workers of the hand and mind," or to "Communists, Socialists, and good democrats," though it was severely constrained in its ability to graft these elements onto the working-class trunk.

This was demonstrated in southern Italy as early as the rural "struggle for the land" that the party tried to dominate in 1949–51. By creating a network of interclass "committees for the land" and refusing to lead the poor peasants onto cultivated lands, the party tried to gain support among poor peasants, small cultivators, and even middle-class absentee landholders. But except in small enclaves where it enjoyed traditional left-wing support, it failed in all three respects.[18] And particularly once the agrarian reform was accomplished, the government proved that it had resources with which to co-opt supporters that the Communists, from their political isolation, could never match.

The problems of the party's alliance strategy were not limited to regions in which it was weak, like the Mezzogiorno, but also emerged where it was strong—for example, in central Italy. But there its appeal to the middle sectors was more likely to take root among

17. Paolo Sylos-Labini has shown that the aggregate size of the "dependent middle class" grew in almost exact proportion to the decline of the "independent middle class" between the 1951 and 1971 censuses. See his *Le classi sociali in Italia* (Bologna: Mulino, 1975), 153–55.

18. For the analysis on which this judgment is based, see Tarrow, *Peasant Communism in Southern Italy*, chap. 13.

traditional artisans and shopkeepers than among the new middle sectors that had arisen in industry and services.[19] This appeal to traditional middle-class groups was more the effect of the traditional leftist subculture of the region than of the progressive interclass strategy that the party claimed to support.

In other words, an important aspect of what Einaudi considered "the Communist Problem"—the support the party offered to a variety of domestic social groups—eventually became a problem for the Communists: how to appeal to groups whose prosperity was linked to capitalism without accepting the essentials of the system that the party was determined to extirpate. This problem, already present in Togliatti's leadership strategy, became overwhelming under Enrico Berlinguer's leadership, especially after 1973.

A second problem was that the interests of these diverse social groups were not always congenial to one another; this was demonstrated as early as the struggle for the land, where the party tried to appeal simultaneously to *braccianti* who wanted to invade middle-class landholdings and to the middle-class landowners who employed them. It was also characteristic of the 1970s, when the party tried simultaneously to restrain a militant industrial proletariat and appeal to middle-class voters who were frightened by its disruptiveness and blamed it for the inflation that was wracking the economy. So diverse were the claims and demands of these various constituencies that the party never succeeded in welding together a unified coalition for reform.

A third problem was generational. The party had much hope for the support of the new generation of educated, middle-class youth who were produced by the economic miracle. The student movement of the 1960s, however, showed that the PCI would be left on the sidelines of the most radical movement to appear in Italian society since the end of the southern land occupations.[20] It was not simply the fact that these young people had not experienced Fascism, Resis-

19. For an in-depth analysis, see Stephen Hellman, "The PCI's Alliance Strategy and the Case of the Middle Classes," in Blackmer and Tarrow, *Communism in Italy and France*, 373–419.

20. Elsewhere I have shown how the student movement in one university, Pisa, developed as an explicit insurgency against the traditional, party-dominated university student movements, particularly against the PCI-dominated Unione Goliardica. See Tarrow, *Democracy and Disorder*, chap. 9.

tance, or the liberation that led them to reject Communist leadership; equally important was the tactical moderation that the party had adopted as a condition of its general strategy of accommodation—a domestic graft that impaired its ability to appeal to a radical new social subject. The consequences of this generational gap were evident both in the frightening appeal of armed struggle to many of the veterans of the 1967–69 period, and in the defection of many young voters from the PCI after the elections of 1976 brought the party into support for the government.

Why was the PCI unable to solve these problem of class alliances? "Objective" factors no doubt had much to do with it. Southern peasants and Emilian shopkeepers simply lacked the potential for mobilization of industrial or agricultural workers; recently politicized students will always choose the most radical over the more moderate political family. But there was also a serious failure of strategy that Stephen Hellman has identified in the PCI. Both in leadership recruitment and in political analysis the party was profoundly tied to the past.

This could be seen in its leadership selection strategy following the end of the war. Its postwar organization, Hellman points out, was built on the basis of "tested veterans forged in exile and clandestinity," [21] and not on the Resistance generations that might have brought broader perspectives to its emerging postwar strategy. This led to a generational monopoly that left the party staffed for many years with people who did not share its moderate policy stance. Only after 1956 did a new generation of "renovators" move into positions of power.

A more basic failure was in the party's political analysis. For from the immediate postwar period on, the party was convinced that Italian capitalism was "utterly moribund" and in crisis.[22] The party was determined to modernize this society—if not from a position of power, then from the opposition, whatever that may mean. Both its alliance strategy and the policies it supported were conceived in response to the need to modernize a backward society on the brink of collapse.

It was therefore natural that the party should appeal to social fig-

21. See Hellman, "Evolution of the Left," 11.
22. Ibid., 3.

ures that it considered marginal or doomed—such as peasants, artisans, and small businesspersons. It was equally logical that it would be unprepared for the dynamic economic development of the late 1950s and 1960s and would grasp only slowly the importance and the concerns of the "new" middle strata that were soon appearing throughout the cities of the north.[23] Though there was much talk from the early sixties on of appealing to the "new middle strata," who made up these strata and where they would fit in an emerging mature capitalism were questions that were never dealt with, because the party could not bring itself to believe that such a society already existed.

How does this relate to Einaudi's polarity of "root and graft"? The party had "grafted" a domestic strategy of broad alliances onto its inherited root; but this was a strategy that was based on the image of an underdeveloped capitalism in crisis which came out of the immediate postwar years. This is perhaps why it was so unprepared for the vast and unruly expansion of participation of the late 1960s and 1970s. Though far more sympathetic to the students of 1968 than the PCF was, the PCI had no tools in its analytical armory to explain the structural sources of student insurgency. Thus while it absorbed a good part of the former student movement during the 1970s, it is only in recent years that it has begun to actively cooperate with some of the mass movements that were the long-term result of 1968. Root and graft may indeed have been opposed; but there were "grafted" elements that—far from facilitating the party's success—contributed to its political problems.

THE INSTITUTIONAL FRAMEWORK OF COMMUNIST SUCCESS

Postwar Italy was born a democracy. But like the French Third Republic, it was not the system most Italians would have chosen; rather it was the institutional compromise that divided them the least.[24] Even many of the new system's most salient characteristics—a

23. Ibid., 7.
24. The parallels between these two seldom compared cases have been brought home by two recent syntheses: Vincent Wright's "Fragmentation and Cohesion in the Nation State: France, 1869–1871," unpublished paper (Nuffield College, Oxford,

weak executive, a constitutional court—were either reactions against the last regime or imitations of the practices of foreign friends. The most innovative characteristics—such as the creation of ordinary regions—were put on the shelf, while many Fascist-era laws were not taken off the books for many years.

For the Communists the nature of the postwar settlement was particularly ambivalent. On the one hand, they had contributed powerfully to the crafting of the constitutional instrument.[25] On the other, they were convinced of the tenuousness of middle-class Italians' commitment to democracy and feared that, under certain circumstances, the disaster that had befallen the workers' movement after the First World War might be repeated.[26] This was an important component in the unity of the Socialist and Communist branches of the Left, but it was also a factor in their commitment to the country's democratic institutions. As Hellman writes, "In the face of impending chaos and breakdown, what truly matters are institutional guarantees and the primacy of the political."[27]

Two characteristics of the postwar settlement, the power of the party system and the weak executive, were particularly crucial to the Left's institutional vocation.[28] Both would later turn out to be the bane of effective decision making, but they were seen as necessary conditions for the establishment of democracy in 1945. Between them, they conspired to bring the PCI deeply into the Italian system and to develop its leadership's political skills.

Consider first the power of the party system. It was the outgrowth

1985); and Gianfranco Pasquino, "The Demise of the First Fascist Regime and Italy's Transition to Democracy: 1943–1948," in Guillermo O'Donnell, Philippe Schmitter, and Laurence Whitehead, eds. *Transitions from Authoritarian Rule* (Baltimore: Johns Hopkins University Press, 1986), 45–69.

25. For a recent analysis, see Roberto Ruffilli, "Quel primo compromesso. I contrasti e le mediazioni all'origine della Repubblica," *Il Mulino* 37 (January–February 1988):99–112.

26. Hellman, "Evolution of the Left," 2.

27. Ibid., 4.

28. It is no accident that both of these engendered deep concern in Einaudi. In *Communism in Western Europe*, he wrote: "First of all, the excessive claims of parties over constitutional life must be abandoned. . . . Second, the persistent suspicion of executive power must be abandoned. . . . What is needed is a simplification of constitutional practices in this field, as well as an acceptance of the legislative, planning and budgetary leadership of the cabinet, since such leadership cannot be found elsewhere" (pp. 52–53).

of a number of factors, from the domination of the mass parties within the anti-Fascist Committee of National Liberation (CLN) to the need for the victorious Allies to have interlocutors who had not been tainted with the brush of Fascism. The Left in particular considered the party system to be a crucial guarantee against a resurgence of Fascism.[29]

The weakness of the executive was also a reaction to Fascism, for it was fear of executive power that constrained the Constituent Assembly from providing the cabinet with effective tools with which to govern. A weak executive was considered a necessary guarantee of democracy in a country just emerging from over two decades of authoritarianism. It was only in the late 1970s that a serious discussion began in the political class to effect the institutional changes that would endow the executive with more effective power.

Both of these tendencies were the source of enormous problems in Italy's postwar development. First, the parties came to dominate parliamentary decision making, to control appointments to a variety of institutions—including normally apolitical ones—and so monopolized representation that new social groups or issues could not easily gain a hearing except through the mass parties. This monopoly of representation was not broken until the late 1960s, but so strong was the party system that, even after mass mobilization declined in the early 1970s, it rapidly recovered its strength.[30]

Second, as Einaudi predicted in 1951, decisional capacity suffered in a system in which governments were frequently changed and ministers seldom remained in power long enough to see their policies through. Einaudi also saw that the surging growth of the economy would make it difficult for public authorities to govern. Ministries were dependent on the groups they were supposed to regulate; urban planning was still regulated by a law passed in 1936; the Fascist-era bureaucracy was never reformed; and the civil servants it left the republic were not encouraged to retire until the 1970s.[31]

29. Hellman, "Evolution of the Left," 3.

30. On the revival of party dominance in the mid-1970s, see Tarrow, *Democracy and Disorder*, chap. 11. For the PCI's capacity to absorb militants from the movements of the 1960s, see Peter Lange, Sidney Tarrow, and Cynthia Ervin, "The Phases of Mobilization," *British Journal of Political Science* 19 (1989).

31. On the problems posed by a Fascist-era civil service in a democratic system, see Robert Putnam, "The Political Attitudes of Senior Civil Servants in Britain, Ger-

The negative consequences of the strong party system and the weak executive were soon apparent. In the context of weak decisional capacity and strong parties, the only kind of policies on which governments could agree and which didn't require detailed implementation were distributional—in simple terms, policies of patronage. And since the DC lacked the strength to govern on its own after the earliest years of the cold war, governments were formed and maintained as *coalitions* for patronage.[32] This had the virtue of easy entry and common coin, but left long-term policy decisions to the market or to politics in the most negative sense.

For these reasons, despite its formal ejection from power in 1947, communism would not remain forever outside the "system" created by the DC. For in a system in which politics is omnipresent and government is weak, players outside the formal circle of power are eventually brought within the system in subtle and not always visible ways. This could occur through local governments' relations with central ministries; through logrolling for the *leggine* which became the stock in trade of parliamentary politics; within the trade unions; and ultimately through direct PCI support for a government in crisis in the late 1970s. Behind the scenes of the baroque drama played out on the public stage, the PCI became part of the continuing *spettacolo* of Italian politics.[33]

But participation in the system meant far more than gaining a share of the patronage pie. It also required the party to develop an efficient class of local administrators, planners, economists; to use the complicated network of conduits for the proposal of projects and the allocation of resources between center and periphery; to work together with Socialist and then Catholic and Social Democratic unionists in

---

many, and Italy," in Mattei Dogan, ed., *The Mandarins of Western Europe: The Political Role of Top Civil Servants* (New York: Sage, 1975). Putnam shows that in the early 1970s, when his data were collected, 86 percent of higher civil servants had entered the national administration before 1939. See page 96 of Putnam's article for these data.

32. The term is from Martin Shefter, "Party and Patronage: Germany, England, and Italy," in *Politics and Society* 7 (1977):403–51.

33. The term *spettacolo* is Joseph LaPalombara's in *Democracy, Italian Style* (New Haven: Yale University Press, 1987), but the notion of a public drama based on ideological divisions overlying a more mundane political game based on political exchange was presented in Sidney Tarrow, *Between Center and Periphery: Grassroots Politicians in Italy and France* (New Haven: Yale University Press, 1977), chap. 12.

hammering out contractual platforms and then bargaining with management. Working within the system meant allocating an independent importance to *politics*—as opposed to the purely organizational skills that would make for a good apparatchik.

In a Stalinist party, there is no iron law that would oblige the leadership to lay aside its revolutionary aspirations; but the nature of the democratic game as it developed in postwar Italy conspired with the PCI's desire to gain power and with its fear of an authoritarian inversion, to develop its institutional vocation. It was this institutional vocation and the political skills that it fostered that explain—better than either Soviet root or domestic graft—the party's political success. But what of its decline?

GROWTH AND DECLINE

It is far too soon to prognosticate about the recent and perhaps temporary reversal of political fortunes of Italian communism. As in explaining its success, we should resist the tendency to see in the PCI a slightly less serious version of its French counterpart. Much of its electoral misfortune is due to external forces, just as much of its electoral success could be explained in the 1960s and 1970s by factors it did not control. Let us conclude this chapter where we began: Mario Einaudi's predictions in 1951.

In two of these predictions, Einaudi was probably mistaken: first, when he predicted that communism grew on poverty and would be defeated by economic growth; and second, when he saw no alternative to the PCI's rooted dependency on the Soviet Union. But these are lessons that only the experience of the last forty years could have taught. What of Einaudi's subtler empirical arguments about Italian communism?

First, was Einaudi correct that "a domestic graft" was responsible for making the Soviet root acceptable to the Italian public? The main problem with this formulation is that, for the working class and that part of the peasantry and lower middle class that was part of traditional left-wing subculture, root and graft were virtually indistinguishable. An anticapitalist subculture actually preceded the October Revolution in Italy and was left intact by the nature of the Italian postwar settlement. It was only in the 1960s, with the changes in both the international system and the domestic political economy, that this patrimony came to the surface. It was not until the 1970s and 1980s that a true political culture of liberal capitalism began to flourish in broad circles of Italian society.

Research since the publication of *Communism in Western Europe* has shown that—whatever was the case in 1945—in the postwar period the constraints of the Soviet tie became increasingly mediated by domestic factors. The Soviet tie eventually ended up more of a cost than a benefit. By the end of the 1970s, in fact, it was the USSR that was the foreign stock grafted onto a domestically rooted strategy, rather than vice versa. And with the coming of *glasnost*, it is possible that the foreign graft will outstrip the domestic root in proposing a "Third Way" to socialism.

Second, the party's social strategy was itself the source of contradictions and ambiguities. How to hold on to proletarian bastions while attracting middle-class support? How to gain allies among peasant cultivators while continuing to favor landless farm laborers? And how to appeal to the new groups and classes that had developed around the transformations in postwar capitalism? These were the dilemmas that the party has faced throughout the postwar period. What began as the Communist problem—the party's appeal to Italians of many social strata—became the major problem of the Communists.

Finally, neither its foreign connections nor its domestic social strategy—nor the combination of the two—was to be the major source of the party's past success. As the Soviet tie loosened and economic development created problems for the party's social strategy, its success came to depend more and more on its involvement in political institutions and on the development of its leaders' political skills. These instincts and capacities would be advantageous in any democratic system; but they were particularly important in the *kind* of system that developed in the Italian political settlement after World War II.

Three aspects of that settlement helped the PCI to survive and to prosper: first, the centrist vocation of the DC was preserved and extended through its involvement of first one, then another political ally in centrist coalitions; second, the constitutional settlement created weak executive power; and third, the parties gained a monopoly of representation. The first and the second factors channeled politics into democratic channels and allowed the PCI to wait out its bleakest period in its strongest bastions; the second and the third denied the government the capacity to hound the party into oblivion and provided the Communists with access to the distributional game of politics. The PCI could thus prosper even as its Soviet tie became a liability and as economic development made it impossible to exploit poverty for partisan purposes.

But institutional involvement brought its own contradictions and its own risks to the PCI. First, specialization and differentiation created cleavages in the party elite—an authentic Italian version of the "red versus expert" dilemma.[34] This became particularly clear in central Italy, and throughout the country after 1975, when the Left gained control of virtually every major city in the country. Second, its institutional involvements weakened the very distinctiveness that made the party historically attractive to many of its lower-class followers. Third, the PCI's initial institutional vocation was most fruitful when it was paired with the unity of the Left.[35] Once that unity broke down, the competition between Socialists and Communists gave an advantage to the PSI within the political institutions which it would never have enjoyed in mass politics.

It was by understanding this basic political fact that Socialist leader Bettino Craxi gained the tremendous advantage he has enjoyed for almost a decade as the PCI's bête noire. Einaudi, with his dislike of political cant, bombast, and trimming, is the last to applaud the ascendency of this type of leader in Italian politics; but with his deep understanding of and belief in liberal institutions, Einaudi would appreciate this fine Italian irony: that the Italian Communist party, which survived the cold war, the economic miracle, the center-Left government, and the terrorism and economic crisis of the 1970s, may be at last outstripped by a small party led by a political tactician whose skills are centered on the manipulation of the political institutions to which the PCI became committed.

34. See Stephen Hellman's *Italian Communism in Transition* for examples of what happened to the party organization in Turin during the height of PCI electoral success.
35. Hellman, "Evolution of the Left," 2.

7

Comparative Political Economy: *Nationalization in France and Italy* Thirty Years Later

PETER J. KATZENSTEIN

OUR UNDERSTANDING of the politics of modern capitalism has been sharpened by our ability to analyze the intersection of capitalist politics with capitalist policies. The detailed analysis of important aspects of economic policy neatly accomplished both purposes. After World War II modern capitalism in all its variants accommodated itself to a political compromise around a mixed economy and a social welfare state that brought the political extremes closer to the center of capitalist politics. Nationalization was a political project that aimed at such a compromise. But nationalization was also the first of a sequence of economic policies—including economic planning, incomes policy, and industrial policy—deemed central to the political legitimacy and economic competitiveness of modern capitalism.

Mario Einaudi, Maurice Byé, and Ernesto Rossi conceived and wrote *Nationalization in France and Italy* thirty years ago in an era dramatically different from the late 1980s. After decades of peace and prosperity the challenge in Europe today is industrial reconversion, not the economic reconstruction required after the Depression and World War II. Today the democratic center has won broad support. Neo-Fascist movements and parties on the Right have remained on the fringe of politics. And the influence of Communist parties has been curtailed sharply. But in the 1950s that center was still lodged between potentially powerful, extremist forces. British representative institutions are no longer the model that Einaudi and his collaborators so clearly admired. Instead these institutions have proven to be inferior to the broad range of political experimentation with economic policies that have been so successful in France, Italy, and elsewhere on the continent. Nationalization and the state's direct intervention in the economy are no longer seen as the main solution to the economic contradictions and political instabilities of modern capitalism. Instead many European governments preach the gospel of deregulation while practicing various forms of indirect economic intervention conveniently summarized under the broad label of industrial policy. While the challenge of the 1950s was the revitalization of the basic infrastructure for Europe's mass production industries, today new production technologies lend new possibilities to the flexible specialization of older, artisanal forms of industrial production. Finally, the 1950s were the dawn of European integration. By the 1980s the political aspirations for a unification of Europe had given way to the recognition that Europe had become too small for some tasks and too big for others. Internationalization no longer refers to the operation of a European cartel such as the European Coal and Steel Community (ECSC). It describes instead rapidly shifting conditions in global markets which create new opportunities while at the same time increasing competitive pressures in established markets.

But these differences in political context should not blind us to the enduring theoretical and methodological contributions that Einaudi and his collaborators made to our understanding of modern capitalism. At the level of theory they insisted forcefully on the primacy of politics. And on questions of methodology they favored the comparative method. This chapter explores the field of comparative political economy from these two perspectives. It concludes with some reflections on the significance of the international dimension for contemporary European politics.

THE PRIMACY OF POLITICS

In his analysis of nationalization policies Einaudi stressed "the primacy of political life over economic life, of political decision over economic policy. The accumulated historical evidence of the last generation supports the validity of the concept. . . . The political climate of each country has everywhere proved to be the decisive factor."[1] Indeed everywhere, Einaudi argued, nationalized industries were subject to overwhelming political influence, by bureaucracies in France and Italy, and by the cabinet and political parties in Britain. The rapidity, casualness, and deliberation that has characterized, respectively, French, Italian, and British nationalization after 1945, Einaudi argued, were not different political tunes but variations on one theme.

Einaudi's insistence on the primacy of politics over economic life anticipated the revival of the study of political economy in the 1970s. Political interpretations of economic processes and events became once again a fruitful analytical perspective. The prolonged postwar boom had led many to believe that capitalist instabilities had been conquered by the self-correcting mechanisms of the market and the fine tuning of an economic policy informed by neoclassical economics. The distributional struggles between business and labor, the tensions between national governments and global markets, or the ecological consequences of capitalist growth had finally been overcome, or so it was thought, by the technical refinements that modern economics had brought to national and international policy. From the perspective of the 1950s and the 1980s this view is curious and must be attributed to the exceptionalism of the prolonged growth of the 1960s. That experience fostered a degree of optimism among economists and economic policy makers which has all but vanished since the mid-1970s. The two oil shocks, stagflation, the global debt crisis, and rising economic tensions throughout the world have driven home the point in the 1980s which was at the center of Einaudi's work in the 1950s, the primacy of politics.

This is illustrated by the transformation of the concept of comparative advantage, a bedrock of the neoclassical theory of international trade. Ricardo had argued that the international division of labor would yield the greatest benefit if countries exploited not their absolute but their relative advantage. But the concept of comparative advantage, as all its critics from Friedrich List to the present have pointed out, is static. In 1780, according to Ricardo's famous ex-

1. Mario Einaudi, Maurice Byé, and Ernesto Rossi, *Nationalization in France and Italy* (Ithaca: Cornell University Press, 1955).

ample, Portugal would specialize in the production of wine, England in the production of cloth. In 1880 Portugal would still export wine while England would export heavy machinery. And by 1980 Portugal would export wine while England would export computer chips. Comparative advantage freezes a set of political relations, expressed in market terms, and advocates a policy leading to a cumulative differentiation between national economies.

During the last decade an explicitly political interpretation of the concept of "competitive advantage" has challenged the traditional notion of comparative advantage.[2] Competitive advantage does not assume fixed resource endorsements (Portuguese sun, British capital). Instead it assumes that national economies everywhere strive to improve their capital stock, the skill of their labor forces, and the application of scientific and technological knowledge to the generation of new products and production processes. This dynamic conception of economic life captures how politics shapes economic choices in the modern world.

The developmental capitalism of East Asia, for example, has been predicated on precisely such a political notion of economic life. Far from being content to specialize in light consumer durables, Japan embarked in the early 1950s on an ambitious buildup of heavy industries, specifically steel and shipbuilding, which became the foundation of its success in global shipping and the automobile industry in the 1960s and 1970s. And in the early 1970s, before the oil shock of 1973, Japanese policy makers announced that the shift to knowledge-intensive industries had become unavoidable. Today astonishing progress in consumer electronics, computers and supercomputers, chips, and telecommunications has propelled Japan into a position from which it hopes to challenge the United States on a broad front as the technological leader of the twenty-first century.

But the notion of competitive advantage can also be applied to the Western European economies. In Einaudi's discussion of nationalization policies Britain appears as a model of representative government and economic common sense. Yet by the 1960s and 1970s Britain was looking across the Channel to discover the political secret to the dy-

2. See Laura Tyson and John Zysman, "American Industry in International Competition," in Zysman and Tyson, eds., *American Industry in International Competition: Government Policies and Corporate Strategies* (Ithaca: Cornell University Press, 1983), 15–59.

namic economic performance of the continental economies. Andrew Shonfield's masterful analysis in *Modern Capitalism* had focused on planning as the key.[3] Yet planning was embedded in different national cultures and required different institutions. The planning commission in France and the universal banks in West Germany evidently suited the requirements of enhancing international competitiveness. Alternatively, John Zysman has suggested that the secret to differential success must be sought in the character of financial systems.[4] Why in the 1960s, Zysman queries, does a left-wing government in Britain fail in its strategy of economic intervention while a right-wing government in France succeeds? Zysman argues convincingly that an important reason lies in the close links between state, finance, and industry in France compared to the arm's-length relationship between the cabinet, the City, and manufacturing industries in Britain. In contrast to Shonfield's emphasis on institutions that are embedded in national culture traditions, Zysman offers a more sharply drawn institutional analysis that succeeds where an ideological explanation fails.

Political accounts of Britain's lagging economy have gone beyond state planning and the character of financial institutions. The contrast between industrial strife in Britain and industrial peace in West Germany has spawned a library of studies that focus on industrial relations as the key to a political interpretation of the economic divergence between these two countries. The power of Britain's militant shop-floor stewards operating within a decentralized industrial relations system contrasts sharply with the centralization of power in the hands of West German union officials cooperating with management in West Germany's system of factory councils on the shop floor and of co-determination in the boardroom. Furthermore, British labor law is much more permissive than West Germany's restrictive approach. Finally, in recent years Michael Piore and Charles Sabel have argued that flexible specialization rather than mass production is the key to success in the unstable and volatile global markets of the 1980s.[5] Northern Italy's economic miracle in the 1970s can be traced to the revival of a dormant mode of artisanal capitalist production. At

3. Andrew Shonfield, *Modern Capitalism* (Oxford: Oxford University Press, 1965).
4. John Zysman, *Governments, Markets, and Growth: Financial Systems and the Politics of Industrial Change* (Ithaca: Cornell University Press, 1983).
5. Michael J. Piore and Charles F. Sabel, "Italian Small Business Development:

the center of this new regional economy are small firms, staffed by highly skilled worker-owners. These firms are tied into dense regional networks of supply and demand and of the diffusion of technological innovations. Because it industrialized early and perhaps for other reasons as well, British industry has probably moved closer to the pattern of Fordist mass production and thus has much greater difficulty in competing in production technologies and markets that in the 1970s and 1980s appear to reward flexible specialization.

The concept of competitive advantage restates in different language the primacy of politics over economic life which Einaudi insisted on thirty years ago. International competitiveness is not the result of a static comparative advantage but of a dynamic competitive advantage. This competitive advantage is to some extent the result of government policy affecting, for example, planning procedures, relations between banks and industry, labor relations, and the economic viability of small firms. But at the same time we can hardly deny the suggestion that Britain's failing economy is not due to any one fatal flaw but must be credited to the complex and not well understood interaction between the political practices, institutions, and ideologies that define what we mean by the generic label of Britain.

Emphasizing the primacy of politics has the distinctive advantage of not letting go of the central point so often forgotten by neoclassical economists. Capitalist markets are politically constructed. Markets cannot be understood apart from states and politics. The recent resurgence in the kind of political economy that Einaudi practiced thirty years ago was possible precisely because established economic models were rendered obsolete as exogenous political variables and parameters could no longer be neglected. This has led to a second kind of political economy. Rather than emphasizing the political explanation of economic events, it searches for economic explanations of political events. This second kind of political economy is an effort by economists to render intelligible through axiomatic reasoning the political forces that have so forcefully and visibly intervened in how markets operate. The theory of the electoral business cycle is a well-known

---

Lessons for U.S. Industrial Policy," in Zysman and Tyson, *American Industry in International Competition*, 391–421, and Piore and Sabel, *The Second Industrial Divide: Possibilities for Prosperity* (New York: Basic Books, 1984).

example.[6] The theory stipulates a strong causal link between the vote-seeking behavior of politicians and programs for fiscal expansion. Like any bold theory, it has received only limited support. The findings in the United States, with its weak party system, are stronger than in Western Europe. But after the second oil shock of 1979 the electorate in many democratic states has preferred deflation, low growth, and rising unemployment to inflation, high growth, and lower unemployment.

An economic explanation of political events is unlikely to displace the usefulness of the political explanations of economic outcomes which Einaudi insisted on. But it is likely to complement political perspectives in the field of political economy. The primacy of politics almost without exception means the primacy of national politics. The political perspective is strong in analyzing how history, national institutions, and politics intersect in shaping economic policies, such as nationalization, at the center of national political life. But the perspective is less useful in elucidating the constraints and opportunities that decision makers face at lower levels of politics. In fact, in the field of political economy few studies even try to gather systematically the data necessary to analyze how national political structures interact with lower levels of politics such as regions, industries, localities, or firms. In preparing to write *Corporatism and Change*, I could in fact not find a single such study in the area of European political economy.[7]

To investigate how politics at different levels interact I relied on the method of "process tracing" familiar to students of decision making in international relations and of public policy.[8] In tracing the policy process in a number of declining industries in Switzerland and Austria I was able to discern, at least to my satisfaction, how stability in national politics was affected by changes in other political arenas. My method was inductive and enormously time-consuming.

Informed by rational-choice theories, economic explanations of

6. See Edward R. Tufte, *Political Control of the Economy* (Princeton: Princeton University Press, 1978).

7. Peter J. Katzenstein, *Corporatism and Change: Austria, Switzerland, and the Politics of Industry* (Ithaca: Cornell University Press, 1984).

8. See Alexander L. George, "Case Studies and Theory Development: The Method of Structured, Focused Comparison," in Paul G. Lauren, ed., *Diplomacy: New Approaches in History, Theory, and Policy* (New York: Free Press, 1979), 43–68.

political outcomes may offer us useful shortcuts for fleshing out the micropolitical foundations of political economy. More important, in manageable research sites economic explanations of politics are most likely to escape their fatal flaw for empirical work. To date much of the rational-choice literature in political science infers from the behavior of actors a rationality in motivation that it assumes in the first place. By this logic whatever decision maxims actors adopt, they will act rationally. It depends on the ingenuity of the theorist to specify the decision rules so that the observed behavior is in fact rational. Since by this procedure there is in fact an infinity of rational actions, once the context and decision rules are properly specified, this is obviously nonsense. Rational-choice theory often forgets the most elementary of all research maxims: the data one collects for measuring the dependent variable (actor behavior) must be different from the data one collects for measuring the independent variable (actor motivation). Otherwise chances are good that, whatever the rigor and elegance of the model, one will not escape the trap of tautology. Future work in political economy is likely to benefit from the complementarities that exist between political explanations of economic events pioneered by Einaudi and the economic explanations of political outcomes proffered by rational-choice theory.

THE COMPARATIVE METHOD

Einaudi's synthetic essay in *Nationalization in France and Italy* is explicitly comparative in placing these two continental countries next to Britain and the United States. In his comparison of France and Italy Einaudi shows sensitivity both to the differences in the circumstances surrounding nationalization and to the similarities in how nationalized industries were administered. But Einaudi goes beyond the comparison of the two continental states. He is also interested in comparing France's and Italy's politicized and ideological style of economic policy to the pragmatic and deliberative style of Britain and the United States. The speed and scope of nationalization as well as the methods of compensation, management, and relative efficiency of nationalized industries all point to enduring differences between the substance and the style of Anglo-Saxon and continental politics.

Einaudi's sophisticated use of the comparative method anticipates subsequent developments in the field of comparative political economy. The social sciences feature different approaches to the task of comparative analysis of capitalist democracies. Some stress similarities, others uniqueness. Political scientists interested in electoral behavior, for example, are likely to emphasize the basic similarity of systems of mass suffrage and regular electoral competition. Similarly, many sociologists will focus on the structural similarities of industrial or postindustrial societies. And economists of liberal and Marxist persuasions agree on the fundamental similarity of national economies conceived of either in terms of market competition or of the private ownership of the means of production.

Anthropologists, by way of contrast, emphasize the uniqueness of national cultures as the result of specific historical developments. A popularized version of this explanation seeks to explain the economic success of the states of Central Europe (West Germany, Switzerland, and Austria) by the Seven Dwarf Theory. West Germans, Swiss, and Austrians are so successful because they depart for work in the morning with a happy yodel. Analogously, the stunning economic performance of Japan and the Gang of Four (South Korea, Taiwan, Hong Kong, and Singapore) is explained by the Asian Ant Theory. Obedient and hardworking to a fault, Asians excel at performing tasks that are clearly specified. These popularized versions of cultural explanations are often ethnocentric and clearly wrong. By international standards absenteeism from the workplace is exceptionally high in the Federal Republic. And during the last decade the Japanese have made stunning technological breakthroughs in a number of high-technology industries. But whatever the particular fault of the popularized versions of cultural explanations, they share with the sophisticated anthropological approaches the insight and assumption that the purpose of comparing the webs of meanings and traditions of different national cultures is to isolate the unique elements that deserve our closest attention.

The comparative institutionalist approach that has evolved in the analysis of political economy combines an analysis that stresses similarity with a perspective that emphasizes uniqueness. Similar are the building blocks of a modern political economy—for example, firms and workers, business associations and labor movements, banks, bu-

176 Peter J. Katzenstein

reaucracies, and parties. These building blocks we find everywhere in the advanced industrial world. But different national histories have created distinctive rather than unique national configurations.

A historically grounded comparative approach has proven very useful for illuminating distinct Italian and French patterns of policy and politics which have appeared since the publication of Einaudi's work in the mid-1950s. Jack Hayward and Michael Watson's analysis of planning, Donald Blackmer and Sidney Tarrow's analysis of communism, Suzanne Berger and Michael Piore's study of traditional sectors, and Tarrow's analysis of center-periphery relations are all exemplars of a style of analysis pioneered by Einaudi.[9] Furthermore, other studies in the field of West European comparative political economy are also indebted to the method of paired comparison, including Peter Hall's and John Zysman's work on Britain and France, Gosta Esping-Andersen's work on Scandinavia, and my own work on Austria, Switzerland, and the small European states.[10] In their insistence on the importance of historically shaped, distinctive national political patterns, these studies differ from a substantial literature relying on cross-national, aggregate economic statistics. These books emphasize that political options and policy choices cannot be understood apart from distinctive national patterns of politics.

One widely accepted explanation of these distinctive national patterns is Alexander Gerschenkron's analysis of economic backwardness.[11] Gerschenkron argues that industrialization requires the mobilization of capital; the amount of capital necessary and the speed with

9. Jack Hayward and Michael Watson, eds., *Planning, Politics and Public Policy: The British, French and Italian Experience* (Cambridge: Cambridge University Press, 1975); Donald L. M. Blackmer and Sidney Tarrow, eds., *Communism in Italy and France* (Princeton: Princeton University Press, 1975); Suzanne Berger and Michael Piore, eds., *Dualism and Discontinuity in Industrial Societies* (Cambridge: Cambridge University Press, 1980); Sidney Tarrow, *Between Center and Periphery: Grassroots Politicians in Italy and France* (New Haven: Yale University Press, 1977).

10. Peter Hall, *Governing the Economy: The Politics of State Intervention in Britain and France* (New York: Oxford University Press, 1986); Zysman, *Governments, Markets, and Growth*; Gosta Esping-Andersen, *Politics against Markets: The Social Democratic Road to Power* (Princeton: Princeton University Press, 1985); Katzenstein, *Corporatism and Change*, and *Small States in World Markets: Industrial Policy in Europe* (Ithaca: Cornell University Press, 1985).

11. Alexander Gerschenkron, *Economic Backwardness in Historical Perspective: A Book of Essays* (Cambridge: Harvard University Press, Belknap Press, 1962), 5–30.

which it had to be mobilized were much less in early industrializers such as Britain than in late industrializers such as Japan. British industrialization coincided with the textile revolution. It created a large number of mechanized textile firms which did not have to mobilize massive amounts of capital to start up production. Furthermore these firms faced virtually no competition in international markets. Japanese industrialization occurred much later, when steel, railways, and engineering industries were defining the technological frontier of capitalism. Massive amounts of capital needed to be mobilized in a relatively short period of time. And Japanese firms faced intensive competition in world markets. Differences in the timing and character of industrialization, Gerschenkron's theory suggests, lead to distinctive national patterns of capitalism. Compared to those of twentieth-century Britain, Japan's state structures were strong. They had to help mobilize capital on a large scale, and they had to protect Japanese producers. Institutional structures distinctive of British and Japanese capitalism—for example, the prominence of London's commercial banks and Japan's groupings of firms (*keiretsu*)—follow from Gerschenkron's explanation. They figure prominently in the analysis of British and Japanese economic policy since 1945.

The political dominance of the City of London has long been analyzed as a major determinant of British economic and foreign economic policy.[12] It was the central political reason British policy makers remained so obsessed with the reserve currency status of sterling. The overseas lobby in the Treasury Department was deeply imbued with the notion—wrong, as we know now through hindsight—that the economic health of the City of London as the hub of international capital markets depended largely on the international role of sterling. The other pillar of the empire, Britain's naval presence east of Suez, could not count on a similarly powerful and persistent defender. As a result, throughout the 1950s and 1960s Britain adhered to a "stop-go" domestic economic policy that took its cues from Britain's balance of payments rather than from the needs of its industrial

12. See Stephen Blank, "Britain: The Politics of Foreign Economic Policy, the Domestic Economy, and the Problem of Pluralistic Stagnation," in Peter J. Katzenstein, ed., *Between Power and Plenty: Foreign Economic Policies of Advanced Industrial States* (Madison: University of Wisconsin Press, 1978), 89–138; and Hall, *Governing the Economy*.

economy. The lack of international competitiveness and an accelerating deindustrialization that has marked British economic life in the 1970s and 1980s cannot be reduced merely to this political constellation. But neither can it be understood fully without it.

Japan's major groups of firms, such as Mitsui or Mitsubishi, have an important structural incentive for pursuing a strategy of competitive advantage. In each of these groups a bank serves primarily the needs of different corporate members producing in each of the major industries: textiles/apparel, steel, shipbuilding, automobiles, and electronics. Although significant exceptions to this broad pattern exist, such as Matsushita and Sony in consumer electronics, the presence of Japan's major corporations across the full spectrum from declining to growth industries is a central characteristic of Japan's political economy. Japan's major firm groupings thus have the ability to anticipate or to react to the structural changes that are affecting and transforming Japan's economy. Reallocation of investment capital among different firms operating in different sectors is one way of anticipating inevitable economic change. Redeploying labor in the form of "temporary" employees is a way of reacting to change, especially in times of crisis. In sum, the institutional differences that Gerschenkron's analysis points to have an evident relation to British and Japanese structures and the economic policies they have pursued since 1945.

This discussion of Gerschenkron, Britain, and Japan illustrates a more general point. It defines two poles, liberalism and statism, which have served as anchors of a historically grounded comparative approach to political economy. Besides Gerschenkron, other theorists have adopted a similar logic to address other questions. Samuel Huntington's comparison of the United States and Britain; Barrington Moore's analysis of America, Europe, and Asia; and Mancur Olson's implicit comparison of America and Britain with Japan and West Germany all have a geographic dimension stretching from West to East.[13]

---

13. Samuel P. Huntington, *Political Order and Changing Societies* (New Haven: Yale University Press, 1968); Mancur Olson, *The Rise and Decline of Nations: Economic Growth, Stagflation, and Social Rigidities* (New Haven: Yale University Press, 1982); Barrington Moore, *Social Origins of Dictatorship and Democracy: Lord and Peasant in the Making of the Modern World* (Boston: Beacon Press, 1966); Katzenstein, *Between Power and Plenty.*

But they also have a chronological dimension that distinguishes between early industrializers with a democratic past and no traumatic defeats in war and late industrializers with an authoritarian past which have experienced great national traumas.

Einaudi's analysis brilliantly demonstrates that France and Italy do not belong to the liberal type. And much recent work on the developmental capitalism in East Asia suggests similarly that, viewed globally, neither do they belong to the second type. While the French and the Italian states are heavily involved in economic life, by and large they lack the talent for exploiting market dynamics to help them achieve their goals. Instead, France and Italy exemplify the primacy of politics in economic policy which Einaudi identified so crisply in his study of nationalization policy. The 1980s provide ample illustration of this point. Political entrepreneurship of the highest order was required to steer the French through their experiment with socialism, the cohabitation of a Socialist president and a Conservative prime minister, and with the election of 1988, the acceptance of cautious Social Democratic policies. The timing and character of nationalization and denationalization policies was shaped primarily by politics. Italy's stunning economic performance in the 1980s was illustrated not only by the success of giant firms such as Olivetti and Fiat but also by the transformation of entire regions in northern Italy. The flexible specialization of industrial production that Piore and Sabel describe, drawing on the works of West European economists and sociologists, occurs within a system of political exchange between the political as well as the territorial centers and peripheries.[14]

But France and Italy must contend in Europe with the Federal Republic, which manifests a less overtly politicized approach to economic policy. As the third strongest capitalist economy and the dominant force in the European economy, West Germany approximates, but does not fully meet, the three criteria that define democratic corporatism: an ideology of social partnership, a centralized and concentrated system of interest groups, and a voluntary and informal coordination of conflicting objectives through uninterrupted bargaining among interest groups, political parties, and state bureaucracies.[15]

14. See Piore and Sabel, *Second Industrial Divide*; and Tarrow, *Between Center and Periphery*.
15. Katzenstein, *Small States in World Markets*.

West German history and its geographic position explain why a consensus ideology was so readily embraced after 1945 and why throughout the postwar era that ideology has been challenged by no more than 10–15 percent of the population. The legacy of the Third Reich and the generational change in West German politics have de-legitimated the radical Right so much that even at the height of its greatest economic crisis, in the early 1980s, the West German elector-ate all but ignored the radical neo-Nazi fringe. And the Communist Left could never make headway in a country divided by barbed wire and cement. Opposition to the consensus ideology came instead from issue-specific movements or parties focusing on rearmament in the 1950s, the Grand Coalition in the 1960s, citizen initiatives and ecology in the 1970s, and peace and ecology in the 1980s. The Greens are the current and to date most durable institutionalized challenge to the ideology of social partnership. Their appeal among younger co-horts of West Germans is, however, much lower than among the twenty-five- to thiry-five-year-olds. And the largest effect of the Greens on West German politics is indirect: by shrinking the electoral base of SPD, they have shifted the political center of gravity right of center. In short, in the foreseeable future the direct appeal of the Greens is unlikely to drastically transform or alter West Germany's consensus ideology.

West German politics also meets the second criterion of a corpo-ratist politics: centralized and concentrated interest groups. Indeed British, French, and Italian observers are often struck by the orderli-ness of West Germany's major producer organizations. The central-ization of business dates back to the late nineteenth century. After 1945 West Germany's labor movement adopted an industrywide or-ganization that is a model of centralization compared to the labor movements of all of the other large industrial states. West Germany's integrated financial structures give the large private banks an impor-tant say in the coordination of strategies in different industrial sectors. Furthermore, West Germany's powerful churches and professional associations illustrate that the centralization and concentration of West Germany's interest groups extend beyond the main producer organizations.

The coordination of conflicting political objectives as the third characteristic of a corporatist politics is facilitated by a set of parapublic institutions that are an important node in West Germany's policy network.[16] These institutions, although heterogeneous, typically are open to interest group elites, party leaders, and senior civil servants. Some of these institutions, such as the social welfare funds, date back to the nineteenth century. Others, such as the Federal Reserve, were creations of the Allies after 1945. Some are active in only one policy arena. Others span a wide range of policy issues. But all of them link the public with the private sector and act like political shock absorbers. They limit political controversies in the implementation of policy; and they also limit the scope of policy initiatives.

In West Germany, as in the small European democracies, these institutional features lead to what Charles Maier has called the politics of productivity—the convergence of political stability with economic flexibility.[17] The gap between the rhetoric of change (*Die Wende*) of the Kohl government and the continuity in political practice is one of the remarkable features of West German politics in the 1980s. Compared to the United States, Britain, France, and even Italy, the broad contours of West German politics have remained unusually constant. At the same time there have been many small-scale changes in society, economy, and politics. The pervasiveness of small changes obviates the pressure for big changes.

West German industry is as good an example as any to illustrate the point. In the early 1980s the prevailing attitude was gloom and doom. The decline of West Germany's international competitiveness and *le défi japonais* seemed to have brought to a screeching halt what a few years earlier had been proudly proclaimed to be "the German model." A few years later West German self-confidence had been restored fully. West German producers found that they could indeed compete effectively under the new and volatile conditions of the 1980s. Their strategy centered not around venture capitalists, large-scale deregulation, supply economics, or other ideological imports from the United States. Instead what mattered was a refinement of existing institutions and practices: a vocational training system im-

16. See Peter J. Katzenstein, *Policy and Politics in West Germany: The Growth of a Semisovereign State* (Philadelphia: Temple University Press, 1987).

17. Charles S. Maier, "The Politics of Productivity: Foundations of American International Economic Policy after World War II," in Katzenstein, *Between Power and Plenty*, 23–50.

parting new skills to a disciplined work force, business willing to invest and capable of doing so, and federal and state governments interested in accelerating the diffusion of new technologies throughout the core of West German manufacturing.

Nonetheless, compared to the smaller democracies in northwest Europe, the Federal Republic approximates rather than epitomizes the politics of democratic corporatism. It does so for two reasons. One is sheer size. In smaller political systems almost everyone deals with almost everyone. Political elites fill multiple roles, encounter one another in numerous settings, and never stop talking to or bargaining with one another. If you give a cocktail party in Oslo or Bern, you have to invite almost everyone. The social psychology of small number systems does not create political harmony. But it facilitates the informal coordination of conflicting objectives. The theory of iterative games leads to similar conclusions.[18] Because of the size of its political system, in West Germany informality is replaced by parapublic institutions that provide a meeting ground for hammering out agreements that in the smaller states are often arrived at more informally by the top political and economic elites.

A strong statist ideology is the second reason the Federal Republic approximates rather than epitomizes democratic corporatist politics. West German politics is imbued with a persistent faith in legal norms and in state "neutrality." The common good is anchored in an orderly process of reaching a consensus. The state, in short, is an integrative concept and a normative order that embraces and reinforces the ideology of social partnership. This legacy of German statism is largely alien to the corporatist politics of the smaller European democracies. There political elites incorporate state norms into their political bargains without, however, accepting them as the supreme normative guides to political action.

THE INTERNATIONAL DIMENSION

The relation between the corporatist politics of West Germany and the small European states and the politicized statism that Einaudi ana-

18. See Robert Axelrod, *The Evolution of Cooperation* (New York: Basic Books, 1984).

lyzed in *Nationalization in France and Italy* illustrates political developments that since the early 1950s have required a fundamental reconceptualization in the study of political economy. Only four of the fifty-nine pages of Einaudi's contribution deal with international developments, specifically the relationship between nationalization and the emergence of supranational agencies such as the European Coal and Steel Community. Since then European integration has evolved in unanticipated directions. Politically Western Europe remains largely dominated by nation-states that have refused to surrender decisive decision-making powers—for example, on questions of foreign and defense policies—to Brussels. But economically European integration has made striking gains, as measured for example by the high rates of penetration of European imports into the different national markets. One authoritative study estimates that in 1980 import penetration in manufacturing in the major European countries was twice as high as in the United States and five times as high as in Japan.[19] There is, however, also a second dimension of internationalization. Europe is closely linked to an international economy that is a mixture of liberal market transactions and politicized exchange relations.

Because of these transformations the most interesting political and theoretical questions now cut across the traditional academic disciplines of comparative and international studies. International relations theorists tell us that in the interest of parsimony we must think about international politics at the level of the international system without specific knowledge of the character of national actors. And students of European politics, a quick glance at any of the major undergraduate textbooks confirms, still view the world largely as a set of discrete political systems. These traditional analytical perspectives are not outmoded. But they are of limited usefulness in exploring policy questions, such as issues of international competitiveness, which cut across established disciplinary boundaries.

The relations between the "depoliticized" corporatist politics of West Germany and the "politicized" approach of France and Italy is a

19. Geoffrey Shepherd, François Duchêne, and Christopher Saunders, *Europe's Industries: Public and Private Strategies for Change* (Ithaca: Cornell University Press, 1983).

case in point. "Politicization" and "depoliticization," it should be understood, are relative terms. Corporatist politics is every bit as political as the politics of nationalized industries which Einaudi wrote about. But the politicization by West Germany's parties in domestic politics and by the West German state in the international system is less overt. The politics of productivity that the West Germans celebrate and recommend to others depends on a number of important political characteristics that can be found in corporatist systems but not in France and Italy—a pliant labor force, unions committed to international competitiveness and technological change, small firms oriented in production and sales to international markets, politicians willing to defer to bankers, Social Democrats committed to fiscal stability in times of crisis. The success that the West Germans have had in international markets with their low political profile makes them prefer a depoliticized approach to the international system—maintaining détente with East Germany as the superpowers intensify their cold war and favoring free trade over politically managed trade in goods, services, and technology. Only on the questions of foreign labor from Turkey and of political or economic refugees from the Third World has the Federal Republic adopted an explicitly political approach.

The politicized approach of France and Italy points in a different direction. In the management of their domestic economies and in their strategy in world markets the political profile, especially of the French, is very marked. Mitterrand's explicit alliance with the United States, against the Soviet Union and the West German Left, his Gaullist-style commitment to pursue a European option to diminish France's technological dependence on the United States, or his preference for a greater role of states in the management of foreign exchange rates (which was belittled by the United States in 1982–83 and embraced in 1985) and trade relations—all exemplify the fact that Mitterrand's socialism is remarkably French. A high political profile of the state is also characteristic in French domestic politics. The nationalizations and reprivatizations in the 1980s are of course a prime example of the explicitly political approach to economic life that Einaudi discerned thirty years ago. And so are the state interventions in declining or growth industries.

These differences between the low political profile of West Ger-

many and the high political profile of France have created complementarities and conflicts that are at the core of European politics and
that raise important questions about the future. West Germany's reli-
ance on market competition in the global economy is secured, in the
eventuality of failure, by France's low threshold for adopting protec-
tionism. The West Germans thus enjoy the best of both worlds.
Where they are strong, they play in global markets; where they are
weak they quietly fall in line witħ the protectionist web the French
are weaving for Europe. Inside Europe, the West Germans dominate
many export markets because of the competitive advantage they enjoy. But at the same time they are held hostage by the subsidies that
the French state decides to pour into particular industries. The cause
of the crisis of West German steel, as West German producers have
pointed out throughout the 1980s, is the lack not of market competitiveness but of political competitiveness. West German rationalization
measures and cutbacks in this industry have been impressive but in-
sufficient to overcome the cost advantage of other European producers, including France, receiving massive state subsidies.

France exploits analogous complementarities and experiences similar conflicts. In the international state system France continues to use
West German economic might to project its own power. Indeed, it
would be only a slight overstatement to argue that the European
Communities serve West Germany's interest in accumulating wealth
and the French interest in accumulating power. Some of this power is
obviously designed to constrain the West Germans. But increasingly
West Germany's economic might has become a resource for project-
ing French power in a world that is experiencing the rapid rise of new
centers of power in Asia. At the same time, though, inside Europe
French producers are exposed to competitive West German firms that
have made deep inroads into French markets.

The political complementarities in European production and trade
are embedded in financial and monetary relations that have had
a substantial impact on West European politics. The European Monetary System (EMS) was the creation of Chancellor Helmut Schmidt
and President Giscard d'Estaing in the late 1970s. The wish to
disengage partially from a volatile dollar and the urge to build
a stronger foundation for Europe's voice in international negotiations pushed Schmidt and d'Estaing to create this international insti-

tution. Eventually their extraordinarily close political relations were superseded by the interaction between the federal government in Bonn, the Bundesbank in Frankfurt, French state officials, as well as the other member states. Through the EMS West Germany's deflationary policy has been slightly diluted and diffused to France and the other European economies. In setting, to different degrees, the monetary parameters for the economic policies adopted by other European states West Germany wields a very substantial and rarely recognized or acknowledged economic power.[20] West German commitment to a low-inflation posture is so strong that it has been one of the major factors that has transformed French socialism into a more conservative Social Democracy. And it has also led to a major political conflict with the United States over the coordination of macroeconomic policies in the major industrial states.

Einaudi's work on political economy was carried by the conviction that European integration and strong ties with the United States would act as an effective barrier against communism. But the political complementarities between France and West Germany which I have sketched in this chapter show that full liberalization of European market relations, now planned for 1992, does not replace but rather complements traditional relations between states. Considering the emphasis Einaudi placed on the primacy of politics in national affairs, this intersection of national politics and international economics is not surprising. Indeed, in his magisterial survey of the international political economy, Robert Gilpin makes this his central point.[21]

Einaudi's work addresses central issues in the study of political economy. This emphasis on the primacy of politics foreshadowed work that subsequently developed into a distinct analytical tradition. His use of the comparative method was exemplary of some of the finest work in West European politics published during the last thirty years. And during the past three decades work in the tradition of Einaudi, Byé, and Rossi's *Nationalization in France and Italy* has provided us with a reasonably secure stock of knowledge about how

20. See Peter Ludlow, *The Making of the European Monetary System: A Case Study of the Politics of the European Community* (London: Butterworth, 1982); and Hugo Kaufmann, *Germany's International Monetary Policy and the European Monetary System* (New York: Brooklyn College Press, 1985).

21. Robert Gilpin, *The Political Economy of International Relations* (Princeton: Princeton University Press, 1987).

the primacy of politics over economic life in domestic affairs shapes
the approach states adopt in the international system. But we know
far too little about how international politics and economics affect
domestic arrangements. Theoretical approaches such as liberalism,
transnationalism, Marxism, early versions of dependency theory, and
world systems analysis offer perspectives that, whatever their limits,
point the field of comparative political economy in new and challenging directions.

8

The Roosevelt Revolution
and the New American State

THEODORE J. LOWI

EINAUDI'S *Roosevelt Revolution* bears the special mark of original intent: it was planned and executed as "a book aimed at those Europeans who think and worry about modern America and are confused about its meaning." His goal was a large and ambitious one: that "the Roosevelt Revolution should become more fully part of the remembered experience of the western world . . . [and] that only a balanced and reasoned understanding of the respective grounds upon which they stand can provide [Europeans and Americans] an authentic basis for the solidarity so needed in their future relationships." Europeans, in Einaudi's view, have "often forgotten that if America is paying a price for its present way of life, this is because America has dared to identify and accept some of the unavoidable conditions for the survival of a democratic community in the 20th century." In effect, the New Deal saved capitalism, as most Europeans do appreciate. But the New Deal did something more, which most Europeans have not appreciated: it saved democracy. In Einaudi's book

> the Roosevelt Revolution is seen, in the first place, as an effort to reestablish the sense of community in a free industrial society and to come to terms with its requirements, and, in the second place, as the most important attempt in the 20th century to affirm the validity and

central role of the political instruments of democracy. . . . While democracy was being routed all over the world by the totalitarians and the technicians, it triumphed in the United States. Those who proclaim their attachment to democracy ought to consider how this was done.[1]

It is only the beginning of analysis, however, to say that capitalism and democracy were saved by the New Deal. One of the most remarkable things about Roosevelt scholarship is the disparity of assessments of the consequences of the New Deal and, especially, the character of the Roosevelt leadership and the Roosevelt legacy. Lincoln is one of the few American leaders who has been more researched than Roosevelt; but there is a good deal less disparity in the range of Lincoln assessments. The Roosevelt assessments are not so much in disagreement with one another as simply not focused on the same things; they are more disparate than they are contradictory. A review of these assessments will make a start toward a clearer sense of the nature of the real contribution that the New Deal made to the "new American state."

WHO WAS THE REAL ROOSEVELT?

A good place to begin is with Einaudi's disagreement with James MacGregor Burns's assessment of Roosevelt's overall leadership. To Burns, Roosevelt failed as a "creative leader." Roosevelt did no more than leaders have to do at a minimum to be leaders, which is to be a strategic role player or "role-taker": "While role-taking is traditionally viewed as a device to enable the leader to present different faces to different publics in the time-honored fashion of the politician, it is also testimony to the influence of environmental factors that compel the leader to recognize their demands and expectations. Roosevelt is an excellent case in point." "The creative leader" must transcend the role-taking requirement and the environmental forces that impose the role:

A test of the more dominant or creative leader . . . is the extent to which his role-taking is a means of implementing a central purpose independent of those roles. . . . Role-taking . . . implies finally the ab-

1. Mario Einaudi, *The Roosevelt Revolution* (New York: Harcourt, 1959), vi, vii.

sence of leadership. . . . [The role-taker] mirrors society rather than
transforms it. The creative leader, on the other hand, stands somewhat
apart from society and assumes roles . . . as a tactical means of realizing
his long-term strategic ends.[2]

It is in this sense that Roosevelt fell short.

Einaudi's response could hardly be more in opposition:

> To deny the central position of Roosevelt throughout the Roosevelt
> Revolution indicates a readiness to go all the way either with a wholly
> chance view of the nature of history . . . or with a deterministic
> view . . . or with an elite theory view. Leadership within this context
> cannot mean the lifting of the leader above and outside society. The
> democratic leader is the man who is able to express the urge of his
> society to achieve common and deeply felt needs. . . . In this sense,
> Roosevelt has been the supreme democratic leader of our time.[3]

Burns carries his assessment into the specifics of policy making,
where he found that on the all-important issue of labor regulation
Roosevelt was neither a lion nor a fox:

> Quite unwittingly [Roosevelt] acted as midwife in the rebirth of labor
> action. Neither he nor Miss Perkins had much to do with [Sec. 7A of
> NRA]. Framed mainly by congressmen and labor leaders, it was sim-
> ply part of a bargain under which labor joined NRA's great "concert
> of interest." . . . Roosevelt failed to see the potentialities of an enlarged
> labor movement. . . . [The Wagner Act of 1935] was the most radical
> legislation passed during the New Deal . . . yet . . . [Roosevelt] threw
> his weight behind the measure only at the last moment, when it was
> due to pass anyway.[4]

Historian William Leuchtenberg begins on a point of agreement
with Burns and then takes a distinctly different tack: "The New Deal
was a Broker State, [yet this] clashed with the fact that [Roosevelt]
was agent, both willingly and unwillingly, of forces of reform that
business found unacceptable."[5] In other words, Roosevelt was a broker among corporate interests and yet a social democrat and leader of
a movement antagonistic to business as a class.

2. James MacGregor Burns, *Roosevelt: The Lion and the Fox* (New York: Harcourt,
1956), 486.

3. Einaudi, *Roosevelt Revolution*, 59.

4. Burns, *Roosevelt*, 215–19.

5. William Leuchtenberg, *Franklin D. Roosevelt and the New Deal* (New York:
Harper Torch Books, 1963), 87–94.

Political scientist Wilfred Binkley jumps in on Einaudi's side, stressing Roosevelt's unprecedented popular leadership, yet when facing a "crucial test" over the economy bill, Binkley was so moved by Roosevelt's party leadership that he was led to stress this element as the aspect of leadership that made the difference: Roosevelt the party leader.[6]

To scholars such as Robert A. Brady, Roosevelt was a centrally placed leader but of a new corporate state of sponsored partnership between labor and capital at the expense of the public at large.[7] Einaudi takes profound exception to the corporatist designation— understandably, given his experience with the real thing in Fascist Italy—yet he agrees with everything else except the label: "The NRA was, on the other hand, an attempt to strike a bargain between government and business . . . [showing] the extent to which the New Deal remained within the framework of what has been loosely called the capitalistic system . . . provided it recognized its social responsibilities."[8]

Other analysts contribute to these disparate and conflicting interpretations of Roosevelt and the New Deal. Paul Douglas's autobiographical account of Social Security shows Roosevelt's power as based in the executive branch, fully in control of Congress, especially in the most creative aspects of policy making.[9] Richard Hofstadter projects a picture of Roosevelt operating at first with "practically dictatorial powers," and beyond that he was operating on the basis of a leadership of the most numerous classes of society against the upper classes, who themselves polarized the situation into class terms: "It has often been said that he betrayed his class; but if by class one means the whole policy-making, power-wielding stratum, it would be just as true to say that his class betrayed him."[10] In contrast, James Landis, in

6. Wilfred Binkley, *President and Congress* (New York: Random House, Vintage Books, 1962), 296–98.

7. See Robert A. Brady, *Business as a System of Power* (New York: Columbia University Press, 1943). See also Grant McConnell, *Private Power and American Democracy* (New York: Knopf, 1966), esp. chaps. 7–8.

8. Einaudi, *Roosevelt Revolution*, 83.

9. Paul H. Douglas, *Social Security in the United States* (New York: Whittlesey House, 1936), 185–96 and passim.

10. Richard Hofstadter, *The American Political Tradition* (New York: Knopf, 1948), 334–35.

his autobiographical account of the Securities Acts and the Public Utility Holding Company Act, is so impressed with Congress's creativity that surely a reborn Woodrow Wilson would have been able to insist, on the basis of Landis's two case studies, that the New Deal was another era of "Congressional Government."[11]

All these characterizations of Roosevelt and the New Deal are accurate and true. But note that each observation tends to be offered in a tone that makes one expect to see the word *yet* following; sometimes, as with Leuchtenberg, it does so within the space of the same paragraph. Roosevelt *was* a mass leader, yet also a broker. He *was* an agent of reform, yet also innocent of the significance of the emerging reform movement. He *was* a social democrat, yet also a corporatist. He *was* a leader of a programmatic administration, yet also head of a completely nonprogrammatic political party. He *was* the supreme leader of an integrated administration, yet made a virtue of pluralistic administration of relatively independent agencies operating with conflicting jurisdictions constantly in need of reorganization. ("The president needs help.") Each characterization simply applies to a different New Deal. Roosevelt was neither lion nor fox. He was an elephant surrounded by blind analysts trying to generalize on the basis of one part of the corpus.

ANTECEDENTS: THE OLD AMERICAN STATE

The best way to put Roosevelt back together is to allow him and the New Deal to emerge out of the state developments that preceded him. Aside from the obvious Great Depression, to what was the New Deal a response? And aside from the economy, which we know was not directly transformed by the New Deal, what was transformed by the New Deal? If it was the state, then from what to what was it transformed?

Table 8.1 presents a quick overview of the old American state. The

11. James Landis, "The Legislative History of the Securities Act of 1933," *George Washington Law Review* 28 (1959): 29–49. A full tabularization of the many Roosevelts can be found in Laurence Chamberlain, *The President, Congress and Legislation* (New York: Columbia University Press, 1946), 58.

Table 8.1   The federal system: Specialization of functions among the three levels of government

The Traditional System, ca. 1800–1933

National Government Policies (Domestic)	State Government Policies	Local Government Policies
Internal improvements	Property laws (including slavery)	Adaptation of state laws to local conditions ("variances")
Subsidies (mainly to shipping)	Estate and inheritance laws	Public works
Tariffs	Commerce laws (Ownership) and exchange	Contracts for public works
Public lands disposal	Banking and credit laws	Licensing of public accommodations
Patents	Insurance laws	Assessible improvements
Currency	Family laws	Basic public services
	Moral laws	
	Public health and quarantine laws	
	Education laws	
	General penal laws	
	Public works laws (including eminent domain)	
	Construction codes	
	Land-use laws	
	Water and mineral resources laws	
	Judiciary and criminal procedure laws	
	Electoral laws (including political parties)	
	Local government laws	
	Civil service laws	
	Occupations and professions laws	

very first impression is how small the U.S. domestic government was (column 1) compared to the state governments (column 2). Leave aside that this was as intended by the Founders. Beyond that, it is important to note two traits common to the policies in column 1: (1) their common purpose was to promote commerce (we were rightly referred to as a "commercial republic"); and (2) the common technique of government was patronage. This is to be understood in the medieval sense of patron and client, where patronage was a relationship between a superior who was in command of resources and a subordinate who sought to share in the allocation of those resources, where the patron could allocate them at his discretion on an individualized and personalized basis. The term was confined in normal American usage to the handing out of jobs to the party's faithful; but that is obviously one very small example of patronage when properly understood. There was discretion in the allocation of these resources as long as the national government stayed away from directly coercive relationships with citizens and with rules of law that bound the resources to a priori conditions of their allocation.

The narrowness of the specialization of policy and function of the national government can be most easily clarified by quick reference to the state government functions during this same period (column 2). These policies are a reflection of the constitutional provision that all powers not explicitly delegated to the national government were "reserved" to the states or to the people, who in their wisdom could vote to delegate any of those retained powers to the states. As a result, the states did most of the fundamental governing, and the states were in particular responsible for those aspects of government that require directly coercive techniques. In our modern parlance we would tend to call this "regulation."

This old American state as outlined in Table 8.1 prevailed for nearly a century and a half. Anyone familiar with U.S. history will immediately interject such famous exceptions of domestic policy as the Fugitive Slave Laws, Reconstruction, the Interstate Commerce Act, and the Sherman Act. But those are so exceptional as to confirm the rule. The Fugitive Slave Laws were the first national intervention and accomplished nothing but the polarization of Congress and the inability of Congress to avoid war. Reconstruction was terminated by congressionally ordained demobilization, and with that, the return completely to the status quo ante bellum. Looking at congressional output in the 1880s, one would hardly be able to recognize that there had been a war at all. The Interstate Commerce and Sherman acts did persist, but were extremely narrowly defined. In fact, the shadow of constitutional doubt was spread so darkly across those acts and the regulatory legislation of the Woodrow Wilson period that all of these exceptions to Table 8.1, column 1, were restricted to an extremely narrow conceptualization of the "interstate commerce clause." Consequently, it was not until the 1930s that Congress began to adopt domestic regulatory policies with such frequency and scope that they put traditional constitutional limits to the test at all.[12] Pre–New Deal exceptions are intimations of a new American state only if we impute to them our post–New Deal knowledge of what ultimately happened.

In sum, for the first 150 years, the national government stayed on the reservation to which it was relegated by the Constitution or by early interpretations thereof. Elsewhere I have covered the implications of this for president-congress relations, for parties, and for pluralism and the group process.[13] At the level appropriate to Einaudi's own inquiry, the most important question is: to what extent did the New Deal produce a new American state?

BUILDING THE NEW AMERICAN STATE[14]

The domestic New Deal was born in 1933 and was buried toward the end of 1939 with the onset of mobilization for war. During those six years, the federal service was expanded from 572,000 to 920,000 employees, a rate of increase of 58,000 employees per year. The budget grew from $4.6 billion in 1933 to $8.8 billion in 1939, a rate of increase of about $700 million per year. But where was the Roosevelt Revolution? In the four preceding years, the Hoover administration expanded the civil service from 540,000 to 572,000 employees, an increase of about 8,000 employees per year. And the Hoover budget expanded from $3.1 billion to $4.6 billion, a rate of increase about half that of the New Deal rate. And for that, Hoover had earned

12. Compare Herman Pritchett, *The American Constitution*, 3d ed. (New York: McGraw-Hill, 1977), 180–81.

13. See for each subject, respectively, Theodore J. Lowi, *The Personal President* (Ithaca: Cornell University Press, 1985); "Party, Policy, and the Constitution," in William Chambers and Walter Dean Burnham, eds., *The American Party Systems* (New York: Oxford University Press, 1967), chap. 9; and *The End of Liberalism—the Second Republic of the United States*, 2d ed. (New York: W. W. Norton, 1979).

14. The title of this section is drawn from an admirable work by Stephen Skowronek, *Building the New American State* (Cambridge: Cambridge University Press, 1982).

the denunciation of candidate Roosevelt as "the greatest spending Administration in peacetime in all our history."

Indeed, where was the revolution? Of the $6.7 billion in the first New Deal budget, $2 billion was allocated to the Works Progress Administration (WPA) and $1 billion to the Public Works Administration (PWA) with another half billion dollars budgeted for the Civil Works Administration (CWA). These three programs alone accounted for nearly 53 percent of the 1934 budget, 46 percent of the 1935 budget, and 41 percent of the 1936 budget. Although these programs were proposed as recovery and relief programs, and indeed did provide a lot of relief work, they were essentially expansions of the patronage state as shown in Table 8.1, column 1.[15]

The Roosevelt administration might well have responded to the Depression by expanding only those types of functions to which the national government had been accustomed during its traditional century and a half. And it is conceivable that such an approach might have been just as effective as the approach Roosevelt ultimately adopted. After all, given the sorry condition of the country in 1939, Roosevelt might have done no worse if he had stuck with traditional means. If he had chosen that approach, however, and even if he had succeeded at it, he would have left no legacy at all and we would hardly concern ourselves with a Roosevelt Revolution.

Table 8.2 shows what the New Deal actually did. In section 1 are the policies adopted by the New Deal which can be considered direct extensions of the traditional system of the national government. These are all essentially patronage policies. Section 2 is made up of policies that definitely do not fit comfortably in the same category with those in section 1. They do resemble the occasional efforts at regulation tried by the national government between 1887 and 1932, but they more closely resemble the kinds of policy traditionally associated with the state governments, because the regulatory policies of the New Deal went well beyond the narrow interpretation of interstate commerce employed in the earlier national efforts and attempted

15. Sources of figures: Herbert Stein, *The Fiscal Revolution in America* (Chicago: University of Chicago Press, 1969), 69–72; and *Report of the Secretary of the Treasury*, Statistical Appendix (Washington, D.C.: Government Printing Office, 1972), 12–13. Some of the prose is taken from Lowi, *Personal President*, 44–45.

Table 8.2   The political economy of the New Deal

(1) *Traditional state*
   Civil Works Administration (CWA) '33
   Civilian Conservation Corps (CCC) '33
   Public Works Administration (PWA) '33
   Rural Electrification Administration (REA) '33
   Tennessee Valley Authority (TVA) '33
   Works Progress Administration (WPA) '33
   Soil Conservation Service (SCS) '35

(2) *Regulatory state*
   Agricultural Adjustment Administration (AAA) '33
   National Recovery Administration (NRA) '33
   Securities Exchange Commission (SEC) '34
   Public Utilities Holding Company Act '35
   National Labor Relations Act (NLRA) '35
   Fair Labor Standards Act (FLSA) '38
   Civil Aeronautics Board (CAB) '38

(3) *Redistributive state*
   Federal Deposit Insurance Corporation (FDIC) '33
   Bank Holiday '33
   Home Owners Loan Corporation (HOLC) '33
   Devaluation Act '34
   Federal Housing Administration (FHA) '34
   Federal Reserve (FED) Reforms '35
   Farm Security Administration (FSA) '35
   Progressive Tax Reforms '35

(4) *Organizational policies*
   Judiciary Reform '37
   Executive Office of the President '39
   Budget Bureau '39
   White House Staff '30's
   Administrative Law '30's
   FBI National Security '40's
   Joint Chiefs of Staff '40's

to go directly to those local conditions that the Supreme Court, until 1937, had definitely put outside and beyond the limits of national government power. We call these regulatory policies because each of them seeks to impose obligations directly on citizens and back those obligations with sanctions. In other words, for the first time in any systematic way, the national government established a direct and coercive relationship between itself and individual citizens.

Section 3 includes New Deal policies that do not fit comfortably in the same category as those of sections 1 or 2. In the first place, these policies are patently different from traditional patronage policies in that they possess an element of direct coercion. Second, although the coercive factor makes them comparable to regulatory policies, they do not work on the conduct of individuals in the same way as regulation. They are called "redistributive" here in order to imply this difference. The best way to convey the difference explicitly is: while regulatory policies seek directly to influence individual conduct, these so-called redistributive policies seek to influence individuals by manipulating the "environment of conduct" rather than "conduct itself." These policies seek to create new structures, to manipulate existing structures in order to change the value of property or money, or to categorize people according to some universalized attribute, such as level of income or age or status of occupation. Call these categoric policies.

Although the Income Tax and the Federal Reserve acts were adopted twenty years before the New Deal, they nevertheless confirmed the distinctiveness of the New Deal in other ways. First, the income tax did not confront the Constitution with any real test, because it was enacted by Congress following an entirely new constitutional amendment adopted precisely to confer on Congress the power to enact an income tax. The Federal Reserve also did not confront the Constitution, because it came clearly within the provisions of article 1, section 8, conferring on the national government the power to coin money and regulate the value thereof. More to the point, both of these policies were given their real scope, scale, and administrative muscle during the New Deal. And by 1939 they were only two of many absolutely fundamental additions to the apparatus of the new national state (as shown in Table 8.2, section 3).

The novelty of the policies in sections 2 and 3 of Table 8.2 can be conveyed by the fact that both put the Constitution itself to the test and required a fundamental adjustment to the Constitution by Supreme Court decisions. The reality of the distinction between the policies in section 2 and those in section 3 can be confirmed by the fact that they required separate constitutional validation. Regulatory policies were validated in a line of cases beginning with *NLRB v. Jones & Laughlin Steel Corporation*, 301 US 1 (1937). The redistributive policies in section 3 required separate testing and validation, in *Helvering v. Davis*, 301 US 619 (1937) and *Steward Machine Co. v. Davis*, 301 US 548 (1937). When validating the regulatory power of Congress, the Supreme Court concentrated on the commerce clause of article I, section 8 and rejected as artificial the distinction between interstate and local, arguing as follows in the *NLRB* case: "When industries organize themselves on a national scale, making their relation to interstate commerce the dominant factor in their activities, how can it be maintained that their industrial relations constitute a forbidden field into which Congress may not enter when it is necessary to protect interstate commerce from the paralyzing consequences of industrial war?" For redistributive policies, the Supreme Court relied on an entirely different part of the Constitution; in fact, for the first time it recognized the "general welfare" clause of the preamble and of clause 1 of article 1, section 8, of the Constitution. The court also based its case on recognition that there is no limit to congressional spending power except Congress's own wisdom, but that was itself colored by the very recognition of the almost unlimited character of the two "general welfare" clauses.

THE ROOSEVELT REVOLUTION 1:
CENTRAL TENDENCY

"Revolution" is a useful exaggeration. It puts the emphasis not merely on change but on discontinuous change, a break from the past. In this context, the Roosevelt Revolution can and should be broken down into four separate aspects, each with its own special relationship with the past: (1) the constitutional revolution; (2) the governmental revolution; (3) the institutional revolution; and (4) the political revolution. The first three concentrate on discontinuities at the broadest, most general level of political phenomena. Although the fourth shares some of that character, it has its own character and will be dealt with separately. In the words of the statistician, the first three changes focus on "central tendency." The fourth focuses primarily on "dispersion" or, more accurately, differentiation. Since the first three have been the focus of most attention, by others as well as myself, I deal with them briefly in this first section. More attention is reserved in the following section for the fourth change, because it has been least recognized.

The Constitutional Revolution

Some constitutional historians actually refer to 1937 as the onset of the First Constitutional Revolution. (The Second Constitutional Revolution usually refers to the period beginning at some point after the 1954 school segregation case.) Although the *NLRB* case (cited above) is the watershed decision, it was reconfirmed in other decisions where Congress reached even further down into local conditions and into situations involving individual farmers and not merely large, essentially interstate corporations.[16] If there was any doubt after the *Filburn* case that economic federalism was dead, it was dispelled in the cases validating the Civil Rights Act of 1964, in which the court argued that Congress could reach a single restaurant in Birmingham for refusing to serve blacks even if it could prove that the restaurant did not serve interstate customers. The court reasoned that Ollie's Barbecue could constitutionally be regulated because a substantial portion of the food served by the restaurant came from outside the state of Alabama.[17]

The Governmental Revolution

The governmental revolution can easily be defined as the addition of the new functions listed in Table 8.2 and by the addition of the directly coercive factor behind those new policies. This is precisely what was being validated in the constitutional revolution. But the

16. See esp. *Wickard* v. *Filburn*, 3317 US 111 (1942). The court validated the Agricultural Adjustment Act (AAA) in a case in which Filburn was allotted 11.1 acres for the growing of wheat but, in violation of the act, put in 23 acres. In his defense, Filburn argued that he was too small a producer to have an effect on interstate commerce, and, besides, his wheat was intended not for trade but for use on his own farm to feed his livestock. A Supreme Court ruling agreed he was small and that his wheat was not intended for market but stated that he came within the AAA because the wheat he grew for his own consumption represented wheat he did *not* purchase from the market!

17. *Katzenbach* v. *McClung*, 379 US 294 (1964).

discontinuity of government goes beyond even that. It includes the fact that all the hundreds of thousands of new civil servants were "covered in" and made permanently tenured employees of the national government. It would take a veritable counterrevolution to return to anywhere near the previous levels of federal employment.

Another aspect of the governmental revolution was the establishment of an elaborate apparatus of overhead agencies for management. A quick glance at section 4 of Table 8.2 will reveal a sense of determination to control all the agencies but, more important, to make them a rational force. In addition, the governmental revolution includes the virtual permanence of all the agencies and functions that had been established in the 1930s. It is extremely significant that not a single important government agency or program established during the 1930s was terminated after World War II, despite the death of Roosevelt, the succession of a very weak President Truman, and the election in 1946 of a very large Republican majority whose leaders were antagonistic to the New Deal.

Finally, the governmental revolution includes the commitment on the part of all the leadership, Republican as well as Democratic, to make the new apparatus a "positive state." With the adoption of the Employment Act of 1946 and its promise to make the national government responsible for getting a job for everyone who wants one, along with its establishment of the Council of Economic Advisors, the national government was determined not to be merely a reactive government but to take initiatives to head off economic disasters and personal injuries.

The Institutional Revolution

The institutional revolution is basically a revolution in the separation of powers. The most prominent institutional feature of the traditional system of national government was the centricity of Congress with its committees and parties. With a few exceptions during emergencies involving military actions, there was legislative supremacy, as intended by the Constitution. Stronger presidents vetoed a lot of legislation, but the source of the legislation, the creativity at the national level, was congressional. Nothing changed more completely or dramatically than this during the 1930s. In order to meet the demands of

the Depression, Congress authorized the executive branch to undertake all the activities identified above, and it delegated those powers
to the president with almost no guidelines on how those powers
would be used. Technically, this practice is called the delegation of
power. And at the beginning, members of Congress and prominent
jurists attempted to rationalize the delegation of power by arguing,
first, that the emergency required it and, second, that administrative
agencies were staffed by experts who were merely "filling in the details" of programs that Congress had constitutionally legislated. But
there came a point fairly soon when most people were willing to admit that these new agencies, especially the regulatory ones, were
making coercive policy decisions about individuals which Congress
itself ought to be making. In 1935 the Supreme Court ruled that such
broad and unguided delegation of power was unconstitutional.[18] That
constitutional rule has never been overturned explicitly by later Supreme Court decisions, but it has never been followed either.

Out of this revolution in institutional relationships the modern
presidency emerged—or sprang.[19] Some would argue, following Ar-
thur Schlesinger, that the modern presidency is based on the rise of
the national security state and the discretion required to run it. Although it is impossible to disagree about the importance of that development, the truth is that the presidency in the new American state
began in the 1930s on the *domestic* side, with the very large number of
domestic policies predicated on broad and unguided delegations of
power from Congress to the executive branch.

The Political Revolution

Part of the political revolution comes under the rubric of central
tendency, so I discuss it briefly here before going on to differentiation. The most dramatic way to put this is the decline of the parties
and the simultaneous rise of interest group politics and mass politics.
There have always been interest groups in American politics. Madison referred to them as "factions" and treated them as a mischievous

18. See in particular *Schechter Poultry Corp.* v. *United States*, 295 US 495 (1935),
invalidating the National Industrial Recovery Act.
19. See Lowi, *Personal President*.

force requiring careful constitutional creativity. But interest groups have become a very special phenomenon in the twentieth century for two reasons. First, with the decline of political parties, interest groups gained direct access to Congress and the executive branch. They are no longer mediated by parties; their demands no longer go through modification and compromise before being processed in congressional committees and executive agencies. Second, the status of interest groups has improved tremendously, from a mischievous force in Madisonian theory to a positive virtue in the liberal theory arising out of the 1930s. Thus, interest groups now not only enjoy access to government unmediated by parties but actually enjoy direct and official sponsorship by government agencies, often in the official statutory obligations of these agencies. Einaudi may be justified in his opposition to the use of the term "corporate" to describe these patterns. (Up to a point, I agree. This is why I coined the alternative concept, "interest-group liberalism.") The practice in the United States, however, at least approximates corporatism to the extent that the government encourages and often sponsors the involvement of organized interests in the policy-making process.

The second central tendency produced by the political revolution, the rise of mass politics, can best be seen in the politics of the presidency. With the decline of political parties and the building of the massive statutory base of presidential power, the presidency itself began in the 1930s to develop its own independent base of power directly among the masses of the American people. President Roosevelt tried to modernize the Democratic party by transforming it into a truly programmatic national party along European lines of programmatic concerns and membership discipline. But it was in this very effort that Roosevelt experienced his most stunning political defeat in 1938, when he tried to purge the disloyal members of his own party. Once he failed to accomplish that, Roosevelt to a large extent abandoned the Democratic party and instead went over the heads of the party and congressional leaders directly to the American people. This has now become a normal and accepted relationship, and it is reflected in the methods of nominating presidential candidates. But this is too obvious a point to belabor here. Let us turn instead to the dispersion or differentiation dimension of the political revolution.

THE ROOSEVELT REVOLUTION 2:
DIFFERENTIATION

Differentiation means simply "the unlikeness of parts." It has been taken by many as a fundamental aspect of modernization, because many of the observable forms of differentiation seem to reflect rational organization of society toward goal achievement. The first entire book of Adam Smith's *Wealth of Nations* is devoted to the division of labor, which for Smith is a manifestation of humankind's ability to use reason. Differentiation can be taken, first, as one of the central tendencies not only in the twentieth-century United States but everywhere that modernization has spread. For example, Samuel Huntington treats "differentiation of structures" as one of three fundamental patterns of modernization throughout the world, in particular in the West.[20]

But applying the general tendency to the specific context of the Roosevelt Revolution brings it down below central tendency to actual and to sustained differences in governmental functions and in political processes and structures. All these were introduced by the New Deal and not before. It is useful to review once again the patterns of policy in Table 8.2. Each of its four sections is a distinguishable category of public policy, and each represents—or one might say each is a measurement of—the differentiation of governmental functions. If differentiation is the mark of modernization, then clearly the New Deal in a scant few years modernized the governmental system of the United States. There were other elements of modernization, such as the reform of the civil service and the introduction of varieties of skills, training requirements, and modern management techniques. All of this could have happened in a government in which virtually all the policies were of the type listed in section 1, the patronage policies that were the tradition of national government. In that case, there would have been a great deal less modernization than in the actual case, which involved sections 2 and 3 as well as an expansion and enhancement of section 4.

20. Samuel Huntington, *Political Order in Changing Societies* (New Haven: Yale University Press, 1968), 93. Huntington is of course not alone in his appreciation of the general significance of differentiation. See, e.g., the great Italian political theorist Gaetano Mosca, *The Ruling Class* (New York: McGraw-Hill, 1959).

This, however, remains modernization by definition only. It is necessary now to look at the cumulative results of this differentiation of functions. The general hypothesis is as follows: each basic function of government, once it is stabilized and repetitive in its policies, becomes a kind of regime and fits the general tendency of any regime, which is to *develop a politics consonant with itself.* Using the terms established here, we can reconstruct Roosevelt and put some order into the disparate assessments of his contribution.

First, take Roosevelt as party leader. This is very much the view of him as seen through the traditional cases of patronage policy. In my own work I generally call it the "patronage state" to dramatize the intimacy of the connection between the type of policy and the type of politics. The so-called Roosevelt coalition or New Deal coalition was indeed an electoral coalition built on logrolling among many different, often conflicting, constituencies and groups. In this matter, Roosevelt might well be understood as a lion, using to the best of his ability as a party leader the large and growing amount of patronage available in both established "internal improvements" policies and newly created ones. Logrolling is a political relationship in which the participants have absolutely nothing in common except their understanding that each will support the other without questioning too hard what the partner is seeking. This was the basis of the political parties and the party system of the nineteenth century. They were patronage parties thriving in a patronage state. Roosevelt inherited this system; he was socialized in it through his recruitment and grooming in the politics of New York State. He had long ago made his peace with the leaders and the politics of New York City, including the best and the worst of Tammany Hall.

This is the Roosevelt the Republicans most feared, because an effective use of all that patronage could possibly enable Roosevelt to create a national machine; after all, it was the same type of resource on which the urban machines were built. No wonder the Hatch Acts were passed in Congress amid expressions of denunciation of Jim Farley and the fear of a dictatorial president. But this national machine failed to happen—not because of the Hatch Acts or the opposition and fears of Republicans, but because Roosevelt became involved in other areas of policy in which a patronage party and a leadership based on it were not effective. As we shall see, when Roosevelt tried to mobilize a large working class or to capitalize on it for the purpose of Social Security and monetary reform (shouting about the "economic royalists" and the "malefactors of great wealth"), he risked losing his party leadership altogether. As pressures of mobilization were mounting, Senator Burton Wheeler (D., Mont.) confronted a White House aide: "Who does Roosevelt think he is? He used to be just one of the barons. I was baron of the Northwest. Huey Long was baron of the South. [Other leaders were also mentioned.] He is like a king trying to reduce the barons."[21]

Roosevelt the broker in a broker state is the definitive characterization of Roosevelt when dealing with group coalitions, and anyone looking at the regulatory category of policies would have seen this kind of leadership rather than party leadership. Perhaps this is Roosevelt the fox, but in any event, this is the view one would get if one limited one's observations to cases of regulatory policy. A good starting point is a review of Burns's interpretation of Roosevelt's role in the passage of the Wagner Act. The same can be said of Roosevelt's role in adoption of the National Industry Recovery Act. This was built on brokerage among trade associations and unions, giving them access to the new agency and the opportunity to write their own tickets—if only they could agree among themselves. Another instance is the adoption of the Agricultural Adjustment Act, giving commodity associations the power to write their own tickets—once again, if they could agree among themselves. Some have called this the pluralistic system and others have called it the corporatist system, but either way, the Roosevelt role is a distinctive one, dealing with organized elements of the capitalists, but never with capitalists as a class. And the public constituency for his operations here was not a general mass constituency at all but a limited, albeit highly intense, constituency of organized leaders, primarily capitalists, contending among themselves, trying desperately to maximize their influence by agreement among themselves, succeeding only a sector at a time.

The third Roosevelt was the anticapitalist Roosevelt, or the savior of capitalism—depending on one's values and point of view. Each view stresses a leadership role in the context of social movements, class politics, and "historic forces." Here we see Roosevelt the Social

21. Quoted in Burns, *Roosevelt*, 341–42.

Democrat. Here we see Roosevelt seeking a constituency among the masses, not among groups or group leaders. Here we see Roosevelt as part of history—responding to it, being led by it; and in fact, at least to some, shaping it.

Those who have seen this Roosevelt have been looking through the spectacles of redistributive policies. This was the Roosevelt as seen by Paul Douglas, Edwin Witte, and Frances Perkins during their experiences with the mobilization of forces necessary to adopt the Social Security Act. It was in cases such as this and cases of monetary reform, devaluation, and agricultural resettlement that Roosevelt was prompted to denounce capitalism's "malefactors of great wealth."

Since the Tennessee Valley Authority (TVA) was one of the gold-star cases of Roosevelt leadership in Einaudi's view, let us take it as a case study in the discontinuity across these differentiated domains of policy or function. Einaudi, more than any other Roosevelt scholar, was impressed by the TVA as a new instrument of government and as an indicator of Roosevelt's leadership. Roosevelt did indeed sincerely view the TVA as a social experiment, in which electric power was to be a "secondary consideration."[22] The true nature of the TVA as a *type of function*, however, won out over Roosevelt's public definition of it. The TVA was really nothing more than an ambitious version of traditional internal improvements policies, and it was aimed at the very core of the traditional constituency of the Democratic party: Tennessee, Alabama, and Georgia. After 1933, as more of the New Deal got into gear, the TVA became the only such regional development, and as a "social experiment" it abruptly ended—in favor of local flood control, local electric power, and local land development—in a word, it ended in favor of local constituency interests.[23] This is typical of politics in the patronage state.

ASSESSMENT

Einaudi's assessment of the Roosevelt Revolution begins with the basic dilemma of democracy, as identified by Alexis de Tocque-

22. Quoted in Einaudi, *Roosevelt Revolution*, 100.
23. For a political assessment of the TVA, see Philip Selznick, *TVA and the Grass Roots* (Berkeley: University of California Press, 1949).

ville exactly one hundred years before the Roosevelt Revolution got under way:

> Tocqueville had no illusions about the advance of the equalitarian movement, to him the essence of democracy. Equality of status was the basic fact of modern times everywhere in the Western world. Democracy, conceived as equality, was both inevitable and desirable in spite of the longings of Tocqueville for the aristocratic societies of the past. "The nations of our time cannot prevent the conditions of men from becoming equal, but it depends upon themselves whether the principle of equality is to lead them to servitude or freedom. . . ." This, then, was the problem to which Tocqueville addressed himself: The problem of the survival of the individual, in a democratic society where essential doctrine was that of the rule of the majority . . . which, no matter how formed and by what issues . . . would strive to assert itself and to stamp out the minority. . . .
> [Also developing] rapidly in a country in which democracy was flourishing was a new and harsh aristocracy, identified by Tocqueville as the aristocracy of industry. The danger was that the business class would first impoverish and debase the men working under it and then abandon them to the charity of the public. . . . Tocqueville remains one of earliest critical commentators of our industrial age to have seen the problems of business controls over the community, and the dangers of the probable failure of the industrial classes to accept the responsibility that went with power and to which earlier aristocracies had submitted. [This] represents a remarkable feat of prophecy.[24]

Einaudi then repeats the theme with which he had opened his book, with a sense that the book had confirmed it:

> Most of the trends forecast by Tocqueville came true in the next century. . . . The vitality of American democracy which Tocqueville had felt joined hands with constitutionalism to subdue the industrial monster to the medium of constitutional principle . . . may well be listed as one of the permanent accomplishments of the Roosevelt Revolution. . . . Democracy had indeed been successful, while at the same time freedom had been able to maintain itself.[25]

Not content with this happy verdict, Einaudi went the long step further with Tocqueville: "Once possessed of the answer, Tocqueville imagined himself ready to advise his countrymen and to help a democratic France and Europe to follow the path of freedom rather than

24. Einaudi, *Roosevelt Revolution,* 337–40.
25. Ibid., 340.

that of despotism." Some sense of Einaudi's purpose can be drawn from the following brief passage:

> American economic policy since 1933 . . . [is a] demonstration of the irrelevance of the theories and practices of the Soviet revolution in the affairs of an industrial society. . . . There have been many and persistent voices in the West bent upon proving our indebtedness to Russia in so far as planning and state intervention were concerned. The belief that the Soviet pattern of action had to be applied in times of trouble was an ingrained one. It took John Maynard Keynes's eloquence and theoretical constructions and Franklin Delano Roosevelt's practical political manipulations to provide proof of the inapplicability of the Soviet experience to the West.[26]

This was a bold and important message for the 1950s. The Soviet model was popular on the Left. The Communist parties of France and Italy were the largest outside the USSR. A Socialist federation with the Communist party was still in the future of France, and Eurocommunism was still to have its brief day. The break between the Socialist and the Communist Left in France was not to come until the 1980s. Andrew Shonfield was writing with the 1950s freshly in mind when he observed that "the United States is indeed one of the few places left where 'capitalism' is generally thought to be an OKAY word."[27]

Thirty years after the publication of *The Roosevelt Revolution*, the European countries (and there is no need to limit this to the European countries) have moved, for them, significantly to the right, but toward Einaudi's precious liberalism rather than toward fascism, as Einaudi feared they might as they fell out of love with the Soviet model. Indeed, by U.S. standards, the move toward liberalism is in a rightward direction only because the European intellectual tradition takes the attitude toward capitalism as its litmus test of Left versus Right.[28] But that is an egregious oversimplification equivalent to the U.S. practice of taking one's attitude toward government as the litmus test to distinguish between conservative (Right) and liberal

26. Ibid., 338, 341.
27. Andrew Shonfield, *Modern Capitalism* (New York: Oxford University Press, 1965), 298.
28. For a discussion of why liberalism is considered left of center in the United States and right of center everywhere else in the world, see Theodore J. Lowi, "Avant-propos," in *La Deuxième République des Etats-Unis* (Paris: PUF, 1987).

(Left). It would be more accurate simply to call the recent European embrace of capitalist methods Americanization. But it would be equally accurate to characterize the U.S. embrace of a Keynesian model as Europeanization. Europeanization refers to the building of a large governmental presence, but with a politics consonant with that. This is the new American state. It is a positive state, one that does not react to but rather attempts to initiate action in regard to social and economic problems. It is a state filled with the rhetoric and a great deal of the reality of mobilization toward social justice and equity. It is also a government whose politics tends toward polarization and mass mobilization.

The United States is far from Europeanized, especially given the long-term decline of organized political parties; but it has been on a Europeanizing course since the New Deal. The growth of the governmental sector and of the public bureaucracy could be seen almost immediately. The political implications were not seen for a while, some indeed not until the 1970s and 1980s, with the emergence of a genuine right wing at the national level. The 1980s has seen a polarization of Right and Left on a national scale in the United States which is certainly unique in this century.

This first aspect of Europeanization has been recognized by many political scientists, and one group has urged a "return to the state" as the proper way to study politics and government.[29] Up to a point this is a good development, but there is a tendency to reify "the state," to approach it as though the state were a particular quality that can be measured as to its strength, its autonomy, and so on. This is an unfortunate extreme. The state, like power, is a term of art, directing the observer toward a certain level of discourse. Moreover, stress on the state as a characteristic more or less present tends to expose the second important dimension of Europeanization (or "state development") in this review of the Roosevelt Revolution. It is a good point on which to conclude.

Differentiation is what is really meant by modernization. Modernization is not to be understood merely in terms of advanced tech-

29. For an inventory of people and ideas in their "return-to-the-state" movement, see Peter B. Evans, Dietrick Rueschemeyer, and Theda Skocpol, eds., *Bringing the State Back In* (New York: Cambridge University Press, 1985).

nology, the increased recruitment of skills, and the elaboration of management techniques. This aspect of modernization was developing before the Roosevelt administration and was not something to which the Roosevelt administration was strongly committed. As a matter of fact, most of the important technological advances made by the Roosevelt administration occurred during World War II, with the integration of science into policy and policy making. In any event, differentiation is the more important dimension of modernization.

Thus, the Roosevelt Revolution opened up two new streets for Americans: the positive state and the modernized or differentiated state. And these should be the main thoroughfares of political science research for the rest of this century and beyond. But for both of these directions there should be a single concern, so well expressed by Einaudi toward the end of *The Roosevelt Revolution*:

> What we have seen in the United States has been the systematic and inventive search for solutions to the difficulties of industrial mass democracy, a search intended to realize the ideals of community without collectivism, the ideal of freedom without anarchy, the advantages of technology without the loss of humanism. . . . What the Roosevelt Revolution has done has been to keep the door open so as to permit to our generation a chance to decide in liberty what we must do.[30]

The research we do today must keep that door open.

30. Einaudi, *Roosevelt Revolution*, 360.

Bibliography of
Mario Einaudi's Work

BOOKS

Edmondo Burke e l'indirizzo storico nelle scienze politiche. Turin: Istituto Giuridico delle Reale Università, 1930.

Le origini dottrinali e storiche del controllo giudiziario sulla costituzionalità delle leggi negli stati uniti d'America. Turin: Istituto Giuridico della Reale Università, 1931.

The Physiocratic Doctrine of Judicial Control. Cambridge: Harvard University Press, 1938.

With Jean-Marie Domenach and Aldo Garosci. *Communism in Western Europe.* Ithaca: Cornell University Press, 1951.

With François Goguel. *Christian Democracy in Italy and France.* Notre Dame, Ind.: University of Notre Dame Press, 1952.

With Maurice Byé and Ernesto Rossi. *Nationalization in France and Italy.* Ithaca: Cornell University Press, 1955.

The Roosevelt Revolution. New York: Harcourt, 1959.

La Rivoluzione di Roosevelt. Turin: Giulio Einaudi, 1959.

Roosevelt et la révolution du New Deal. Paris: Armand Colin, 1961.

The Early Rousseau. Ithaca: Cornell University Press, 1967.

Il Primo Rousseau. Turin: Piccola Biblioteca Einaudi, 1979.

213

ARTICLES

"Interpretazioni europee della dottrina americana del sindacato di costituzionalità delle leggi." *Studi urbinati* 6 (1932):7–30.

"The British Background of Burke's Political Philosophy." *Political Science Quarterly* 49 (December 1934):576–98.

"La collaborazione del Conte di Cavour al 'Risorgimento.'" *Rivista di storia economica* 2 (1937):1–22.

"Le Prime ferrovie piemontesi ed il Conte di Cavour." *Rivista di storia economica* 3 (1938):1–38.

"The Economic Reconstruction of Italy." *Foreign Affairs* 22 (January 1944):3–13.

"Political Issues and Alignments in Italy Today." *Review of Politics* 6 (October 1944):484–515.

"What Is the Future of Italy?" *GI Roundtable* 28 (December 1945):1–47.

"Christian Democracy in Italy." *Review of Politics* 9 (January 1947):16–33.

"Nationalization in France and Italy." *Social Research* 15 (March 1948):22–43.

"The Italian Elections of 1948." *Review of Politics* 10 (July 1948):346–61.

"The Constitution of the Italian Republic." *American Political Science Review* 42 (August 1948):661–76.

"The Italian Land: Men, Nature, and Government." *Social Research* 17 (March 1950):8–34.

"Nationalization of Industry in Western Europe: Recent Literature and Debates." *American Political Science Review* 44 (March 1950):177–91.

"Burke on Rousseau." *Review of Politics* 12 (April 1950):247–72.

"Italy." In *Encyclopedia Americana* (1951), 429–557.

"Western European Communism: A Profile." *American Political Science Review* 45 (March 1951):185–208.

"The Crisis of Politics and Government in France." *World Politics* 4 (October 1951):64–84.

"Communism in Western Europe: Its Strengths and Vulnerability." *Yale Review* 45 (December 1951):234–46.

"L'Influence des idées et des institutions religieuses sur la politique extérieure de l'Italie, de 1870 à 1953." *La Politique étrangère et ses fondements.* Cahiers de la Fondation Nationale des Sciences Politiques, no. 55 (1954):62–79.

"Alcune riflessioni sullo sviluppo del pensiero politico di Rousseau." In Institute of Political Science of the University of Turin, ed., *Studi in memoria di Gioele Solari*. Turin: Ramella (1954):219–42.

"The Crisis of Communism." *Political Quarterly* 28 (1957):260–70.

"Foreign Aid in the Mediterranean." *Current History* (August 1957):101–4.

"Problems of Freedom in Postwar Europe, 1945–1957." In Milton R. Konvitz and Clinton Rossiter, eds., *Aspects of Liberty: Essays Presented to Robert E. Cushman*. Ithaca: Cornell University Press, 1958.

"Les Idées de George Kennan et l'évolution de la politique étrangère des Etats-Unis." In *Les Affaires étrangères* (1959):417–30.

"Fascism." In *International Encyclopedia of Social Sciences*. New York: Macmillan, Free Press, 1968.

"Rousseau." In Luigi Firpo, ed., *Storia delle idee politiche, economiche, e sociali*. Turin: Unione Tipografico-Editrice Torinese, 1974.

Index

Library of Congress Cataloging-in-Publication Data

Comparative theory and political experience / Peter J. Katzenstein,
    Theodore Lowi, Sidney Tarrow, editors.
        p. cm.
    Outgrowth of a conference held Nov. 1987 at the Society for the
    Humanities at Cornell University in honor of Mario Einaudi,
    sponsored by Cornell's Western Societies Program.
    Includes bibliographical references.
    ISBN 0-8014-2368-6 (alk. paper)
        1. Einaudi, Mario, 1904– —Contributions in political science—
    Congresses.   2. Political science—Congresses.   I. Katzenstein,
    Peter J.   II. Lowi, Theodore J.   III. Tarrow, Sidney G.
    IV. Einaudi, Mario, 1904– .   V. Cornell University. Western
    Societies Program.
    JC251.E35C65   1990
    320.5—dc20   89-39112